THE ROUGH GUIDE TO

LISBON

by Matthew Hancock

with additional research by Amanda Tomlin
and Bob Taylor

ROUGH
GUIDES

We set out to do something different when the first Rough Guide was published in 1982. Mark Ellingham, just out of university, was travelling in Greece. He brought along the popular guides of the day, but found they were all lacking in some way. They were either strong on ruins and museums but went on for pages without mentioning a beach or taverna. Or they were so conscious of the need to save money that they lost sight of Greece's cultural and historical significance. Also, none of the books told him anything about Greece's contemporary life – its politics, its culture, its people, and how they lived.

So with no job in prospect, Mark decided to write his own guidebook, one which aimed to provide practical information that was second to none, detailing the best beaches and the hottest clubs and restaurants, while also giving hard-hitting accounts of every sight, both famous and obscure, and providing up-to-the-minute information on contemporary culture. It was a guide that encouraged independent travellers to find the best of Greece, and was a great success, getting shortlisted for the Thomas Cook travel guide award, and encouraging Mark, along with three friends, to expand the series.

The Rough Guide list grew rapidly and the letters flooded in, indicating a much broader readership than had been anticipated, but one which uniformly appreciated the Rough Guide mix of practical detail and humour, irreverence and enthusiasm. Things haven't changed. The same four friends who began the series are still the caretakers of the Rough Guide mission today: to provide the most reliable, up-to-date and entertaining information to independent-minded travellers of all ages, on all budgets.

We now publish more than 150 titles and have offices in London and New York. The travel guides are written and researched by a dedicated team of more than 100 authors, based in Britain, Europe, the USA and Australia. We have also created a unique series of phrasebooks to accompany the travel series, along with an acclaimed series of music guides, and a best-selling pocket guide to the Internet and World Wide Web. We also publish comprehensive travel information on our website: **www.roughguides.com**

5 Belém 76

6 Avenida da Liberdade to the Gulbenkian 87

7 Outer Lisbon 100

8 Parque das Nações 105

Listings

9 Accommodation 115

10 Eating 136

11 Cafés 167

12 Bars and clubs 176

13 Gay Lisbon 190

14 Live music 194

15 Cinema and theatre 205

16 Sport and outdoor activities 208

17 Shopping 216

18 Kids' Lisbon 228

19 Festivals 233

20 Directory 240

Out of the city

21 Sintra, Queluz and Mafra 247

22 Estoril and Cascais 272

23 South of the Tejo 285

Contexts

History	303
Books	316
Language	324
Index	330

MAP LIST

Lisbon Metro	12
Museu Nacional de Arte Antiga	70
Fundação Calouste Gulbenkian	96
Parque das Nações	106
Sintra	250
Around Sintra	256
Cascais	276
South of the Tejo	286

Colour maps (at back of book):

1 Around Lisbon

2 Greater Lisbon

3 The Baixa and Around

4 Alfama and Castelo

5 Bairro Alto, Chiado and Cais do Sodré

6 Alcântara, Lapa and Estrela

7 Belém

8 Avenida da Liberdade and Around

9 Parque Eduardo VII and the Gulbenkian

Introduction

For me no flowers can match the endlessly varied colours of Lisbon in the sunlight.

Fernando Pessoa, *The Book of Disquiet* (1933).

Lisbon (Lisboa), Europe's most westerly capital, is fast becoming one of the continent's most vibrant cities. Set on a series of hills overlooking the broad estuary of the Rio Tejo (River Tagus), most visitors are struck by its stunning location and effortless beauty. But its historic significance and faded charm also embrace a modern and forward-thinking lifestyle. Old men still grill sardines on cobbled streets in front of crumbling mansions, but alongside you'll find cosmopolitan bars and restaurants, many of them influenced by the tastes of African and Brazilian immigrants from Portugal's former colonies. It's an immediately likeable place, perhaps gentler than any capital should be; a big city that remains human in pace and scale.

Lisbon is officially the European Union's least expensive capital city, with a cost of living half that of London's. Once, however, it was one of Europe's wealthiest cities, controlling a maritime empire that stretched from Brazil in the west to Macau in the east. Many of its grandest buildings were destroyed in the Great Earthquake of 1755, and much of today's city dates from the late eighteenth and nineteenth centuries. At its heart is the eighteenth-century grid of the lower town, the **Baixa** (Chapter 1), enclosed by a switchback of hills and linked to surrounding districts by a network of cobbled streets. Its elegant, mosaic-studded squares – filled with cafés, buskers, businesspeople and streetwise dealers – form the hub of central Lisbon's daily activity, while to the west is **Chiado**, Lisbon's most elegant shopping area. East of the Baixa, the leafy shell of the **Castelo de São Jorge** commands superb views from a craggy hill, with the **Alfama** district (Chapter 2) sprawling below. This is the oldest, most traditional part of Lisbon, a village within a city, whose steep, whitewashed streets are so narrow that vehicles fear to enter.

At night the focus shifts to the **Bairro Alto** (Chapter 3), the upper town, west of Chiado, and best reached by one of the city's unique *elevadores* (funicular railways), which – along with the city's trams – crank their way up outrageous gradients. The Bairro Alto shelters some of the city's best restaurants, bars and clubs, while to the west of here (Chapter 4) lie the wealthy districts of **Estrela** and **Lapa**, the **Museu Nacional de Arte Antiga**, effectively Portugal's national art gallery, and the **Alcântara docks**, a former industrial port area now given over to cafés and nightlife.

Heading further west, out along the Tejo, brings you to the historical suburb of **Belém** (Chapter 5), 6km from the centre, from where many of Portugal's great maritime explorers set sail to explore the new world. The extraordinary **Mosteiro dos Jerónimos** is the most impressive of Belém's maritime monuments, while the turreted **Torre de Belém** is perhaps Lisbon's most recognizable landmark. Heading north instead from the Baixa, the tree-lined **Avenida da Liberdade** (Chapter 6) runs to the city's central park, **Parque Eduardo VII**, just beyond which is the outstanding **Fundação Calouste Gulbenkian** – a museum and cultural complex with an extraordinary rich collection of ancient and modern art. The suburbs of **outer Lisbon** (Chapter 7) stretch to the north and west, containing – among other sights – the city's zoo and perhaps its finest palace, the Palácio dos Marquêses de Fronteira.

It's to the east, however, where Lisbon is fast developing its contemporary credentials. Five kilometres east of the capital, the futuristic **Parque das Nações** (Chapter 8) occupies the former Expo 98 site, and has developed into a hugely popular theme park, with a whole host of restaurants, bars and attractions, including Europe's largest **oceanarium**.

The individual sights aside, Lisbon's big attraction is its daily **street life**, and nothing beats watching the city's comings and goings from a pavement café over a powerful *bica* coffee or Portuguese beer. Getting around is half the fun, whether taking one of its ancient trams, riding a ferry across the breezy Rio Tejo, or speeding across town on the metro, whose stations are decorated with adventurous contemporary art. And if you're fit enough to negotiate its hills, Lisbon is a great place to explore on foot: get off the beaten track and you'll find atmospheric neighbourhoods sheltering aromatic *pastelarias* (patisseries), traditional shops, and shuttered houses faced with beautiful azulejo tiles. There's a buoyant **nightlife** – some say the most hip in Europe at present – which ranges from the traditional fado clubs of Alfama to the glitzy clubs in Lisbon's redeveloped docklands. You're just as likely to hear music from Brazil and Africa as the latest club sounds, while Lisbon's **bars** and **restaurants** stand comparison with the best in any European city.

If you want to escape from the city for a while, the beautiful hilltop town of **Sintra** (Chapter 21), northwest of the city, is a must. Easily reached by train, its lush wooded heights and royal palaces formed Byron's "glorious Eden" and remain a UNESCO World Heritage site. If you're interested in Portuguese architecture, there are also the Rococo delights of the **Palácio de Queluz** or the extraordinary convent at **Mafra** to the north to visit. The sea is also close at hand, with the lively beach towns of **Estoril** and **Cascais** (Chapter 22) just half an hour's journey away. The best nearby beaches, however, are **south of the Tejo** (Chapter 23), along the **Costa da Caparica**, where Atlantic breakers crash on miles of superb dune-backed sands. Further south still lie the more sheltered waters off **Sesimbra**, a popular summer resort which sits at the edge of the craggy **Parque Natural da Arrábida**.

When to visit

Lisbon is comfortably warm from April to October. The cooling Atlantic breezes mean it is less hot than Mediterranean cities on the same latitude, especially after sundown, though in terms of hours of sunshine it is one of Europe's brightest capitals. Most Lisbon residents take their holidays in July and August, which means that some shops, bars and restaurants close for the period, while the local beaches are heaving. September and October are good times to go, as is June, when the city enjoys its main saints' festivals. Lisbon's westerly position means that it gets its fair share of rainfall, most of which falls in the winter months (November to March), when the whole city seems to become saturated. However, when the sun does appear, it can be gloriously warm, even in mid-winter. It is also worth noting that weather conditions can be extremely localized – it can be pouring in Sintra but clear in Lisbon, or cloudy in Lisbon and sunny south of the Tejo.

	°F		°C		RAINFALL	
	AVERAGE DAILY		AVERAGE DAILY		AVERAGE MONTHLY	
	MAX	MIN	MAX	MIN	IN	MM
Jan	57	46	14	8	4.3	111
Feb	59	47	15	8	3.0	76
March	63	50	17	10	4.2	109
April	67	53	20	12	2.1	54
May	71	55	21	13	1.7	55
June	77	60	25	15	0.6	16
July	81	63	27	17	0.1	3
Aug	82	63	28	17	0.2	4
Sept	79	62	26	17	1.3	33
Oct	72	58	22	14	2.4	62
Nov	63	52	17	11	3.7	93
Dec	58	47	15	9	4.1	103

BASICS

Arrival	3
Information and maps	7
City transport	10
Costs, money and banks	19
Communications	21
Crime and personal safety	24

Arrival

When you arrive in Lisbon the most central places to head for are either **Rossio** – which lies close to the Portuguese Tourist Office in neighbouring Praça dos Restauradores – or the riverfront **Praça do Comércio**, home to the main tourist office, the Lisbon Welcome Centre. Both squares can be reached easily by bus, metro or taxi from the airport and main train stations (though note that the Santa Apolónia and Terreiro do Paço metro stations aren't due to open until 2004).

BY AIR

The **airport** (Map 2, G2; ☎ 218 413 700, ⓦ www.lisboa-airport.com) is just twenty minutes north of the city centre and has a tourist office (daily 6am–midnight; ☎ 218 450 657), a 24-hour exchange bureau, currency exchange machines, ATMs and left-luggage facilities.

The easiest way into the centre is by **taxi** and, depending on traffic conditions, a journey to Rossio should cost €7–10. Note that you'll be charged €1.50 extra for baggage and that fares are slightly higher between 10pm and 6am, as well as at weekends and on public holidays. The tourist office at the airport sells **taxi vouchers**, priced according to the zone you are travelling to (€11 for the central zone, €14 for zone 2, including Belém; and €33 for Estoril and Cascais; extra supplements are payable for night travel). The vouchers allow you to jump the queue for taxis at the airport and avoid the faint possibility that the taxi driver is ripping you off, but otherwise they work out more expensive than regular fares.

Alternatively, catch the #91 **Aerobus** (☎966 298 558) which departs every twenty minutes between 7am and 9pm from outside the terminal, and runs to Praça do Marquês de Pombal, Praça dos Restauradores, Rossio, Praça do Comércio and Cais do Sodré train station. The ticket, which you buy from the driver, gives you one day's travel on the city's buses and trams for €2.50 (available free from the Welcome Desk for TAP passengers), or three days' for €5.50. **Local buses** (#44 or #45) leave from outside the terminal – a little beyond the Aerobus stop – to Praça dos Restauradores and Cais do Sodré station every ten to fifteen minutes between 6am and midnight and cost only €0.85, though these are less convenient if you have a lot of luggage.

Direct Stagecoach buses to Estoril and Cascais (taking 30–40 minutes) depart from the airport hourly (on the hour from 7am, last departure 10.30pm), costing €6.25.

BY TRAIN

Long-distance trains from Coimbra, Porto and the north (and also from Madrid and Paris) use **Santa Apolónia station** (Map 4, K6; ☎218 884 142), on the Gaivota metro line (from 2004), about fifteen minutes' walk east of Praça do Comércio or a short ride on bus #9, #39, #46 or #90 from Praça dos Restauradores or Rossio. There's a helpful **information office** (Mon–Sat 9am–7pm; ☎218 821 604) at the station, an exchange bureau and left-luggage facilities. An increasing number of trains also call at **Oriente station** (Map 1, G5; ☎218 920 307), east of the centre at the Parque das Nações, on the red Oriente metro line. This station is more convenient for the airport or for the north and east of Lisbon.

There are plans to open a new rail bridge over the Rio Tejo and to extend the commuter rail route under the Ponte 25 de Abril so it links up with the Algarve line. However, for the time being, trains from the Algarve and the south of Portugal still terminate at **Barreiro station** (Map 1, G7; ☎212 073 028), on the south bank of the Tejo. From here, you catch a ferry (included in the price of the train ticket) to **Estação Fluvial** (Map 3, L3; ☎212 729 710), the ferry terminal next to Praça do Comércio. Buses #9, #39, #80 and #90 run up from Fluvial to Rossio, through the Baixa (and from 2004 Estação Fluvial will also be on the Gaivota metro line).

Local trains from Sintra or Queluz emerge right in the heart of the city at **Rossio station** (Map 3, C8; ☎213 465 022), complete with shops, currency-exchange counters, ATMs and left-luggage lockers. Trains to Belém, Estoril and Cascais leave from the fairly central **Cais do Sodré station** (Map 5, B8; ☎213 470 181), to the west of the Baixa. This can be reached on the Gaivota metro line, or any one of buses #1, #2, #7, #32, #35, #43, #44 or #45 from Praça do Comércio.

BY BUS

Various bus companies have terminals scattered about the city, but the main one is at **Avenida João Crisóstomo** (Map 9, G5), a short walk from metro Saldanha (or around 1km northeast of Praça Marques de Pombal and 2km north of the Baixa). This terminal is also where most international bus services arrive. Each bus company has its own information number (see "Directory", p.240); the most useful is that of the main national carrier, Rede Expressos ($\textcircled{T}$213 581 470). There's a left-luggage office at the bus terminal.

Many bus services also stop at the **Oriente station** at Parque das Nações (Map 1, G5) on the Oriente metro line.

Leaving Lisbon, you can usually buy tickets if you turn up half an hour or so in advance, though for summer express services to the Algarve it's best to book a seat (through any travel agent) a day in advance.

BY CAR

Don't even think of **driving** in Lisbon: it takes years off your life and, particularly at the beginning or end of public holiday weekends, is to be avoided at all costs. Heading to or from the south on these occasions, it can take over an hour just to cross the Ponte 25 de Abril, a notorious traffic bottleneck that the Vasco da Gama bridge to the northeast of the city has done little to alleviate.

Parking is very difficult in central Lisbon. Pay-and-display spots get snapped up quickly and some of the local unemployed get by on tips for guiding drivers into empty spots; reports suggest that scratches suddenly appear on cars whose drivers do not leave tips. So you'd be wise to head for an official **car park**, for which you can expect to pay around €8 per day: central locations include underground car parks at Praça dos Restauradores (Map 8, G7), Praça Luis de Camões (Map 5, E5), Praça do Município (Map 5, F9), Largo Martim Moniz (Map 3, B3), and Praça da Figueira (Map 3, D5). Further out there are underground car parks at Parque Eduardo VII (Map 9, B9 and Map 9, C5), on Rua Marquês de Sá da Bandeira near the Gulbenkian (Map 9, D3); and in the Amoreiras complex on Avenida Eng. Duarte Pacheco (Map 2, D7). Wherever you park, do not leave valuables inside: the break-in rate is extremely high.

If you're **renting a car**, it's best to wait until the day you leave the city to pick it up; see p.241 for car rental companies. When depositing a rental car at the airport at the end of your stay, follow the signs to the special rental car park and allow plenty of time for the paperwork. If you're driving your own car, the **Automobile Clube de Portugal** (☎219 429 103, ⓦwww.acp.pt) is a useful contact as it has a reciprocal agreement with motoring organizations in other EU countries.

Information and
maps

The **Portuguese Tourist Office** is in Praça dos Restauradores in the Palácio da Foz (Map 3, A9; daily 9am–8pm; ☎213 463 314, ⓦwww.portugalinsite.pt), and is useful for general information. However, far more helpful is the **Lisbon Welcome Centre** at Rua do Arsenal 15, by Praça do Comércio, near the riverfront (Map 3, J6; daily 9am–8pm; ☎210 312 700, ⓦww.atl-turismolisboa.pt), which can supply accommodation lists, bus timetables and maps.

LISBON ON THE INTERNET

Ⓦ **www.atl-turismolisboa.pt**
The Lisbon Welcome Centre's comprehensive site, with details (in English) of hotels, restaurants, news and events.

Ⓦ **www.ccb.pt** The Cultural Centre of Belém's official site, highlighting its full programme of forthcoming concerts, exhibitions and events.

Ⓦ **www.paginasamarelas.pt**
Portuguese version of the Yellow Pages, in Portuguese and English.

Ⓦ **www.parquedasnacoes.pt**
Details the main attractions, conferences and events at the Parque das Nações.

Ⓦ **www.portugalinsite.pt** The official Portuguese website, run by ICEP (Investments, Trade and Tourism of Portugal), containing information about various tourist attractions and some practical advice, most of it on the superficial side.

Ⓦ **www.portugalvirtual.pt**
Comprehensive directory of everything Portuguese from hotels to shops, tourist sites to businesses.

Ⓦ **www.portuguesesoccer .com** Independent soccer magazine in English with the latest soccer news, fixtures and gossip, reports on games and links to official club websites.

Ⓦ **www.portuguesewine.com**
A rundown of the best ports and madeiras, and reviews of the different wine-producing regions of Portugal.

There are also tourist offices at the airport and Santa Apolónia which can help you find accommodation; and a few smaller **"Ask Me" kiosks** dotted around town, like the ones in Largo Martim Moniz, on Rua Augusta, and within the Castelo de São Jorge, though these tend to be only open in the summer (usually daily 10am–2pm & 3–6pm). A free **telephone information line** dispenses basic information in English (Mon–Sat 9am–midnight, Sun 9am–8pm; ☎800 296 296).

Our colour **maps** will guide you around the city, though you might as well pick up the free maps and plans from the various tourist offices. Michelin's *Lisboa Planta Roteiro*, available in most good Lisbon bookshops, is the closest you'll find to an A-to-Z of the city.

The best **listings magazine** is *Agenda Cultural*, a free monthly produced by the town hall, which details current exhibitions and shows (in Portuguese). *Follow me Lisboa* is a watered-down English-language version produced by the local tourist office. They also publish *Lisboa Step by Step*, a quarterly magazine with articles about the area and a brief listings section. All publications are available from the tourist offices and larger hotels. For **exhibitions and concerts**, pick up a schedule of events from the reception desks at the Gulbenkian Foundation or the Cultural Centre in Belém.

For other news of forthcoming events and reviews of concerts, bars, clubs and restaurants, get hold of the Lisbon-based **newspaper** *Diário de Notícias* (ⓦ www.dn.pt), whose daily editions contain good listings, accessible with only a very sketchy knowledge of the language. The stylish *Público* (ⓦ www.publico.pt) newspaper also has fairly easy-to-read listings.

FREE LISBON

The following museums and attractions have **free admission on Sunday** (from 10am to 2pm, unless otherwise stated): Centro de Arte Moderna (all day); Igreja de Santa Engrácia; Igreja de São Roque; Mosteiro dos Jerónimos; Museu Antóniano (all day); Museu de Arqueologia; Museu de Arte Popular; Museu do Chiado; Museu da Cidade (all day); Museu dos Coches; Museu Calouste Gulbenkian (all day); Museu Militar (all day Wed); Museu Nacional de Arte Antiga; Museu Nacional do Azulejo; Museus da Teatro e Traje; Palácio da Ajuda; Palácio de Queluz (until 1pm); Torre de Belém.

City transport

Central Lisbon is compact enough to explore on foot, but don't be fooled by the apparent closeness of sights and streets as they appear on two-dimensional maps. There are some very steep hills to negotiate, especially around the castle, and in the Alfama and Bairro Alto neighbourhoods, although the city's quirky **elevadores** (funicular railways) save you the steepest climbs around the Bairro Alto and Avenida da Liberdade. Lisbon's **trams** (*electricos*) ply the narrow streets around Alfama, the Baixa and out to Estrela. They're hardly the fastest form of transport (the modern tram to Belém being the exception) but, along with the *elevadores*, they are undoubtedly the most fun way to get around. The city also has a comprehensive network of **buses**, although they often get snarled up in Lisbon's growing traffic congestion. Tram, bus and *elevador* stops are indicated by a sign marked **paragem**, which carries route details.

The most efficient way to get around, however, is on the **metro**, with stations sited close to most of the main sights. Suburban **trains** run from Rossio out to Sintra and Queluz and from Cais do Sodré to Belém, Estoril and Cascais, while **ferries** link Lisbon to Cacilhas, with bus connections to the beach resort of Caparica, south of the Rio Tejo. Otherwise, there are plenty of inexpensive **taxis**, which can be hailed or telephoned for in advance, 24 hours a day.

Trams and buses in the city are operated by the public transport company **Carris** (☎213 632 044, ⓦwww.carris.pt). You're unlikely to get much help on the phone in English, but the website carries timetable information. **Operating hours** for most forms of public transport are from around 6.30am to midnight (1am for the metro). You can just buy a ticket each time you ride, though you may find a travel pass (see below) saves you money.

TRAVEL PASSES

A one-day **Bilhete Turístico** (Tourist Ticket; €2.50) allows unlimited travel on buses, trams, the metro and *elevadores* until midnight of that day. You can also buy a three-day *bilhete turístico* (€5.50) but, confusingly, this is not valid on the metro. The **Passe Turístico** (Tourist Pass; €9.25 for four days, €13.10 for seven days) is also good value. It's valid on buses, trams, the metro and *elevadores*, and is obtainable – like the one- and three-day passes – from the kiosks next to the Elevador Santa Justa, in Praça da Figueira and inside Restauradores metro station, among other places. There's also a three-day pass on the **Cascais train line** (€5.10), which is worth considering if you are staying in the resorts of Estoril or Cascais and travelling into Lisbon.

If you're planning some intensive sightseeing, the **Cartão Lisboa** (Lisbon Card; €11 for one day, €18 for two, or €23 for three) is a good buy. The card entitles you to unlimited rides on buses, trams, *elevadores* and the metro, as well as entry to around 25 museums, including the Gulbenkian and Museu de Arte Antigua, plus discounts of between 25 and 50 percent at other main sites. It's available from all the main tourist offices, including the one in the airport.

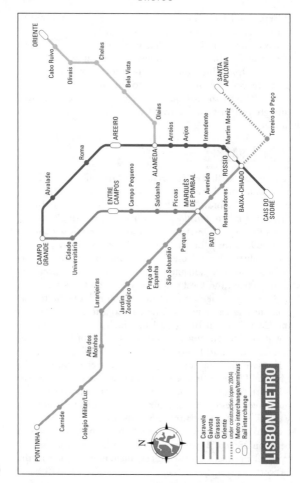

LISBON METRO

Caravela
Gaivota
Girassol
Oriente
······ under construction (open 2004)
○ Metro interchange/terminus
○ Rail interchange

N

ORIENTE
Cabo Ruivo
Olivais
Chelas
Bela Vista
SANTA APOLÓNIA
Terreiro do Paço
Olaias
AREEIRO
Arroios
Anjos
Intendente
Martim Moniz
ROSSIO
Roma
ALAMEDA
Avenida
BAIXA-CHIADO
Alvalade
ENTRE CAMPOS
Campo Pequeno
Saldanha
Picoas
MARQUÊS DE POMBAL
Restauradores
CAIS DO SODRÉ
CAMPO GRANDE
Cidade Universitária
Parque
RATO
Laranjeiras
Praça de Espanha
São Sebastião
Jardim Zoológico
Alto dos Moinhos
Colégio Militar/Luz
Carnide
PONTINHA

THE METRO

Lisbon's **metro** – the *Metropolitano* – (☎ 213 558 457, ⓦ www.metrolisboa.pt) is the most efficient way of reaching the city's outlying districts. Its four colour-coded lines provide access to many useful sights and destinations (see map opposite and information below). Hours of operation are from 6.30am to 1am, and you rarely have to wait more than five to ten minutes for a train, with peak time trains running every couple of minutes. **Tickets** cost €0.50 per journey, or €4.50 for a ten-ticket *caderneta* – sold at all stations. If you think you're going to use the metro a lot, buy a **bilhete diário** (one-day metro pass; €1.40).

USEFUL METRO STOPS

Linha da Caravela (green line)

Cais do Sodré, for the riverfront, ferries to Cacilhas and trains to Belém, Estoril and Cascais.

Baixa-Chiado, for the main shopping streets and the Elevador Santa Justa.

Rossio, for Praça da Figueira and the Baixa.

Martim Moniz, for tram connections to the Castelo de São Jorge and Alfama.

Alameda, for interchange to Linha do Oriente (red line) to Parque das Nações.

Roma, for the shops along Avda de Roma.

Campo Grande, for Sporting Lisbon football club, Museu da Cidade and Museu Rafael Bordalo Pinheiro.

Linha da Gaivota (blue line)

Santa Apolónia (from 2004), for the main Lisbon railway station.

Terreiro do Paço (from 2004), for Praça do Comércio, the Lisbon Welcome Centre, the Baixa, the riverfront and ferries to Cacilhas.

Restauradores, for the Portuguese Tourist Office, the Elevador da Glória and trains to Sintra.

Marquês de Pombal or **Parque**, for Parque Eduardo VII.

S. Sebastião or **Praça de Espanha**, for the Gulbenkian (and **Praça de Espanha** for buses to Caparica).
Jardim Zoológico, for the zoo.
Colégio Militar-Luz, for Benfica football club and Colombo Shopping Centre.

Linha do Girassol (yellow line)
Saldanha, for the main bus station.

Campo Pequeno, for the bull-ring.
Campo Grande, for Sporting Lisbon football club, Museu da Cidade and Museu Rafael Bordalo Pinheiro.

Oriente (red line)
Oriente for Parque das Nações, the Oceanarium, national bus connections and national and international train connections.

BUSES, TRAMS AND ELEVADORES

Buses (*autocarros*) run just about everywhere in the Lisbon area, and can prove useful for getting to and from outlying attractions (see "Useful bus routes", below). A couple of **open-top bus tours** run year-round, departing from Praça do Comércio; details are given on p.17.

Trams (*eléctricos*) run on five routes, serving the area around the Castelo de São Jorge and west to Belém. Ascending some of the steepest urban gradients in the world, most are worth taking for the ride alone, especially the cross-city **tram #28** (see p.52). Another picturesque route – covering some of the same route as #28 but with fewer tourists – is **#12**, which circles the castle area east of the city centre, via Alfama, Praça da Figueira and Largo Martim Moniz. Other useful routes are the air-conditioned "supertram" **#15** from Praça da Figueira to Belém (signed Algés), and **#18**, which runs from Rua da Alfândega (next to Praça do Comércio) via Praça do Comércio and Cais do Sodré to the Palácio da Ajuda. The remaining route, **#25**, runs from Rua da Alfândega to Campo

Ourique via Praça do Comércio, Cais do Sodré, Lapa and Estrela. There's also a year-round **tourist tram tour** (see p.17) in an historic vehicle – though you can follow virtually the same route for less money and in the company of locals by taking tram #28 from Largo Martim Moniz to Estrela and then hopping onto tram #25 back to Praça do Comércio

Also particular to Lisbon are the city's four **elevadores** – three funicular railways offering quick access to the heights of Bairro Alto (see p.58) and to the eastern side of Avenida da Liberdade (p.37); and one giant lift, the Elevador da Santa Justa (p.33), connecting the Baixa to the Chiado.

The same **tickets** are valid on buses, trams and *elevadores* (though not on the metro or ferries), and can be bought either individually (€0.93) or in blocks of ten (€9.30) from kiosks in Praça do Comércio, Praça da Figueira and other bus terminals. These **advance tickets** are valid for two journeys within a single travel zone or one journey across

USEFUL BUS ROUTES

#1 Cais do Sodré to Charneca via Lumiar, the Baixa, Avda da Liberdade, Picoas (for the youth hostel), Saldanha (for the bus station), Campo Pequeno and Campo Grande.

#8 Outside the airport to Largo Martim Moniz via Avda Almirante Reis and the Baixa.

#27 Marquês de Pombal to Belém via Rato, Estrela, Lapa and Alcântara.

#37 Praça da Figueira to Castelo de São Jorge via the Sé and Alfama.

#44/45 Outside the airport to Cais do Sodré via Entrecampos, Saldanha, Marquês de Pombal, Avda da Liberdade and the Baixa.

#46 Santa Apolónia station to near Palácio dos Marquêses de Fronteira via Praça do Comércio, the Baixa, Avda da Liberdade, Praça Marquês de Pombal and the Fundação Gulbenkian.

two travel zones (such as from the city centre to Belém). Tickets are validated by punching them into the machine next to the driver when you board.

Individual tickets for buses, trams and *elevadores* can also be **bought on board** (the modern tram #15 has an automatic ticket machine and does not issue change). These cost €0.90, but are only valid for one journey within a single travel zone – thus costing more than those bought in advance. Advance-purchase travel passes (see "Travel passes" above) can save you even more money.

FERRIES

Ferries cross the Rio Tejo from various departure points and are worth taking for the terrific views of Lisbon alone.

The traditional route for a quick trip is the service from **Praça do Comércio** (Estação Fluvial, Map 3, L4) to the fish restaurants of Cacilhas (every 15min, Mon–Fri 6.10am–9.45pm, Sat & Sun 6.15am–9.50pm, last return 9.30pm; €0.55 one-way). However, this service is currently suspended because of tunnelling work associated with the metro system. In the meantime, you'll have to use the car and passenger ferries to Cacilhas from **Cais do Sodré** (Map 2, E10; every 5–10min, daily 5.30am–2.30am; €0.55). The remaining cross-Tejo services from Praça do Comércio (Estação Fluvial) are unaffected by the metro tunnelling: namely ferry services to **Barreiro**, for train connections to the Algarve (every 20–30min, Mon–Fri 6.10am–9.45pm, Sat & Sun 6.15am–9.50pm, last return 9.30pm; €1); and to the industrial port of **Montijo** (every 30min, Mon–Fri 6.30am–11.30pm, Sat 7am–10pm, Sun 9.45am–10pm; €1.50).

Ferries run on from Cacilhas to **Parque das Nações** (Mon–Fri 6 daily, Sat & Sun 8 daily; €1.10), while from **Belém** (Map 7, I6) there are services to the fishing villages of Porto Brandão and Trafaria (every 30min–1hr, Mon–Sat 6.30am–11.30pm, Sun 7.30am–11.30pm; €0.55), from where you can catch buses to the beaches at Caparica.

SIGHTSEEING TOURS

Guided walks The Portuguese Tourist Office in Palácio Foz, Praça dos Restauradores, is the starting point for a privately run three-hour guided walk through the districts of Chiado and Bairro Alto. Additional walks through "Old Lisbon" take in Alfama and the castle area, beginning from Casa dos Bicos on Praça da Ribeira. Minimum of six people required, price €13 per person; book two weeks in advance. Information on ⓣ & ⓕ 213 906 149, ⓔ jcabdo@ip.pt.

Open-top bus tour The one-hour "Circuito Tejo" (hourly 11am–4pm; €12.50) takes passengers around Lisbon's principal sights; a day-ticket allows you to get on and off whenever you want. The "Oriente Express" tour departs three times daily to Parque das Nações for the same price. Both tours depart from Praça do Comércio. Tickets can be bought on board. Information from Carris ⓣ 213 632 021.

River cruises Two-and-a-half-hour cruises along the Tejo depart from Praça do Comércio's Estação Fluvial (daily at 11am & 3pm), stopping at Parque das Nações (11.45am and 3.45pm, though only when tides permit) and Belém (1pm and 5pm). The price (€15) includes a drink and commentary, and tickets are valid for returns on the later boats. Reservations advised on ⓣ 218 820 348.

Tourist tram tour The "Circuito Colinas" (Hills Tour) takes passengers on a ninety-minute ride in an early twentieth-century tram, departing from Praça do Comércio and touring around Alfama, Chiado and São Bento. March to October, departures hourly from 9am to 6pm; November to February, departures at 11am, 1.30pm & 3.30pm; price €15. Information on ⓣ 966 298 558.

TAXIS

Lisbon's cream – or the older black-and-green – **taxis** are inexpensive for journeys within the city limits. There's a minimum charge of €1.80 and an average ride will run to around €5. Fares are higher from 10pm to 6am, at weekends and on public holidays, when the minimum charge is €2.10. All taxis have meters, which should be switched on, and tips are not expected; a green light means the cab is occupied. Outside the rush hour taxis can be flagged down quite easily in the street or, alternatively, head for one of the ranks in various central spots, including outside the train stations; at Rossio and Praça da Figueira (Map 3, D6); at the southern end of Avenida da Liberdade (Map 8, G6); and at Praça do Comércio's Estação Fluvial (Map 3, L3). You can expect to have to queue during morning and evening rush hours. At night it's usually best to get a restaurant or bar to phone a taxi for you, or call yourself (which attracts an extra charge of €0.80): try Rádio Taxis ☏218 119 000, Autocoope ☏217 932 756 or Teletáxi ☏218 111 100.

Costs, money and banks

Lisbon remains one of the cheapest capital cities in Europe. Accommodation, public transport, food and drink are all better value than in northern Europe, and the only things that are markedly more expensive are telephone calls and petrol. On average, excluding your hotel bill, you can expect to spend from around €30–40 per day in Lisbon, which is enough for all local transport costs, visiting a sight or two, three square meals and a night out; for around €50–60 per day you could be eating in the best restaurants and taking taxis everywhere.

Portugal's currency is the **euro** (€), with notes issued in **denominations** of 5, 10, 20, 50, 100, 200 and 500 euros, and coins in denominations of 1, 2, 5, 10, 20 and 50 cents, and 1 and 2 euros. The **exchange rate** fluctuates around €1.6 to £1 or €1.10 to $1.

Usual **bank opening hours** are Monday to Friday 8.30am to 3pm. Most main branches are located in the Baixa and feature automatic exchange machines for various currencies and denominations. Changing cash in banks is easy too, and shouldn't attract more than €3 commission, though not all banks offer an exchange service. As ever, it's unwise to carry all your money as cash, so consider the alternatives.

By far the easiest way to get money in Portugal is to use your debit or credit card to withdraw cash from any of the large number of ATM cash machines, called **Multibanco**. You'll find them all over Lisbon – including on arrival at the airport – and you can withdraw up to €200 per day. English-language instruction options are usually available. All major **credit cards** are also accepted for payment in most hotels and restaurants.

BUDGET LISBON

Lisbon is officially the EU's least expensive capital city, but with a little planning you can save even more money.

• When eating, look for the *prato do dia* (daily special) or the *ementa turística* (set meal) - these are usually the cheapest options, especially at lunchtime.

• *Um jarro com água* (a jug of tap water) is cheaper than bottled water – and perfectly OK to drink.

• In a café or bar, drinks are often cheaper when you stand at the bar, while esplanade service adds further to the bill.

• Stick to national brands of beer, wines and spirits (ask for *uma cerveja nacional* if you want a Portuguese beer).

• Buy a travel pass or individual public transport tickets in advance – both are much cheaper than buying tickets on board.

• Use telephone kiosks in post offices and phone offices for international calls.

• See p.9 for days when Lisbon's main sights and attractions have free entry.

• Most of Lisbon's sights give discounts to holders of European youth/under-26 cards and to senior citizen cardholders.

It's probably worth taking a supply of **travellers' cheques** in case your plastic is lost, stolen or swallowed by an ATM. However, banks charge an outrageous commission for changing them (upwards of €13 per transaction in some cases), though more reasonable fees are charged in **caixas** – savings banks or building societies – and exchange bureaux, like *Novacâmbios* (branches at Rua Augusta 283; Map 3, E6; daily 9am–9pm; and Rossio 42; Map 3, D7; daily 8.30am–9pm). Larger hotels are also sometimes willing to change travellers' cheques at low commission.

Communications

You'll have no trouble keeping in touch while in Lisbon. Stamps are widely sold, public telephones and telephone offices are plentiful, and there is a growing number of internet cafés where you can check your email.

MAIL

The Portuguese postal service is reasonably efficient. Letters or cards take three or four days to arrive at destinations in

Europe, a little longer to the US. The *Correio Azul* system guarantees European delivery in two or three days and to the US in no more than six days, but, naturally, you pay for it – €1.80 for a letter to Europe compared to the standard €0.55.

Post offices (*correios*) are normally open Monday to Friday 8.30am to 6.30pm. The main Lisbon office is at Praça dos Restauradores 58 (Map 3, A8; Mon–Fri 8am–10pm, Sat & Sun 9am–6pm ☎213 238 971). This also has a poste restante service; take your passport and go to the counter marked *encomendas*. There's also a 24-hour post office at the airport. **Stamps** (*selos*) are sold at post offices and anywhere that has the sign of a red horse on a white circle over a green background and the legend "Correio de Portugal – Selos". To send a postcard to Europe costs €0.55, to the rest of the world €0.62.

TELEPHONES

All calls, whether local or international, are most easily made using card-operated **public telephones** called *credifones*, which you'll find all over Lisbon. Cards cost either €3, €6 or €9, and are available from post offices and the larger newsagents, tobacconists and street kiosks. Using these cards is far cheaper than making calls from hotels, whose telephone services can be extortionately priced.

You'll also find pay phones in bars and cafés, usually indicated by the sign of a red horse on a white circle over a green background and the legend "Correio de Portugal – Telefone". The minimum charge is €0.20 for a local call, €0.30 for an international call and €0.80 for calls to a mobile.

If you need quieter surroundings you'd be better off in the **telephone office** (Mon–Fri 8am–10pm, Sat & Sun 9am–6pm) next to the main post office in Praça dos Restauradores (see "Mail" above). There's a second office on the northwest corner of Rossio at no. 65 (Map 3, C7;

daily 8am–11pm). Simply tell the clerk where you want to phone, go to the cabin indicated and pay for your call afterwards. The cheap rate for international and national calls is between 9pm and 9am Monday to Friday, and all day weekends and holidays.

Most European-subscribed **mobile phones** will work in Lisbon, though if you are planning to take your phone with you, it is worth checking with your phone provider whether you need to get international access switched on and what the call charges will be: you are likely to be charged extra for incoming and outgoing calls when abroad. You may also have to ask your provider for a new access code if you want to retrieve voice messages while you're away. Those with a non-European subscribed mobile phone should check with their provider to see if it will work in Portugal.

TELEPHONE CODES

To phone Lisbon from abroad
Dial 00 + 351 (country code) + nine-digit number

To phone abroad from Lisbon
Dial 00 + country code (UK, 44; US/Canada, 1) + area code (minus initial zero) + number

EMAIL

There are lots of **internet points and cyber-cafés** where you can browse the web and send or receive email. Most places charge around €3–4 per hour for internet use.

Useful options in each main neighbourhood include: *Ask Me Lisboa*, above the Lisbon Welcome Centre in Praça do Comércio, Baixa (Map 3, J6; daily 9am–8pm; ☎210 312 815); *Web Café*, Rua do Diário de Notícias 16, Bairro Alto (Map 5, E4; daily 4pm–2am, ☎213 421 181); *Cyberica*, Rua Duques de Bragança 7, Chiado (Map 5, E7; Mon–Thurs

9am–midnight, Fri 9am–2am, Sat 7pm–2am; ☎213 421 707); and in the Forum Picoas building, Avda Fontes Pereira de Melo 38, by metro Picoas (Map 9, F7; Mon–Fri 9am–7pm, ☎213 142 527).

Crime and personal safety

Although Lisbon is one of the safer European capitals, you should take care in certain districts after dark, including Alfama, the top of Avenida da Liberdade and in Parque Eduardo VII. If you are robbed, whatever you do, don't resist. Hand over your valuables and run. Watch out also for pickpockets on public transport, something for which Lisbon is developing a bit of a reputation. On crowded trams and metro trains in particular, keep wallets and purses out of back pockets, hold handbags in front of you and take day-packs off your back. It's always best to take out only the cash you'll need for that day and use hotel safes where available.

If you are robbed, go to the **tourist police station** in the Foz Cultura building in Palácio Foz, Praça dos Restauradores (Map 3, A9; daily 24 hours; ☎213 421 634) primarily to file a report, which your insurance company will require before they'll pay out for any claims made on your policy.

Portugal has recently decriminalized the use of soft **drugs** (and even heroin), although drug-pushing remains a crime. You may well be approached by dope peddlers in the Baixa area, though it would be a mistake to think Lisbon is a liberal haven for drug users. Portugal remains one of the major entry ports for drugs into Europe and the liberalization measures were taken in an attempt to persuade the growing number of addicts to seek treatment rather than fear prosecution. Any blatant use of drugs is unlikely to go down well in any establishment.

THE GUIDE

2	The Baixa, Chiado and Cais do Sodré	29
3	Alfama and around	43
4	The Bairro Alto	58
5	West to Alcântara	65
6	Belém	76
7	Avenida da Liberdade to the Gulbenkian	87
8	Outer Lisbon	100
9	Parque das Nações	105

THE GUIDE

The Baixa, Chiado and Cais do Sodré

Early eighteenth-century prints show a Lisbon of tremendous opulence and mystique, its skyline characterized by towers, palaces and convents. Then, in November 1755, the greater part of the city was devastated by what came to be known as the Great Earthquake. Given orders following the disaster to "Bury the dead, feed the living and close the ports", the king's minister, the Marquês de Pombal, first restored order, then embarked on a complete rebuilding of the heart of the city on the plan of a Neoclassical grid, an austerely impressive example of eighteenth-century town-planning.

This central area, the **Baixa**, adheres to Pombal's ideals of simplicity and economy. Individual streets were assigned to particular crafts and trades, and the whole enterprise shaped around public buildings and squares. Only **Rossio**, the city's main square since medieval times, remains in its original place, slightly off-centre in a symmetrical design that runs between it and the adjacent **Praça da Figueira** and **Largo Martim Moniz** at its northern end, and the arcaded **Praça do Comércio** at its southern.

West of here is the affluent **Chiado** district, housing some of Lisbon's most famous cafés and designer boutiques. By contrast, the streets around **Cais do Sodré** station, south of Chiado, retain their earthy origins in a bustling commercial district epitomized by the **Mercado da Ribeira**, one of Lisbon's most colourful markets.

The area covered by this chapter is shown in detail on colour maps 3 and 5.

THE GREAT EARTHQUAKE

The Great Earthquake – which was felt as far away as Scotland and Jamaica – struck Lisbon at 9.30am on November 1, 1755, All Saints' Day, when most of the city's population was at Mass. Within the space of ten minutes there had been three major tremors. Fires – spread by the candles of a hundred church altars – raged throughout the capital, and a vast tidal wave swept the seafront, where refugees had sought shelter. In all, 40,000 of a population of 270,000 died. The destruction of the city shocked Europe, with Voltaire, who included an account of it in his novel *Candide*, leading an intense debate with Rousseau on the operation of providence. For Portugal, and for the capital, it was a disaster that in retrospect seemed to seal an age and marked the end of Lisbon's role as arguably the most active port in Europe. Many people feel that it is only a matter of time before a quake of similar magnitude strikes Lisbon again – a soothsayer's recent prediction that an earthquake was imminent virtually emptied the city for a weekend.

THE BAIXA

The **Baixa** (pronounced *bye-sha*) houses many of the country's government departments, banks and business offices, as well as some of its most interesting shops. As Europe's first great example of Neoclassical urban planning, it remains an imposing quarter of rod-straight streets, some streaming with traffic, although an increasing number – concentrated around the broad Rua Augusta – have been cobbled underfoot and turned over to pedestrians, street performers and pavement artists. It's where tourists new to Lisbon find their feet and is the area you're most likely to be offered a shoe shine, lottery ticket, dodgy watch or "hasheesh".

For listings of the Baixa's best hotels and restaurants, see p.118 and p.138.

Praça do Comércio

Map 3, J5–K6.

At the southern end of the Baixa, on the waterfront, the **Praça do Comércio** represents the climax of Pombal's design, surrounded by classical buildings – once a royal palace, now government offices – and centred on an exuberant bronze equestrian statue of Dom José, monarch during the earthquake and the capital's rebuilding. Two of Portugal's last royals came to a sticky end in the square: in 1908, King Carlos I and his eldest son were shot dead here, clearing the way for the declaration of the Republic two years later.

Praça do Comércio's riverfront provides a natural focus for the area. In the hour or two before sunset, people linger in the golden light to watch the orange ferries ply between the Estação Fluvial and Cacilhas on the opposite side of the Tejo, while the square is one of the main venues for the city's New Year's Eve festivities, when there's a midnight firework display.

On the square's western side, the **Lisbon Welcome Centre** (Map 3, J6; daily 9am–8pm) houses a tourist office, café, internet centre, shops, restaurant and exhibition hall, all buried in a series of rooms between the square and neighbouring Rua do Arsenal, where there is another entrance. On the opposite side of the square, under the arcades, the old-world café-restaurant **Martinho da Arcada** – one of the haunts of Portugal's greatest twentieth-century poet, Fernando Pessoa – makes a fine coffee or lunch stop. Two blocks east, along Rua da Alfândega, you'll encounter the church of **Conceição Velha** (Map 3, J3; Mon–Fri 8am–5pm, Sat 8am–1pm, Sun 10am–1pm; free), severely damaged by the earthquake but still in possession of its flamboyant fifteenth-century Manueline doorway, an early example of the brilliant style that later emerged at Belém.

For more on Fernando Pessoa, see p.68.

Just to the northwest of the praça lies a smaller square, the attractive **Praça do Município** (Map 3, J7), site of the Neoclassical nineteenth-century Câmara Municipal, or **City Hall**, where the Portuguese Republic was declared in 1910. Flatteringly described by Pessoa as "one of the finest buildings in the city", it houses Pombal's plans for rebuilding Lisbon after the earthquake (sadly not on view to the public). From here, it's a short walk west to Cais do Sodré, down **Rua do Arsenal**, which is packed with pungent shops selling dried cod and grocers selling cheap wines, port and brandies.

North from Praça do Comércio

The largely pedestrianized route north from Praça do Comércio along Rua Augusta is marked at its southern end by a huge arch, the **Arco da Rua Augusta** (Map 3, J5). It's adorned with statues of historical figures, including the Marquês de Pombal and Vasco da Gama, and is fronted by a bronze statue dedicated to Fernando Pessoa – his head a book – by Belgian artist Jean-Michel Folon. The lower town north of here has always been the core of Lisbon: building work on the BCP bank in Rua dos Correeiros revealed the remains of a Roman fish-preserving industry, a fifth-century Christian burial place and Moorish ceramics. These varied exhibits can be seen in the tiny **Núcleo Arqueológico** at Rua dos Correeiros 9 (Map 3, H5; Thurs 3–5pm, Sat 10am–noon & 3–5pm; free; advance bookings required ☏213 211 700), with most viewed through glass floors, providing a fascinating insight into the lives of Lisbon's early inhabitants.

Pombal intended many of the streets in the Baixa grid to take their names from the crafts and businesses carried out there, like Rua da Prata (Silversmiths' Street), Rua dos Sapateiros (Cobblers' Street), Rua do Ouro (Goldsmiths' Street, now better known as Rua Aurea) and Rua do Comércio (Commercial Street). Modern businesses have interrupted these cosy divisions, though there are still some traditional shops in the Baixa, like those along the central section of Rua da Conceição selling beads and sequins. Their tiled Art Deco shop-fronts are a visual delight, as are the surviving mosaic-embellished squares and elaborately decorated *pastelarias* (pastry shops). The best streets to explore are the pedestrianized ones running south to north – Rua Augusta, Rua dos Correeiros and Rua dos Douradores (where Pessoa set his novel *The Book of Disquiet*) – and the smaller Rua de Santa Justa, Rua da Assunção, Rua da Vitória and Rua de São Nicolau, which run east to west.

At the western end of Rua de Santa Justa, it's hard to avoid Raul Mésnier's **Elevador de Santa Justa** (Map 3, E7; May–Sept Mon–Fri 8.30am–10.30pm, Sat & Sun

THE BAIXA ●

9am–10.30pm; Oct–April daily 9am–7pm), one of the city's most extraordinary and eccentric structures. Built in 1902 by a disciple of Eiffel, its giant lift whisks you 32m up the innards of a latticework metal tower before depositing you on a platform high above the Baixa, where there's a rooftop **café** with great views over the city. Note that there's currently no exit from the top of the *elevador* to the Largo do Carmo (see p.61).

Rossio

Map 3, C7–D6.

Until the beginning of the twentieth century, Praça Dom Pedro IV, popularly known as **Rossio**, sat at the edge of the city limits; beyond were the vineyards of Palhavã and the wine estates of Campo Pequeno and Campo Grande. During the nineteenth century Rossio's plethora of cafés attracted Lisbon's painters and writers and, though many of the artists' haunts were converted to banks in the 1970s, it remains very much the focus of the city's daytime life. Despite the traffic, the outdoor seats of the square's cafés are popular vantage points for taking in the sparkling Baroque fountains and mosaic-cobbled pavements.

For reviews of the best Baixa cafés, see p.168.

The square's single concession to grandeur is the **Teatro Nacional de Dona Maria II** (Map 3, B7), built along its north side in the 1840s, though heavily restored after a fire in 1964. A statue of Gil Vicente, Portugal's sixteenth-century equivalent of Shakespeare, sits atop the facade, while inside is a good café (see p.170). On this site, prior to the earthquake, stood the Inquisitional Palace, in front of which public hangings and *autos-da-fé* (ritual burnings of heretics) took place.

The nineteenth-century statue topping the central column of Rossio is officially of Dom Pedro IV – after whom the square is named – though in fact it was cast originally as Emperor Maximilian of Mexico. The statue just happened to be in Lisbon en route from France to Mexico when news came through of Maximilian's assassination in 1867, and it was decided that since Maximilian would have no further use for it, it would do just as well for Dom Pedro. The statue is now the focus of a weekly **flower market** (Sat 7am–2pm). On the northwestern side of the square, there's a horseshoe-shaped entrance to **Rossio station**, a mock-Manueline complex with the train platforms an improbable escalator-ride above the street-level entrances.

The **Igreja de São Domingos** (Map 3, C6; daily 8am–7pm; free), immediately to the east of Rossio, stands on the site of the thirteenth-century Convento de São Domingos, where the Inquisition read out its sentences – one terrible pronouncement in 1506 instigated the massacre of much of the city's Jewish population. The convent was destroyed in the earthquake of 1755, though its portal was reconstructed soon after as part of the current Dominican church, which was built on the same spot. For over a century it was the venue for royal marriages and christenings, though it lost this role after the declaration of the Republic and was then gutted by a fire in the 1950s. It was reopened in 1997 after partial restoration replaced the seats and some internal statues; the rest of the cavernous interior and the scarred pillars remain powerfully atmospheric.

Largo de São Domingos outside the church, is a popular meeting place: the local African population hangs out on the street corner; commuters get their shoes cleaned at the rank of small metal booths; while everyone from businessmen to Lisbon's lowlife frequent the various *ginginha* (cherry brandy) bars (see p.178).

Praça da Figueira and Largo Martim Moniz

Heading south from São Domingos or east from Rossio, it is a short walk into **Praça da Figueira** (Map 3, D5), another historic square that has recently been spruced up. It is much quieter than Rossio, despite being one of the city's main bus and tram stops. Its western side is lined with shops and cafés, including the famous **Café Suiça**, whose outdoor seats are particularly appealing, with views of the green slopes of the Castelo de São Jorge above. On the south side, meanwhile, **Confeitaria Nacional** is one of the city's oldest cafés, opened in 1829.

From the northeastern corner of Praça da Figueira, Rua da Palma leads through to **Largo Martim Moniz** (Map 3, B3–A3), once the gateway to the medieval city and named after a Christian knight who died trying to keep the gates open during a crusade against the occupying Moors. Nowadays the square is a sparse concrete expanse, not much improved by its water features and odd modernist craft kiosks.

From Largo Martim Moniz, it's possible to reach the Mouraria district and the eastern entrance to the Castelo de São Jorge using tram #12.

Praça dos Restauradores

Map 3, A8.

The northern end of the Baixa, beyond Rossio, broadens out into the long expanse of the **Praça dos Restauradores**, which takes its name (Square of the Restorers) from the renewal of independence from Spain in 1640. The square is dominated by the pink **Palácio de Foz** (Map 3,

A9), on the western side, which housed the Ministry of Propaganda under the Salazar regime but is now home to the Portuguese Tourist Office and tourist police station. To the north lies the **Elevador da Glória** (Map 3, A9), offering access to the Bairro Alto (see p.58); south sits the superb Art Deco frontage of the old **Eden** cinema, now an apartment-hotel (see p.131).

Parallel to the square, one block to the east, is **Rua das Portas de Santo Antão** (Map 3, A7–B6), a pedestrianized drag well known for its seafood restaurants. Despite the tourist trappings – this is the only place in town you're likely to get waiters trying to smooth-talk you into their premises – the street does have some fine local haunts and, provided you choose carefully, it is worth eating here at least once (see p.141 for restaurant reviews). The street is also home to several theatres and the domed **Coliseu dos Recreios**: opened in 1890 as a circus, it's now one of Lisbon's main concert venues. Rua das Portas de Santo Antão ends at the tiny **Largo da Anunciada** (Map 8, G6), where another of the city's classic *elevadores*, **Elevador do Lavra**, begins its ascent; see p.89 for details of a walk that embraces this route.

CHIADO

On the west side of the Baixa, stretching up the hillside towards the Bairro Alto, lies the area known as **Chiado** (pronounced *she-ar-doo*) – it's said that the district was named after the sixteenth-century poet António Ribeiro, who was known as "O Chiado" (literally "squeaking" or "hissing"). The area was greatly damaged by a fire in August 1988, which destroyed all but the facade of the Grandella department store and many old shops in Rua do Crucifixo. After years of dallying, the authorities have restored most of the area's gutted buildings under the direc-

CHIADO

tion of eminent Portuguese architect Álvaro Siza Vieira, in keeping with Chiado's traditions; soaring marble facades consciously mimic those destroyed in the fire.

At the top end of Rua Garrett, you can take tram #28 to São Bento and Estrela (see p.67) or head up Rua Nova da Trindade to the Bairro Alto (see p.58).

Despite the fire damage, Chiado remains one of the city's most affluent quarters. From Rossio, the easiest approach is along **Rua do Carmo** (Map 3, F7), virtually rebuilt from scratch after the 1988 fire and home to some of the area's best shops, including the plush **Armazéns do Chiado** shopping complex. Rua do Carmo also offers an alternative route to the Elevador de Santa Justa (see p.33). At the southern end of Rua do Carmo, you turn into **Rua Garrett** (Map 3, F8–F9), boasting more fashionable shops and several old café-tearooms, of which **A Brasileira**, at no. 120, is the most famous, having been frequented by generations of Lisbon's literary and intellectual leaders – Fernando Pessoa and novelist Eça de Queiroz among them. While on Rua Garrett, take a stroll past **Igreja dos Mártires** (Map 3, G9; daily 8am–7pm; free), built on the site of a burial ground created for English Crusaders killed during the siege of Lisbon. Fernando Pessoa was baptized here in 1888.

Just west of the Igreja dos Mártires, Rua Serpa Pinto veers steeply south and downhill, past Lisbon's main opera house, the **Teatro Nacional de São Carlos** (Map 3, H9). Heavily influenced by the great Italian opera houses, it was built shortly after the original Lisbon opera house on Praça do Comércio was destroyed in the Great Earthquake. There's a sumptuous Rococo interior, but you can only see it during performances.

DEVELOPMENT AND DESTRUCTION

In recent years Lisbon has experienced some of the most radical **redevelopment** since the Marquês de Pombal rebuilt the shattered capital after the 1755 earthquake. This building boom began in the wake of Portugal's joining the European Community (now the European Union) in 1986, when grants and foreign investment poured into the capital. Work continued during the lead-up to Expo 98, which saw chunks of old Lisbon disappearing under new roads and train lines, while tramlines were removed to provide space for faster roads. Metro extensions and the digging of a series of underground car parks have continued to disrupt the city centre – one of the locals' biggest complaints is about *obras* (building works).

Ironically, it is beyond Pombal's statue at Praça Marquês de Pombal that most of the redevelopment work is being done, with some fairly grim housing developments taking shape out in the newer suburbs. Most of these are a result of a long-standing chronic housing problem that has made new property in Lisbon among the most expensive in Europe.

Fortunately, most of Lisbon's historic quarters have experienced renovation rather than redevelopment. The facades of older buildings are protected by law – though developers often tack modern structures onto them, such as the extraordinary Heron Castillo building at Rua Braacamp 40, near Rato. Meanwhile, EU funding continues to help upgrade many historic buildings, particularly in Lisbon's oldest quarters, including **Alfama** (many of whose houses previously had no bathrooms) and the **Bairro Alto**, while much of the **Tejo river-front** has been transformed from industrial wasteland to a thriving area of cafés and clubs. The most obvious sign of renovation is in the streets of **Chiado**, burned out in the 1988 fire but now beautifully restored to their original design.

CHIADO

●

Museu do Chiado

Map 3, H9. Tues 2–6pm, Wed–Sun 10am–6pm; €3, free on Sun until 2pm. Metro Baixa–Chiado, or bus #58 or #100 from Cais do Sodré.

Opposite the Teatro Nacional de São Carlos on Rua Serpa Pinto, the **Museu do Chiado** is Lisbon's contemporary art museum. Opened in 1994 and constructed around a nine-teenth-century biscuit factory, it's a stylish building with a pleasant courtyard café and rooftop terrace. Temporary art exhibitions often take up some of the gallery space, while the museum displays a permanent collection of works by some of Portugal's most influential artists since the nine-teenth century. Highlights include António Costa Pinheiro's portrait of Fernando Pessoa and a beautiful sculpture, *A Viúva* (The Widow), by António Teixeira Lopes. There are also some evocative early twentieth-century Lisbon scenes by water-colourist Carlos Botelho, and you should keep an eye out for the wonderful Art Deco decorative panels by José de Almada Negreiros, recovered from the long-gone São Carlos cinema. There is also a small collection of French sculpture, including Rodin's *The Bronze Age*.

CAIS DO SODRÉ

Ten minutes' walk west of the Baixa along the riverfront, or a steep walk down Rua do Alecrim from Chiado, is **Cais do Sodré** (pronounced *kaiysh doo sodray*) metro and station (Map 5, B8), from where trains run out to Estoril and Cascais, and car-ferries cross to Cacilhas. It's not the most elegant of areas, though its waterfront warehouses are slowly being converted into upmarket cafés and restaurants and by day, in particular, a stroll along its atmospheric riverfront is very enjoyable. Outside the station look out for the *varinas* – colourfully dressed fishwives from Cape Verde – with giant baskets of fish on their heads, who usually appear from dawn to around midday, scuttling off when the police arrive.

Just north of Cais do Sodré, beyond the domed Mercado da Ribeira (see below), is the bottom end of the precipitous **Elevador da Bica** (Map 5, A6–C4; Mon–Sat 7am–10.45pm, Sun 9am–10.45pm), one of the city's most atmospheric funicular railways; the entrance is tucked into an arch on Rua de São Paulo. Built in 1892 – and originally powered by water counterweights, but now electrically operated – the *elevador* leads up towards the Bairro Alto, via a steep residential street with drying laundry usually draped from every window. Get off at the top, take a left and then the second left down Rua M. Saldanha and you'll reach the **Miradouro de Santa Catarina** (Map 5, B4) from where there are spectacular views back over the city. At the viewpoint, in the shadow of the statue of the Adomastor – a mythical beast from Luís de Camões's *Lusiads* – a mixture of oddballs and guitar-strumming New Age hippies often collects around the handy drinks kiosk, which has a few outdoor tables. Back at the top of the *elevador*, it's a short walk up Rua da Rosa to the Bairro Alto or you can hop on tram #28 to Alfama.

Mercado da Ribeira

Map 5, A7–B7. Market Mon–Sat 6am–2pm; flower market Mon–Sat 3pm–7pm; Loja de Artesanato daily 10am–10pm; food stalls daily 10am–11pm; live music Fri–Sat 10pm–1am. Metro Cais do Sodré or tram #15 from Praça da Figueira.

Just north of Cais do Sodré station, take the time to look inside Lisbon's best market, the **Mercado da Ribeira**, built originally on the site of an old fort at the end of the nineteenth century, though the current structure dates only from 1930. Downstairs is an impressive array of food – fish of all shapes and sizes, as well as some gruesome slabs of flesh and innards – along with flowers, spices, and fruit and vegetable displays. In the past it was traditional for Lisboetas to enjoy a *cacau da Ribeira* (cocoa) here after a night out on the town, and the local council recently decided to renovate the market in an attempt to restore this social aspect to the building. The upper level is now a centre for regional arts and gastronomy and, although squarely aimed at tourists, the **Loja de Artesanato** (craft shop), specializing in art and crafts from Lisbon and the Tejo valley, at least keeps traditional crafts alive. There are also various food stalls on this level selling produce from the Portuguese regions, including superb fresh breads, cheeses, wines and *petiscos* (snacks); and there's a restaurant specializing in regional food. A central stage hosts live music at weekends, ranging from jazz to folk.

Alfama and around

The **Castelo de São Jorge** – high on a hill to the east of the Baixa – was originally founded by the Moors and remodelled by the Christians after their reconquest of the city in 1147. During the Middle Ages it became the hub of a walled city that spread downhill as far as the river, and the ancient districts of **Alfama**, **Mouraria** and **Santa Cruz** are still the oldest and most interesting areas of Lisbon. These neighbourhoods retain a quiet, village-like quality, particularly Alfama, whose maze-like streets remain largely devoid of traffic and free of tourist boutiques. Fado, the mournful Portuguese music style, emerged from the Alfama alleys and the **Casa do Fado** museum has found a fitting place here.

To the south of the castle are the city's cathedral, the **Sé**, and a handful of historic sights and museums, including the applied-art collections in the **Museu Escola de Artes Decorativas**. To the east, around the **Campo de Santa Clara**, are the churches of **São Vicente de Fora** and **Santa Engrácia**, best visited on a Tuesday or Saturday to coincide with the chaotic Feira da Ladra flea market. On the Tejo riverside, the **Doca do Jardim do Tobaco** is a dockside development of restaurants and bars that's rapidly becoming a favoured night out. Finally, east along the river, museum buffs can indulge themselves in three very different collections: weapons and uniforms in the **Museu da Militar** (Military Museum); historical machinery in the **Museu da Água** (Water Museum); and – best of all – the beautiful decorated tiles of the **Museu do Azulejo**.

- -

The area covered by this chapter is shown in detail on colour map 4.

- -

THE SÉ AND AROUND

Map 4, B8. Cathedral: daily 8.30am–6pm; free. Cloisters: Mon & Sun 9am–5pm, Tues–Sat 9am–7pm; €0.50. Sacristy: same hours as cloisters; €2.50. Tram #28 from Rua da Conceição in the Baixa.

Lisbon's cathedral – the **Sé** – stands solidly on a hill overlooking the Baixa. Founded in 1150 to commemorate the city's reconquest from the Moors (and occupying the site of the principal mosque of Moorish Lishbuna), it's a Romanesque structure with a suitably fortress-like appearance, yet is extraordinarily restrained in both size and decoration. The great rose window and twin towers form a simple and effective facade, although there's nothing very exciting inside: the building was once splendidly embellished on the orders of Dom João V, but his Rococo whims were swept away by the 1755 earthquake and subsequent restorers. All that remains is a group of Gothic tombs behind the high altar and the decaying thirteenth-century **cloister**.

You need to buy a ticket for admission to the cloister and the Baroque **sacristy**. The latter holds a small museum of treasures including the relics of Saint Vincent, brought to Lisbon in 1173 by Afonso Henriques in a boat that, according to legend, was piloted by ravens. Ravens were kept in the cloisters for centuries, but the tradition halted when the last one died in 1978. To this day, however, the birds remain one of the city's symbols.

Opposite the Sé, on Largo da Sé, is the church of **Santo António** (Map 4, B8; daily 9am–7.30pm; free), said to have been built on the spot where the city's most popular saint was born. If you want to find out more about Saint Anthony of Padua, as he is more commonly known, the neighbouring **museum** (Tues–Sat 10am–1pm & 2–6pm; €1) chronicles the saint's life, including his enviable skill at fixing marriages. During the Festa de Santo António in June, the council sponsors free televised weddings here, in an attempt to keep young Lisboetas living in the area.

Two hundred or so metres south of the Sé, on Rua dos Bacalhoeiros, stands the curious **Casa dos Bicos** (Map 4, B9; Mon–Fri 9.30am–5.30pm; free), the "house of points", whose walls – set with diamond-shaped stones – offer an image of the richness of pre-1755 Lisbon. It was built in 1523 for the son of the Viceroy of India, though only the facade of the original building survived the earthquake. It sees fairly regular use for cultural exhibitions; at other times, you can look around the remains of Roman fish-preserving tanks and parts of Lisbon's old Moorish walls (demolished in the fifteenth century), which were excavated during renovation work in the 1980s.

ALFAMA

The oldest part of Lisbon, tumbling from the walls of the castle down to the Tejo, **Alfama** was buttressed against significant damage in the 1755 earthquake by the steep, rocky mass on which it's built. Although none of its houses dates from before the Christian Reconquest, many are of Moorish design and the *kasbah*-like layout is still much as the English priest Osbern of Bawdsley described it in the twelfth century, with "steep defiles instead of ordinary streets . . . and buildings so closely packed together that,

ALFAMA

except in the merchants' quarter, hardly a street could be found more than eight foot wide".

In Moorish times, this was the grandest part of the city, but as Lisbon expanded the new Christian nobility moved out, leaving it to the local fishing community. Today, it is undergoing extensive renovation, the latest scheme being to reintroduce fado houses into the area that helped give birth to the music. Although antique shops and restaurants are also moving in, they are far from taking over – indeed the tourist office still cautions against wandering around the area alone at night. Certainly the quarter retains a largely traditional life, with cheap local cafés, the twice-weekly flea market at Campo de Santa Clara and, during June, the "Popular Saints" festivals, above all the Festa de Santo António on June 12, when makeshift tavernas appear on every corner.

From the Sé, Rua Cruzes de Sé leads into **Rua de São João da Praça** – just about the only road hereabouts wide enough for cars – which runs into the heart of Alfama. The steep alleys and passageways are known as *becos* and *travessas* rather than *ruas*. Along these streets and alleys, life continues much as it has done for years: kids playing ball in tiny squares; people buying groceries and fish from hole-in-the-wall stores; householders stringing washing across narrow defiles and stoking small outdoor charcoal grills; and elderly men idling away the hours on decrepit wooden benches. It would be futile to try to follow any set route – indeed half the fun is getting lost. At some point in your wanderings around the quarter, though, head for **Rua de São Miguel** – off which run some of the most interesting *becos* – and for the lower, parallel **Rua de São Pedro**, where *varinas* (fishwives) sell the catch of the day from tiny stalls. East of here, you can wind down to **Largo do Chafariz de Dentro**, at the bottom of the hill, once site of the area's main springs and now home to a museum dedicated to fado music.

ALFAMA

Casa do Fado e da Guitarra Portuguesa

Map 4, G7. Daily 10am–1pm & 2–5pm; €2.50. Bus #9 from Praça dos Restauradores to Doca do Jardim do Tobaco, then a short walk. Set in the renovated Recinto da Praia, a former water cistern and bathhouse on Largo do Chafariz de Dentro, the **Casa do Fado e da Guitarra Portuguesa** is an engaging museum detailing the history of fado and Portuguese guitar. It provides an excellent introduction to the music and is well worth visiting before you experience the real thing. The museum also contains a good shop for buying fado CDs and a small café.

Fado (literally "fate") is often described as a kind of working-class blues – something like a flamenco Billie Holiday sung to a Portuguese guitar and viola accompaniment. It is believed to derive from music that was popular with eighteenth-century immigrants from Portugal's colonies who first settled in Alfama. Famous singers like Maria Severa and Amália Rodrigues grew up in Alfama, which since the 1930s has hosted some of the city's most authentic fado houses.

A series of rooms in the museum contains wax models, pictures and descriptions of fado's leading characters. Press buttons to hear the different types of fado (Lisbon has its own kind, differing from that of the northern city of Coimbra), which vary from mournful to positively racy. The museum also traces the history of the Portuguese guitar, an essential element of the fado performance. It derives from the Italian "cittern", a sixteenth-century instrument that was introduced to Portugal by its English community. The guitars, which are still handmade in Lisbon and Coimbra, remained in use in Portugal long after they had lost popularity elsewhere.

See p.195 for more on fado and fado houses.

ALFAMA

47

Doca do Jardim do Tobaco

Map 4, G9. Bus #9 from Praça dos Restauradores or any bus heading east from Praça do Comércio.

On the riverfront, just southeast of Largo do Chafariz de Dentro, across the busy Avenida Infante Dom Henrique, lies the dockland development of the **Doca do Jardim do Tobaco**. Its name, "Tobacco Garden Dock", refers to its previous role as the city's main depot for storing tobacco. The old warehouses have been spruced up and, sited only a kilometre or so from the Baixa's Praça do Comércio, it's a great place for a sunset drink or an evening meal (see p.152). Facing one of the broadest sections of the Rio Tejo, the views from the outdoor tables of its restaurants attract a largely local crowd.

TOWARDS THE CASTELO DE SÃO JORGE

Returning from Alfama to the Sé, it's an uphill walk towards the Castelo de São Jorge along Rua Augusto Rosa. En route, you'll pass the sparse ruins of a **Roman theatre** (Map 4, B7), dating from 57 AD, set behind a grille just to the left at the junction of Rua de São Mamede and Rua da Saudade. The finds excavated from the site can be seen at the adjacent **Museu do Teatro Romano** (entrance on Patio de Aljube; Tues–Sun 10am–1pm & 2–6pm; free), which also has video and computer-generated exhibits telling the story of the theatre's history. Further uphill, the church of Santa Luzia marks the entry to the **Miradouro de Santa Luzia** (Map 4, D7), a spectacular viewpoint where elderly Lisboetas play cards and tourists gather their breath for the short, steep final ascent to the castle.

Just beyond here, at Largo das Portas do Sol 2, is the Espírito Santo Silva Foundation, home of the **Museu Escola de Artes Decorativas** (Map 4, D6; Tues–Sun

10am–5pm; €4.50; ⓦwww.fress.pt). Set in the seventeenth-century Azurara Palace, this fascinating museum contains some of the best examples of seventeenth- and eighteenth-century applied art in the country, taken from what was once the private collection of banker Ricardo do Espírito Santo Silva, who gave it to the nation in 1953. The rambling building has unique pieces of furniture, major collections of silver and porcelain, and paintings and textiles on five floors, set around a stairway decorated with dazzling azulejos. Highlights include a stunning sixteenth-century tapestry depicting a parade of giraffes; beautiful carpets from Arraiolos in the Alentejo district; and oriental-influenced quilts that were all the rage during the seventeenth and eighteenth centuries. Look out, too, for the lavish Chinese Kangxi cutlery case, commissioned by the Portuguese Viceroy of India in the eighteenth century.

The museum has a small café with a patio garden, while over the road, the views from the terrace-café in **Largo das Portas do Sol** are tremendous: a solitary palm rising from the stepped streets below, the twin-towered facade of Graça convent, the dome of Santa Engrácia, and the Tejo beyond.

CASTELO DE SÃO JORGE

Map 4, C4. March–Oct daily 9am–9pm; Nov–Feb daily 9am–6pm; free. Tram #28 to Miradouro de Santa Luzia then follow the signs uphill, or bus #37 from Praça do Comércio.

Reached by a confusing – but well-signposted – series of twisting roads, the **Castelo de São Jorge** is perhaps the most spectacular building in Lisbon, though as much because of its position as anything else. Beyond the small statue of Afonso Henriques, triumphant after the siege of Lisbon (see box on p.51), the entrance leads to gardens, walkways and viewpoints within the old Moorish walls.

The first Portuguese kings took up residence in the Alcáçova, the old Muslim palace within the castle, although by the time of Manuel I they had moved to the new royal palace on Praça do Comércio. After this, the castle was used as a prison for a time and then as an army barracks until the 1920s, although the walls were partly renovated by Salazar in the 1930s and further restored for Expo 98. It's an enjoyable place in which to wander about for a couple of hours, looking down on the city from its ramparts and towers. One of these, the Tower of Ulysses, now holds a **Câmara Escura** (daily every 30min, weather permitting, 10am–1.30pm & 2.30–6.30pm, until 5.30pm from Nov–May; €2), a kind of periscope which projects sights from around the city onto a white plate with commentary in English. Unless you like being holed up in darkened chambers with up to fifteen other people, you may prefer to see the view in the open air.

Olisipónia

Map 4, B5. March–Oct daily 10am–1pm & 2–6pm, Nov–Feb daily 10am–1pm & 2–5.30pm; €3.

Of the old Moorish Alcáçova, only a much-restored shell remains. This now houses **Olisipónia** (the Roman name for the city), a multimedia history show in three underground chambers, including the one in which Vasco da Gama was once received by Dom Manuel. Portable headsets provide a 35-minute commentary on aspects of Lisbon's development presented through film, sounds and images. The presentations overlap somewhat and gloss over a few of Lisbon's less savoury chapters, such as slavery and the Inquisition, but are a useful introduction to the city. The final, 36-monitor "Quadroscope" show is the best part, offering insights into Salazar's regime and some interesting archive footage.

THE SIEGE OF LISBON

The siege of the Moorish castle and walled city of Lisbon remains an uneasy episode in the city's history. Although an important victory, which led to the Muslim surrender at Sintra and throughout the surrounding district, it was not the most Christian or glorious of Portuguese exploits. A full account survives, written by one Osbern of Bawdsley, an English priest and Crusader, and its details, despite the author's judgemental tone, direct one's sympathies to the enemy.

The attack, in the summer of 1147, came through the opportunism and skilful management of Afonso Henriques, already established as "king" at Porto, who persuaded a large force of French and British Crusaders to delay their progress to Jerusalem for more immediate goals. The Crusaders – scarcely more than pirates – came to terms and in June the siege began. Osbern records the Archbishop of Braga's demand for the Moors to return to "the land whence you came" and, more revealingly, the weary and contemptuous response of the Muslim spokesman: "How many times have you come hither with pilgrims and barbarians to drive us hence? It is not want of possessions but only ambition of the mind that drives you on." For seventeen weeks the castle and walled inner city stood firm, but in October its walls were breached and the citizens – including a Christian community coexisting with the Muslims – were forced to surrender.

The pilgrims and barbarians, flaunting the diplomacy and guarantees of Afonso Henriques, stormed into the city, cut the throat of the local bishop and sacked, pillaged and murdered Christian and Muslim alike. In 1190 a later band of English Crusaders stopped at Lisbon and, no doubt confused by the continuing presence of Moors, sacked the castle and city a second time.

CASTELO DE SÃO JORGE

Santa Cruz and Mouraria

Crammed within the castle's outer walls is the tiny medieval quarter of **Santa Cruz**, very much a village in itself, with kids playing in the streets and women chatting on doorsteps – though the area is currently undergoing substantial redevelopment, with a new hotel due for completion shortly. Leaving Santa Cruz, a tiny arch at the end of Rua do Chão da Feira leads through to Rua dos Cegos and down to Largo Rodrigues de Freitas, which marks the eastern edge of **Mouraria**, the district to which the Moors were relegated after the siege of Lisbon – hence the name. Today Mouraria is an atmospheric residential area with some of the city's best African restaurants (see p.148), especially around **Largo de São Cristóvão** (Map 3, E4), which lies on the western side of the castle, a ten-minute walk along Costa do Castelo and then Rua das Farinhas.

TRAM #28

The picture-book **tram #28** is one of Lisbon's greatest rides, though its popularity is such that at times it carries more tourists than Lisboetas and chances are you'll have to stand. With a travel pass (see p.11), you can hop on and off at no extra cost. The central section of its route runs from Rua da Conceição in the Baixa, past the Sé and up Rua Augusto Rosa, before rattling through some of Lisbon's steepest and narrowest streets – at times you are so close to the shops you could almost take a can of sardines off the shelves. The route is of less interest after you reach Rua de Voz do Operário, from where it's a short walk down to the church of São Vicente and the Feira da Ladra market; or get off at the next stop, in Largo da Graça, where you can admire the superb views over Lisbon and the castle from the Miradouro da Graça.

From Largo Rodrigues de Freitas, catch tram #12 down the
steep Calçada de Santo André to Largo Martim Moniz in
central Lisbon.

EAST TO SANTA ENGRÁCIA

Five hundred metres east of the castle, the church of **São
Vicente de Fora** (Map 4, G4; Tues–Fri 9am–6pm, Sat
9–7pm, Sun 9am–12.30pm & 3–5pm; free) provides a
neat reminder of the extent of the sixteenth-century city;
its name means "Saint Vincent of the Outside". An older
church, where Saint Anthony of Padua took his religious
vows in 1210, was built here in 1185 on the site of a
Crusader burial ground, while Afonso Henriques pitched
camp on this spot during his siege and conquest of
Lisbon.

The current church was built during the years of
Spanish rule by Philip II's Italian architect, Felipe Terzi
(1582–1629); its severe geometric facade was an important Renaissance innovation. Through the cloisters,
decorated with azulejos, you can visit the old monastic
refectory, which since 1855 has formed the **pantheon of
the Bragança dynasty** (Tues–Sun 10am–5.30pm; €2).
Here, in more or less complete (though unexciting)
sequence, are the bodies of all Portuguese kings from João
IV, who restored the monarchy in 1640, to Manuel II,
who lost it and died in exile in England in 1932. Among
them is Catherine of Bragança, the widow of England's
Charles II, who is credited as having introduced the concept of teatime to the Brits. There's a café at the church,
whose roof terrace provides spectacular Alfama views.

A couple of hundred metres further east of the church,
Campo de Santa Clara (Map 4, I3–K3) is home to the

twice-weekly **Feira da Ladra** ("Thieves' Market"), Lisbon's rambling and ragged flea market (Tues & Sat 7am–6pm; tram #28 from Rua da Conceição in the Baixa to Rua da Voz do Operário, or bus #12 from Santa Apolónia station or Praça Marquês de Pombal). It's not the world's greatest market, but it does turn up some interesting things, like oddities from the former African colonies and old Portuguese prints. Out-and-out junk – from broken alarm clocks to old postcards – is spread on the ground above Santa Engrácia, and half-genuine antiques at the top end of the *feira* around the covered market building, whose upstairs restaurant (see p.151) is particularly lively on market days.

The dome of nearby **Santa Engrácia** (Map 4, J4; May–Oct Tues–Sun 10am–6pm; Nov–April Tues–Sun 10am–5pm; €2, free on Sun 10am–2pm) makes it one of the most recognizable buildings on the city skyline. The loftiest and most tortuously built church in the city, it has become synonymous with unfinished work – begun in 1682, it was finally completed in 1966. Since 1916, the church has doubled as the **Panteão Nacional**, housing the tombs of eminent Portuguese figures, including writer Almeida Garrett, and former presidents, notably Sidónio Pais, president during World War I. You can ride the lift up to the dome, from where there are great views over the flea market, port and city.

SANTA APOLÓNIA AND AROUND

A couple of blocks south of Santa Engrácia stands **Santa Apolónia** (Map 4, K6), Lisbon's main train station, whose new metro station is due to open in 2004, providing easier access to this side of the city. Lisbon's most fashionable club, *Lux*, is sited by the docks opposite the station.

PORTUGUESE AZULEJOS

You'll see **azulejos** – decorative ceramic tiles – wherever you go in Lisbon: inside and outside houses, shops, monuments and even metro stations. The word derives from the Arabic *al-zulecha*, "small stone", and the craft was brought to Iberia by the Moors in the eighth century. As the Koran prevents the portrayal of living forms, early Portuguese tiles were produced using Moorish-influenced geometric techniques, with thin ridges of clay being used to separate the lead-based colours. The ridges prevented the depiction of complex patterns and Portuguese azulejos didn't develop their own style until the mid-sixteenth century when a new method of tin-oxide coating allowed images to be painted directly onto the clay. At first, religious imagery was the favoured form – such as those in the Igreja de São Roque (see p.60) – but during the seventeenth century, more decadent images were all the rage: the wealthy commissioned large panels displaying battles, hunting scenes and images influenced by Vasco da Gama's voyages. Later, new Dutch Delftware techniques allowed individual tiles to be immensely detailed, with tiny figures of birds, boats and flowers on every tile. Huge tiled walls in churches came to be known as *tapetes* (rugs), because of their resemblance to a giant Persian carpet.

Dutch artisans also began producing blue-and-white tiles, a form influenced by Chinese pottery, and in the late seventeenth century this style was the most popular with Portugal's aristocracy, who favoured images of flowers and fruit – such as those at the Palácio dos Marquêses de Fronteira (see p.103). The early eighteenth century saw artist "masters" producing highly decorated multi-coloured ceramic mosaics, culminating in Rococo themes which can be seen, for example, in Madre de Deus church (now the Museo do Azulejo).

After the Great Earthquake of 1755 more prosaic tiled facades – often with Neoclassical designs – were considered good insulation devices, as well as protecting buildings from rain and fire. By the mid-nineteenth century, azulejos were being produced in factories to decorate shops and industries – such as the tiles on the front of the Fábrica Viúva Lamego (p.218), – while the end of the century saw the reappearance of figures on tiles, typified by the work in the *Cervejaria da Trindade* (p.157). The nineteenth century also saw the arrival of individualists such as Rafael Bordalo Pinheiro (p.101), who used azulejos for comical and satirical purposes. The art continues today, but although some artists maintain the hand-painted tradition, the majority of today's tiles are less impressive mass-produced items, pale imitations of the old figurative or geometric designs.

West of the station, across Largo dos Caminhos de Ferro, rises the imposing Corinthian facade of the city's military museum, the **Museu Militar** (Map 4, J6; Tues–Sun 10am–5pm; €2, free Wed; bus #9 from Praça do Comércio or #39 from Restauradores), set in a seventeenth-century munitions factory. There are some lavish azulejos and paintings of battles, though this is very traditional in layout – old weapons in old cases – and lacks appeal unless you've an unusual interest in historical military campaigns and weaponry.

Some ten minutes' walk east of the Museu Militar at Rua do Alviela 12, a side street off Calçada dos Barbadinhos, the **Museu da Água** (Map 2, H8; Mon–Sat 10am–6pm; €2; bus #105 from Praça da Figueira or #107 from Cais do Sodré) is a limited, but surprisingly engaging, museum devoted to the development of the city's water supply. It is housed in an attractive old pumping station, built in 1880 to force water up Lisbon's steep hills. If you get a kick out of watching demonstrations of nineteenth-century beam engines, this is the place for you. While here, you can arrange a visit to the Aqueduto das Águas Livres (see p.91).

MUSEU NACIONAL DO AZULEJO

Map 2, H8. Tues 2–6pm, Wed–Sun 10am–6pm; €2.25, free on Sun. Bus #104 from Praça do Comércio or bus #105 from Praça da Figueira.

A little over 2km to the east of Alfama stands one of Lisbon's most interesting small museums, the **Museu Nacional do Azulejo**, which traces the development of the distinctive Portuguese azulejo tiles from Moorish styles to the present day. It is installed in the church and cloisters of **Madre de Deus**, whose eighteenth-century tiled scenes of the life of Saint Anthony are among the best in the city. Upstairs there are temporary exhibitions usually related to tiles. The highlight, however, is Portugal's longest azulejo – a wonderfully detailed forty-metre panorama of Lisbon, completed in around 1738. Look out, too, for the meat-and-game imagery on the tiled walls of the museum **café-restaurant**. This is a great spot for lunch, with meals taken in the leafy garden. There is also a good museum shop selling high-quality azulejos.

The Bairro Alto

High above and to the west of the city centre is the **Bairro Alto**, the upper town. After the 1755 earthquake, this relatively unscathed district became the favoured residence of the aristocracy and the haunt of Lisbon's young bohemians, who made it the cultural heart of the city – a status it retains today. By day, the quarter's narrow seventeenth-century streets feel essentially residential, with grocery stores open to the pavement, children playing in the cobbled streets and old people sitting in doorways. However, behind the facades sit the city's Faculty of Fine Arts, the Institute of Art and Design, and scores of fashionable shops, boutiques and cafés; while after dark the area is thronged with drinkers, clubbers and diners visiting its fado houses, bars and restaurants.

The most exciting way to approach the Bairro Alto is via the **Elevador da Glória**, the steep funicular ride which links the quarter directly with Praça dos Restauradores in the lower town. There's an alternative approach, using the Elevador da Bica (see p.41), which runs up to the southern fringes of the Bairro Alto from behind Cais do Sodré station. Highlights in the *bairro* itself include the city's **Instituto do Vinho do Porto** (Port Wine Institute) and two of its most interesting churches, the **Convento do**

Carmo and **São Roque**. Heading north, towards the district of Rato, the leafy **Praça do Príncipe Real** is a foretaste of the exotic **Jardim Botânico** botanical gardens, which roll down the hill below the **museums of science and natural history**.

The area covered by this chapter is shown In detail on colour maps 5 and 8. For listings of the Bairro Alto's best restaurants, see p.153; for bars and clubs, see p.176.

ELEVADOR DA GLÓRIA

Map 5, G2. Daily 7am–1am.

Everyone should ride the **Elevador da Glória** at least once to experience one of the city's most amazing feats of engineering. From the bottom of Calçada da Glória (off Praça dos Restauradores, behind the Portuguese Tourist Office), funicular-like trams climb the gut-bustingly steep street in a couple of minutes, leaving the lower city behind as you ascend above its rooftops. Built in 1885, the tram system was originally powered by water displacement and then by steam, until electricity was introduced.

At the top of the Elevador da Glória, most people pause at the gardens, the **Miradouro de São Pedro de Alcântara** (Map 5, G1), from where there's a superb view across the city to the castle. Immediately over the road is the **Instituto do Vinho do Porto** (Map 5, G2), the Port Wine Institute, set in the eighteenth-century Palácio Ludovice, the former home of the architect of Mafra's convent (see p.296). The Institute, based in the northern city of Porto, regulates and promotes the production of port wine. It opened its Lisbon headquarters here in 1944 and the bar (open to the public, see p.183) is the best place in the city to sample the famous beverage.

IGREJA DE SÃO ROQUE

Map 5, G3. Church: daily 8.30am–5pm; free. Museu de São Roque:
May–Oct Tues–Sun 10am–5pm, Nov–April daily 10am–noon &
1–5pm; €1, free on Sun. Bus #58 from Cais do Sodré.

Take a left turn at the top of the Elevador da Glória and
it is a short walk to the **Igreja de São Roque**, in Largo
Trindade Coelho, a square with a diminutive statue of a
postman loping across it. From the outside, this looks like
the plainest church in the city, its bleak Renaissance
facade (by Filipo Terzi, architect of São Vicente) having
been further simplified by the earthquake. But inside lie
an astonishing succession of side chapels, lavishly crafted
with azulejos, multicoloured marble and Baroque painted
ceilings.

The highlight is the **Capela de São João Baptista**.
This chapel, one of the most extravagant commissions of
its age, is estimated for its size to be the most expensive
ever constructed. It was ordered from Rome in 1742 by
Dom João V to honour his patron saint and, more dubi-
ously, to gratify the pope, whom he had persuaded to
confer a patriarchate upon Lisbon. Designed by the papal
architect, Vanvitelli, and using the most costly materials
available, including ivory, agate, porphyry and lapis lazuli,
it was erected at the Vatican for the pope to celebrate
Mass in, before being dismantled and shipped to Lisbon
at the then vast cost of £250,000. If you take a close look
at the four "oil paintings" of John the Baptist's life, you'll
find that they are in fact intricately worked mosaics.
Today, the lapis lazuli and more valuable parts of the altar
front are kept in the adjacent **museum**, which also displays sixteenth- to eighteenth-century paintings and the
usual motley collection of vestments, chalices and bibles
which have been bequeathed to the church over the
centuries.

CONVENTO DO CARMO

Map 3, E8. April–Sept Tues–Sun 10am–6pm; Oct–March Tues–Sun 10am–5pm; €2.50, free on Sun. Metro Baixa-Chiado.

Further south of São Roque, it's a couple of minutes' walk down Rua Nova da Trindade – past the famous *Cervejária da Trindade* beer-hall (see p.157) – and Rua da Trindade to the pretty, enclosed **Largo do Carmo**, with its outdoor café. Opposite here stand the ruined Gothic arches of the beautiful **Convento do Carmo**. Built between 1389 and 1423, and once the largest church in the city, this was half-destroyed by the 1755 earthquake but is perhaps even more striking as a result. In the nineteenth century its shell was adapted as a chemical factory but today it houses the splendidly capricious **Museu Arqueológico do Carmo**, home to many of the treasures from monasteries that were dissolved after the 1834 Liberal revolution. The entire nave is open to the elements, with columns, tombs and statuary scattered in all corners. Inside, on either side of what was the main altar, are the main exhibits, centring on a series of tombs of great significance. Largest is the beautifully carved, two-metre-high stone tomb of Ferdinand I; nearby, that of Gonçalo de Sousa, chancellor to Henry the Navigator, is topped by a statue of Gonçalo himself, his clasped arms holding a book to signify his learning. Other noteworthy pieces include a fifteenth-century alabaster relief, made in Nottingham, and sixteenth-century Hispano-Arabic azulejos. There's also a model of the convent before it was ruined, an Egyptian sarcophagus (793–619 BC), whose inhabitant's feet are just visible underneath the lid; and, even more alarmingly, two pre-Columbian mummies which lie curled up in glass cases, alongside the preserved heads of a couple of Peruvian Indians. Elsewhere there are flints, arrowheads, prehistoric ceramics, coins dating back to the thirteenth century, Roman inscriptions, church architecture and much more.

CONVENTO DO CARMO

The Elevador de Santa Justa (see p.33) has its exit at the side of the Convento do Carmo – but this has been closed for structural works for some time. To reach the Convento from the Baixa on foot, head up the steep steps of Calçada do Carmo (Map 3, D8), off the southwest side of Rossio, or take the gentler route from metro Baixa-Chiado (Map 3, F7), along Rua do Carmo into Rua Garrett, then first right up Calçada do Sacramento. Both walks take about five minutes.

WEST OF RUA DA MISERICÓRDIA

Many of the Bairro Alto's most interesting streets lie in the squeezed grid to the west of **Rua da Misericórdia**, itself a couple of blocks west of the Convento do Carmo. The narrow, cobbled streets have undergone extensive renovation in the last few years, with parking and traffic access restricted (though many of the buildings are still liberally defaced with grafitti). The area is the focus of the Bairro Alto's famed nightlife and it's in these streets – particularly those running north to south: Rua do Norte, Rua Diário de Notícias, Rua da Atalaia and Rua da Rosa – that you'll find many of the city's best bars, restaurants and fado clubs. A little further west, running steeply downhill towards São Bento, **Rua do Século** is one of the city's most historic streets; a sign at number 89 marks the **birthplace of the Marquês de Pombal**, while the basement of the modernizing minister's former home is now occupied by the restaurant *Consenso* (see p.155).

PRAÇA DO PRÍNCIPE REAL AND AROUND

Heading north from the Miradouro de São Pedro de Alcântara at the top of Elevador da Glória, along Rua Dom Pedro V, brings you to **Praça do Príncipe Real** (Map 8,

D7). It's one of the city's loveliest squares, laid out in 1860 and surrounded by the ornate homes of former aristocrats – now largely turned into offices. At weekends the square is full of elderly locals playing cards around a superb cedar tree, whose extensive branches are propped up to form a natural shelter. By night, the square takes on a somewhat different air as the focal point of Lisbon's best gay nightclubs (see p.191).

The central pond and fountain is built over a covered reservoir that houses the **Museu da Água Príncipe Real** (Mon–Sat 10am–6pm; €1). Steps lead down inside the nineteenth-century reservoir, where you can admire both the water and temporary art exhibits from a series of walkways winding among the columns, usually accompanied by ambient music. This is part of a network of underground water supplies that link up with the Aqueduto das Águas Livres (see p.91); one of the tunnels from this reservoir heads down through what is now the *Enoteca* wine bar on nearby Rua Mãe d'Água (see p.185).

The square has a handy play area for children, near the outdoor tables of the *Esplanada do Príncipe Real* café.

Continuing 250 metres along the busy Rua Escola Politécnica towards the district of Rato, you'll come to the Neoclassical former technical college, now housing museums of natural history and science. The **Museu da Historia Natural** (Map 8, D6; Mon–Fri 10am–noon & 1–5pm, closed Aug; free; bus #15 or #58 from Cais do Sodré), houses a rather sorry collection of stuffed animals, eggs and shells representing plant and animal life in the Iberian peninsula, though temporary exhibitions held in the adjacent rooms can be more diverting. The **Museu da Ciência** opposite (Map 8, D6; Mon–Fri 10am–1pm & 2–5pm, Sat 3–6pm, closed Aug; free) has more absorbing geological exhibits and a low-tech interactive section where you can balance balls on jets of air and swing pendulums among throngs of school kids.

JARDIM BOTÂNICO

Map 8, D5. May–Oct Mon–Fri 9.30am–7pm, Sat & Sun 10am–8pm; Nov–April Mon–Fri 9.30am–6pm, Sat & Sun 10am–6pm; €1.30. Bus #58 from Cais do Sodré or Rato.

Just beyond the museums lies the entrance to the city's nineteenth-century **Jardim Botânico** (botanical gardens). Almost entirely invisible from the surrounding streets – there's another entrance tucked into Rua da Alegria (Map 8, E6; closed weekends) – the gardens are an oasis of greenery and provide a tranquil escape from the city bustle. The Portuguese explorers helped introduce many plant species to Europe and these gardens, laid out between 1858 and 1878, are packed with twenty thousand neatly labelled species from around the world. Steep, shady paths lead downhill under overbearing palms and luxuriant shrubs.

To get back into town from here, leave through the gardens' lower exit into Rua da Alegria and walk downhill to Avenida da Liberdade. Alternatively, from the top of the gardens it's five minutes' walk north along Rua da Escola Politécnica to Rato metro, itself a short walk from the Amoreiras shopping centre and the Mãe d'Agua aqueduct.

West to Alcântara

West of the Bairro Alto extend some of Lisbon's most affluent areas. Beyond **São Bento** – home to the impressive Palácio da Assembléia, Portugal's parliamentary building – lies the leafy district of **Estrela**, best known for its **gardens** and enormous **basilica**, whose white dome can be seen from much of the city. To the north are the **Cemitério dos Ingleses** – the English Cemetery – and the **Casa Museu Fernando Pessoa**, former home of one of Lisbon's greatest writers, now a cultural centre.

To the south of Estrela is the opulent suburb of **Lapa**, whose tranquil streets are the favoured homes of diplomats and Lisbon's rich. The key sight here is the wonderful collection of paintings and artefacts in the **Museu Nacional de Arte Antiga** (National Museum of Ancient Art). West of Lapa, a tangle of busy roads leads towards Ponte 25 de Abril, near which the **Doca de Alcântara** and **Doca de Santo Amaro** have been developed into Lisbon's liveliest dockside bar and restaurant zones. A short hop on the tram from Alcântara takes you to the **Palácio da Ajuda**, one of Lisbon's more eccentric palaces.

The area covered by this chapter is shown in detail on colour map 6.

MULTICULTURAL LISBON

Lisbon is one of southern Europe's most cosmopolitan cities, with over 120,000 people of African or Asian descent living in the Greater Lisbon area, most hailing originally from Portugal's former colonies, especially Cape Verde and Angola and, to a lesser extent, Mozambique, Brazil, Goa and Macau. The first Africans in Lisbon arrived in the fifteenth century, shipped over as slaves during Portugal's maritime explorations. By the sixteenth century, a remarkable thirteen percent of the city's population was already of African descent, and almost all were involved in menial work. But over the following centuries black people began to assert a more profound influence over Lisbon society, with many becoming intellectuals, academics, priests and artists, while African musical forms probably influenced the development of fado. The 1974 revolution and the subsequent independence of former Portuguese colonies saw a large number of immigrants settling in the capital, a trend which has continued to the present day – either legally or otherwise. Nowadays, African and Brazilian culture permeates Lisbon life, influencing its music, food, television and street slang. Most Lisboetas are rightly proud of their cosmopolitan city and few Portuguese are openly racist. Nevertheless, inevitably, underlying racism persists and most blacks and Asians continue to be employed in menial labour. Unlike white Brazilians, who easily climb up the career ladder, few people from ethnic minorities have managed to break through the glass ceiling into the top jobs. Those that have been successful tend to be musicians or sports stars, such as the great footballer Eusébio. Extreme right-wing groups do exist, but fortunately, examples of racist violence are rare.

SÃO BENTO

En route to Estrela, the district of **São Bento** is worth a brief stopover to peer at the **Palácio da Assembléia** (Map

6, H3), Portugal's parliament building. The Neoclassical facade was originally that of the Mosteiro de São Bento, a Benedictine monastery, which the government took over in 1834 after the abolition of religious orders. You're not allowed inside, though you get a good view from tram #28 as it rattles along Calçada da Estrela.

The parliament building has been spruced up in recent years, making it stick out like even more of a sore thumb in an otherwise down-to-earth residential area which houses some good ethnic restaurants and clubs (see p.160). In fact, São Bento was home to one of the city's first black communities, whose inhabitants were primarily slaves, brought back by the Portuguese maritime adventurers. Their lives were held so cheap that, in the sixteenth century, a mere ditch was dug to bury the countless numbers who died in an epidemic – an event commemorated by the name of the road, **Rua do Poço dos Negros** (Map 6, I5; "road of the blacks' well"), which lies 500 metres south of parliament, off Rua de São Bento.

ESTRELA

Estrela is one of Lisbon's more attractive and traditional districts. Tramlines from Campo de Ourique, Lapa and Chiado converge at the spacious Praça da Estrela, overlooked by the impressive **Basílica da Estrela** (Map 6, G3; daily 8am–1pm & 3–8pm; free; tram #28 from the Baixa or #25 from Praça do Comércio), a vast monument to late-eighteenth-century Neoclassicism, constructed by order of Queen Maria I (whose tomb lies within) and completed in 1790. Opposite is the **Jardim da Estrela** public garden (Map 6, G2). Lisbon takes its gardens seriously and this is among its most enjoyable: a quiet refuge with a pond-side café, a well-equipped children's playground and even a library kiosk for those who fancy a spot of Portuguese literature under the palms.

●

FERNANDO PESSOA

Portugal's most celebrated modern poet, **Fernando Pessoa** was largely unrecognized until after his death. Born in Lisbon in 1888, Pessoa spent most of his childhood in South Africa with his mother and subsequently wrote many of his poems in English. Returning alone to Lisbon aged seventeen, he lived mostly in spartan rented rooms, contributing poetry to literary magazines. He soon became known as a modernist, influenced by the European avant-garde, Cubists, Futurists and others. With his distinctive gold-rimmed glasses, bow tie and hat, the quirky poet was a conspicuous figure in the Baixa cafés where he wrote. Unfortunately, his need to smoke and drink while he worked contributed to a short life and he died in 1935, a year after the appearance of *Mensagem* (Message), the only one of his books published during his lifetime. Since his death, researchers have unearthed several intriguing but previously unpublished works, many written under pseudonyms including Alberto Caeiro, Alvaro de Campos, Ricardo Reis and, for his prose, Bernardo Soares. Each pseudonym represented a different persona and a different literary style; but each one was equally learned and inspired, embodiments of the different personalities the enigmatic Pessoa believed we all possess.

North of the park on Rua de São Jorge you'll find the gate to the **Cemitério dos Ingleses**, or English Cemetery (Map 6, G2; ring loudly for entry), actually a Protestant cemetery founded in 1717. Here, among the cypresses and tombs of various expatriates, lie the remains of Henry Fielding, author of *Tom Jones*, whose imminent demise may have influenced his verdict on Lisbon as "the nastiest city in the world".

A little further uphill from here at Rua Coelho da Rocha 16 stands the **Casa Museu Fernando Pessoa** (Map 6, G1;

Mon–Wed 10am–7pm, Thurs 1–8pm; Fri 10am–6pm; free), where Fernando Pessoa lived for the last fifteen years of his life. The heavily restored interior contains a few of Pessoa's personal belongings, including his diaries. There are also exhibitions of works by artists influenced by Pessoa, a library of his own works, and Almada Negreiros's famous painting of the writer, showing his distinctive spectacles (on display in the museum) and black hat.

MUSEU NACIONAL DE ARTE ANTIGA

Map 6, F6. Tues 2–6pm, Wed–Sun 10am–6pm; €3. Bus #40 or #60 from Praça do Comércio, or bus #27 or #49 from Belém.

The **Museu Nacional de Arte Antiga** at Rua das Janelas Verdes 95 is, in effect, Portugal's national gallery. It features the largest collection of Portuguese fifteenth- and sixteenth-century paintings in the country, European art from the fourteenth century to the present day and a rich display of applied art showing the influence of Portugal's colonial explorations. All of this is well displayed in a beautifully converted seventeenth-century palace, once owned by the Marquês de Pombal, with a **café** (same hours as museum) complete with outdoor tables in attractive formal gardens overlooking the Tejo. The palace was built over the remains of the Saint Albert monastery, most of which was razed during the 1755 earthquake, although its chapel can still be seen today.

Gonçalves and the Portuguese School

Starting on the top floor (level 3), **Nuno Gonçalves** and other painters of the so-called **Portuguese School** span that indeterminate and exciting period in the second half of the fifteenth century when Gothic art was giving way to the Renaissance. Their works, exclusively religious in

MUSEU NACIONAL DE ARTE ANTIGA

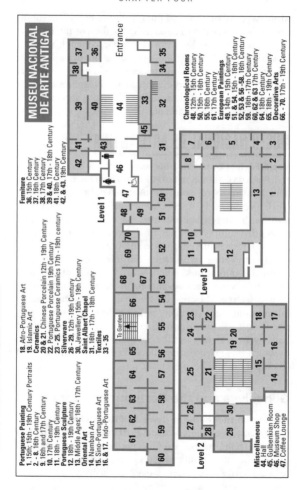

MUSEU NACIONAL DE ARTE ANTIGA

Portuguese Painting
1. 15th; 15th - 19th Century Portraits
2. 15th - 16th Century
9. 16th and 17th Century
10. 17th Century
11. 18th - 19th Century
Portuguese Sculpture
12. 18th - 20th Century
13. Middle Ages; 16th - 17th Century
Oriental Art
14. Nambam Art
15. Sino-Portuguese Art
16. & 17. Indo-Portuguese Art

18. Afro-Portuguese Art
19. Islamic Art
Ceramics
20 & 21. Chinese Porcelain 12th - 19th Century
22. Portuguese Porcelain 19th Century
23 - 25. Portuguese Ceramics 17th - 19th century
Silverware
26 - 29. 12th - 19th Century
30. Jewellery 15th - 19th Century
Saint Albert Chapel
31. 16th - 17th - 18th Century
Textiles
33 - 35

Furniture
36. 16th Century
37. 16th Century
38. 17th Century
39. & 40. 17th - 18th Century
41. 18th Century
42. & 43. 19th Century

Chronological Rooms
48. 12th - 15th Century
50. 15th - 16th Century
55. 16th Century
61. 17th Century
European Paintings
49. 14th - 15th Century
51. & 54. 15th - 16th Century
52. 53 & 56 - 58. 16th Century
59. 16th - 17th Century
60. 62 & 63 17th Century
64. 18th Century
65. 18th - 19th Century
Decorative Arts
66 - 70. 17th - 19th Century

Entrance

Level 1

Level 3

Level 2

To Garden

Miscellaneous
44. Hall
45. Gulbenkian Room
46. Museum Shop
47. Coffee Lounge

70

concept, are particularly interesting in their emphasis on portraiture, transforming any theme into a vivid observation of local contemporary life (notably Gregório Lopes's *Martyrdom of São Sebastião*, and Frei Carlos's *Annunciation*). Stylistically, the most significant influences upon them were those of the Flemish Northern Renaissance painters: Jan van Eyck, who came to Portugal in 1428, Hans Memling and Jan Mabuse (both well represented here), and Roger van der Weyden. As two of the main maritime powers of the time, there were close trade links between Portugal and Flanders, and many Flemish painters visited or settled in Lisbon.

The acknowledged masterpiece is Gonçalves's **altarpiece for Saint Vincent** (1467–70) in room 1, a brilliantly marshalled composition depicting Lisbon's patron saint receiving homage from all ranks of its citizens. It was painted for Lisbon's cathedral, then disappeared for a time before being rediscovered in the church of São Vicente de Fora in 1882. On the two left-hand panels are Cistercian monks, fishermen and pilots; on the opposite side the Duke of Bragança and his family, a helmeted Moorish knight, a Jew (with book), a beggar, and a priest holding Saint Vincent's own relics (a piece of his skull, still kept by the cathedral). In the epic central panels the moustachioed Henry the Navigator, his nephew Afonso V (in black and green), and the youthful (future) Dom João II, pay tribute to the saint. Among the frieze of portraits behind them, that on the far left is reputed to be Gonçalves himself; the other central panel shows the Archbishop of Lisbon. **Later Portuguese painters** – from the sixteenth to the eighteenth century – are displayed too, most notably António de Sequeira and Josefa de Óbidos. The latter, though born in Seville (in 1634), is considered one of Portugal's greatest women painters, spending most of her life as an etcher, miniaturist and

MUSEU NACIONAL DE ARTE ANTIGA

●

religious painter in the convent of Óbidos, around 70km north of Lisbon.

The rest of the collection

After Gonçalves and his contemporaries, the most interesting exhibits are on the bottom floor (level 1), where there are works by **Flemish and German** painters – Lucus Cranach, Hieronymus Bosch and Albrecht Dürer. The highlight for most people is Bosch's stunningly gruesome *Temptation of St Anthony* in room 57. Elsewhere on this level there are miscellaneous gems: an altar panel depicting the Resurrection by Raphael, Francisco de Zurbarán's *The Twelve Apostles* and a small statue of a nymph by Auguste Rodin. Look out, too, for the Baroque Saint Albert Chapel in room 31, beautifully decorated with azulejos.

Level 2 contains extensive applied art sections. Here, you'll find Portuguese **furniture** and **textiles** to rival the European selection in the Gulbenkian, and an excellent collection of **silverware** and **ceramics**. The **Oriental art collection** shows the influence of Indian, African and Oriental designs derived from the trading links of the sixteenth century. Other colonially influenced exhibits include inlaid furniture from Goa and a supremely satisfying series of late sixteenth-century **Japanese namban screens** (room 14), showing the Portuguese landing at Nagasaki. The Japanese saw the Portuguese traders as southern barbarians (*namban*) with large noses – hence their Pinocchio-like features.

For details of the Museu da Marioneta, a puppet museum ten minutes' walk east of the Museu Nacional de Arte Antiga, see Kids' Lisbon, p.228.

MUSEU NACIONAL DE ARTE ANTIGA

A STROLL THROUGH LAPA

From Estrela, **tram #25** passes through the well-heeled suburb of Lapa en route to Praça do Comércio, stopping at the end of Rua das Janelas Verdes, which houses the Museu Nacional de Arte Antiga. If you want to explore Lapa's opulent streets more close- ly, you could walk all the way from Estrela to the museum in around thirty minutes (allow an hour for the detour via the *Lapa Palace Hotel*).

From Praça da Estrela (Map 6, G3) head along the tramlines to the top of Rua de São Domingos à Lapa (Map 6, F4). A detour to the left along Rua da Lapa reveals steep side streets offering lovely **views over the Tejo** below. You can continue downhill along Rua de São Domingos à Lapa all the way to the museum (take a right along Rua do Prior and left along Rua do Conde).

Alternatively, for a real taste of Lapa opulence, head right along Rua do Sacramento à Lapa (Map 6, F4), past grand embassy buildings and stunning mansions. Turn left into Rua do Pau da Bandeira where you'll find the luxurious **Lapa Palace Hotel** (Map 6, E5; see p.128) at no. 4. It's worth saving some euros for a drink here in one of Lisbon's most tasteful hotels. From here, it's a ten- minute walk (from Rua do Pau da Bandeira, go left into Rua do Prior and then first right into Rua do Conde), downhill all the way, to the Museu Nacional de Arte Antiga.

ALCÂNTARA

Steps beside the Museu Nacional de Arte Antiga lead down to **Avenida 24 de Julho**, where you can brave the pedes- trian crossing over the railway lines to reach the **Doca de Alcântara** (Alcântara docks; Map 6, C6–E7), where an increasing number of luxury cruise ships dock alongside an expanding series of clubs and bars. Since the mid-1990s, the once run-down warehouses here have been transformed into an alternative nightclub zone, setting in motion a development boom that has turned many of Lisbon's river-front warehouses all the way from Belém to Santa Apolónia into smart bars and restaurants.

To reach Alcântara and the docks from the centre, catch an Oeiras train from Cais do Sodré to Alcântara Mar station (Map 6, C6). Alternatively, tram #15 from Praça da Figueira goes along Avenida 24 de Julho, just north of the docks, via Praça do Comércio and Cais do Sodré.

The Doca de Alcântara is liveliest at night, when its boat-bars and restaurant-clubs like *Queens* (see p.188) come into their own. A better bet by day is to head west to the more intimate **Doca de Santo Amaro** (Santo Amaro docks; Map 6, B7), nestling right under the humming traffic and rattling trains crossing Ponte 25 de Abril. This small, almost completely enclosed dock is filled with bobbing sailing boats and lined with tastefully converted warehouses. There's the odd restaurant around here, but many more cafés, with prices considerably higher than usual in Lisbon. For more on these, see p.161. Leaving Doca de Santo Amaro at its western side, you can pick up the pleasant **riverside path** that leads along the Tejo all the way to Belém (see p.76), twenty minutes' walk away.

A few hundred metres inland, over the busy Avenida da Índia, the suburb of **Alcântara** itself is a traditional district of shops and houses wedged between railway lines and the major traffic arteries that pass along and over the river – a suitably grungy zone for some of Lisbon's coolest clubs (see p.186) and restaurants (see p.161).

Just northeast of here are the steep, green expanses of the **Jardim da Tapada das Necessidades** (Map 6, D4–E3; Mon–Sat 10am–6pm; free; bus #13 from Praça do Comércio to Rua Possidónio, then a short walk). The gardens belong to the Palácio Real das Necessidades, a former royal residence now used by the government (and not open to the public). The gardens have somewhat hard-to-find entrances on Rua do Borja and Calçada das Necessidades: inside, the wooded slopes – eerily deserted and unkempt – offer some impressive semi-tropical plants and fine views over the Ponte 25 de Abril.

PALÁCIO DA AJUDA

Map 1, F6. Mon, Tues & Thurs–Sun 10am–4.30pm; €3, free on Sun 10am–2pm. Tram #18 from Praça do Comércio and Alcântara, or bus #60 from Praça da Figueira or #14 from Belém.

From Alcântara it's a short ride on tram #18 from Avenida 24 de Julho to the **Palácio da Ajuda**, sited around 1.5km northwest of the Ponte 25 de Abril. Construction of the palace began in 1802, but was incomplete when João VI and the royal family fled to Brazil to escape Napoleon's invading army in 1807. The original plans were therefore never fulfilled, though the completed section was used as a royal residence after João returned from exile in 1821. The surviving decor was commissioned by the crashingly taste-less nineteenth-century royals, Dona Maria II (João's grand-daughter) and Dom Ferdinand (1834–1853) and, like their Pena Palace folly at Sintra, is all over-the-top aristocratic clutter. The banqueting hall, however, is quite a sight, as is the lift, decked out with mahogany and mirrors.

Next to the palace is the attractive **Jardim Botânico d'Ajuda** (Mon, Tues & Thurs–Sun 9am–dusk; €1.50), one of the city's oldest botanical gardens. Laid out in 1768 by an Italian botanist, it was extensively restored in the 1990s. The garden is divided into eight parts representing plant species from round the world, all arranged round a system of terraces, statues and fountains – a fine example of formal Portuguese gardening and boasting some great views over Belém.

PALÁCIO DA AJUDA

75

Belém

I t was from **Belém** (pronounced *ber-layng* and derived from the Portuguese for "Bethlehem") that Vasco da Gama set sail for India in 1497, and here too that he was welcomed home by Dom Manuel "the Fortunate" (O Venturoso), bringing with him a small cargo of pepper which was enough to pay for his voyage sixty times over. The monastery subsequently built here – the **Mosteiro dos Jerónimos** – stands as a testament to his triumphant discovery of a sea route to the Orient, which initiated the beginning of a Portuguese golden age.

The Rio Tejo at Belém has receded with the centuries. When the monastery was first built it stood almost on the beach, within sight of the caravels moored ready for expeditions and of the **Torre de Belém**, which guarded the entrance to the port. This, too, survived the earthquake and is, along with the monastery, Lisbon's other showpiece of the Manueline style (see p.79). Both monastery and tower lie in what is now a pleasant waterfront suburb, close to a small group of museums, most of them set up by Salazar during the wartime (1940) Belém Expo, though the best of the lot, the **Museu do Design**, opened in 1999 inside the landmark **Centro Cultural de Belém**. There are also some fine cafés and restaurants, most of them within sight of the large **Padrão dos**

Descobrimentos (Monument to the Discoveries), which celebrates the exploits of the Portuguese explorers. Heading east, back into the city, you might want to find time to visit another couple of museums, the **Museu da Electricidade**, set in an amazing former generating station by the Tejo, and the **Museu do Centro Científico e Cultural de Macau**, recording Portugal's trading links with its former colony.

Belém lies 6km west of the city centre (and 2km west of the Ponte 25 de Abril) and is easily reached by **public transport**. The fast supertram #15 (signed Algés) runs from Praça da Figueira via Praça do Comércio, taking about twenty minutes – the route goes through Alcântara (via Rua Fradesso da Silveira and Rua 1° de Maio) and not along the riverfront. Bus #51 runs to and from the Gulbenkian (weekdays only); while Belém train station, five minutes' east of the main sights, is on the Oeiras line from Cais do Sodré.

The area covered by this chapter is shown in detail on colour map 7. Note that many of Belém's sights are closed on Mondays.

MOSTEIRO DOS JERÓNIMOS

Map 7, F4. Monastery: June–Sept daily 10am–6.30pm; Oct–May daily 10am–5pm; restricted access on Sat mornings and during Mass; free. Cloisters: same hours; €3, free on Sun 10am–2pm.

Even before the Great Earthquake, the **Mosteiro dos Jerónimos**, flanking the northern side of Praça do Império, was Lisbon's finest monument: since then, it has stood quite without comparison. Begun in 1502, the monastery is the most ambitious and successful achievement of Manueline architecture. It was built on the site of the

Ermida do Restelo, a hermitage founded by Henry the Navigator at which Vasco da Gama and his companions spent their last night ashore in prayer before leaving for India. Dom Manuel made a vow to the Virgin that he would build a monastery should da Gama return successfully. And successful he was: the monastery's funding came from a five percent tax on all spices imported from the East other than pepper, cinnamon and cloves, whose import had become the sole preserve of the Crown.

The daring and confidence of the monastery's design is largely the achievement of two outstanding figures: **Diogo de Boitaca**, perhaps the originator of the Manueline style with his Igreja de Jesus at Setúbal, and **João de Castilho**, a Spaniard who took charge of construction from around 1517.

The church and cloisters

It was Castilho who designed the **main entrance** to the church, a complex hierarchy of figures clustered around Henry the Navigator (on a pedestal above the arch). In its intricate and almost flat ornamentation it shows the influence of the then current Spanish style, Plateresque (literally, the art of the silversmith). Yet it also has distinctive Manueline features – the use of rounded forms, the naturalistic motifs in the bands around the windows – and these seem to create both its harmony and individuality. The style is also unmistakably outward-looking, evoking the new forms discovered in the East, a characteristic that makes each Manueline building so new and interesting, and so much a product of its particular and expansionist age. Appropriately, just inside the entrance lie the stone **tombs** of Vasco da Gama (1468–1523) and the great poet and recorder of the discoveries, Luís de Camões (1527–70).

The breathtaking sense of space inside the church places it among the great triumphs of European Gothic, though Manueline developments add two extraordinary fresh dimensions. There are tensions, deliberately created and carefully restrained, between the grand spatial design and the areas of intensely detailed ornamentation. And, still more striking, there's a naturalism in the forms of this ornamentation that seems to extend into the actual structure of the church. Once you've made the analogy, it's difficult to see the six central columns as anything other than palm trunks, growing both into and from the branches of the delicate rib-vaulting. The basic structure is thoroughly Gothic, though Castilho's ornamentation on the columns is much more Renaissance in spirit. So, too, is the semicircular apse (around the altar), added in 1572, beyond which is the entrance to the remarkable double cloister.

MANUELINE ARCHITECTURE

This elaborate architectural style known as **Manueline** was a development of the Gothic and evolved during the reign of Manuel 1 (1495–1521), after whom it is named. This was the age of Portugal's maritime explorations, and it was these that supplied the inspiration for the distinctive Manueline motifs, drawn from ropes, anchors, ships' wheels and the exotic plant and animal life encountered abroad, and which typically adorn Manueline buildings' windows, doors and columns. It would be hard to imagine an art more directly reflecting the achievements and preoccupations of an age. Another peculiarity of Manueline buildings is the way in which they can adapt, enliven, or encompass any number of different styles. João de Castilho's columns in the Mosteiro dos Jerónimos, for example, show the influence of the Renaissance, while the Torre de Belém has Moorish touches.

Vaulted throughout and fantastically embellished, the **cloisters** form one of the most original and beautiful pieces of architecture in the country, holding Gothic forms and Renaissance ornamentation in an exuberant balance. The rounded corner canopies and delicate twisting divisions within each of the arches lend a wave-like, rhythmic motion to the whole structure, a conceit extended by the typically Manueline motifs drawn from ropes, anchors and the sea.

The monastery museums

In the wings of the monastery are two museums (Map 7, E4). The **Museu de Arqueologia** (Tues 2–6pm, Wed–Sun 10am–6pm; €3, free on Sun 10am–2pm), a Neo-Manueline extension to the monastery added in 1850, has a small section on Egyptian antiquities, but concentrates on Portuguese archeological finds. It's a sparse collection and, apart from a few fine Roman mosaics unearthed in the Algarve, thoroughly unexceptional, though its temporary exhibits can be rewarding.

In contrast, the enormous **Museu da Marinha** (June–Sept Tues–Sun 10am–6pm; Oct–May Tues–Sun 10am–5pm; €2.50), in the west wing, is an absorbing maritime museum, packed not only with models of ships, naval uniforms and a surprising display of artefacts from Portugal's oriental trade and colonies, but also with real vessels – among them fishing boats and sumptuous state barges – a couple of seaplanes and even some fire engines. There's also a **Museu das Crianças** (Children's Museum) within the museum – see p.230 for details.

A comboio turístico (toy train) departs roughly every half hour in summer (May–Sept daily 10am–noon & 2–5pm; €3) from in front of the Mosteiro dos Jerónimos, running up to the Torre de Belém and back. At other times of year it runs roughly hourly in good weather only.

MOSTEIRO DOS JERÓNIMOS

AROUND PRAÇA DO IMPÉRIO

Outside the monastery, the expanse of **Praça do Império** (Map 7, E5), a square with an impressive fountain laid out during World War II, soaks up with ease the hundreds of daily visitors to Belém. It's especially busy on Saturday mornings, when there seems to be an endless procession of flamboyant weddings at the monastery, whose photo-calls invariably spill out into the square.

The pink marble **Centro Cultural de Belém** (Map 7, D5; Mon–Fri 11am–8pm, Sat & Sun 10am–7pm; event information on ☎213 612 400, ⓦwww.ccb.pt), on the square's western side, was built to host Lisbon's 1992 presidency of the European Union. It's now an arts complex containing a design museum (see overleaf) and hosting regular photography and art exhibitions, as well as concerts and live entertainment at weekends – jugglers, mime artists and the like. For the best views of the surroundings, drop into *Café Quadrante* on the first floor, whose roof-garden overlooks the river and the Padrão dos Descobrimentos.

Just east of the square down **Rua de Belém** are the seemingly never-ending rooms of the **Antiga Confeitaria de Belém** (map 7 G4; see p.174), which bills itself as the only producer of *pastéis de Belém* – delicious flaky tartlets filled with custard-like cream. If you want something more to eat, head for the attractive traditional buildings along nearby **Rua Vieira Portuense**, where there's a row of restaurants with outdoor seating; as a rule, the further east you head, the less touristy the restaurants become (see p.162 for details). North of here lies the leafy **Jardim do Ultramar** (Map 7, H3; daily 10am–5pm; free), a green oasis with hothouses, ponds and towering palms – the entrance is on Calçada do Galvão. In the southeastern corner of the gardens lies the Portuguese President's official residence, the pink **Presidência da República** (Map 7, H4).

Museu do Design

Map 7, D5. Daily 11am–8pm (last entry at 7.15pm); €3.

Housed in the rather soulless rooms of the Centro Cultural's Exhibition Centre, the **Museu do Design** (Design Museum) is the first in the city dedicated to contemporary household design and is already touted as being one of the most important in Europe. The collection was amassed by former stockbroker and media mogul Francisco Capelo (who also helped found the Museu de Arte Moderna in Sintra) and contains over 600 design classics embracing furniture, glass and jewellery from 1937 to the present day. The collection is so big that exhibits are changed over every now and then, though the most important items usually remain on display. These are shown chronologically in three sections entitled "Luxo" (Luxury), "Pop" and "Cool". "Luxo" contains one-off luxury and, later, industrially produced designs from the 1930s to the 1950s, including classic fibreglass chairs from Charles and Ray Eames, and Marshmallow and Coconut chairs by the American George Nelson. "Pop" features fun designs from the 1960s and 1970s, including bean-bags, kitsch moulded plastic furniture and an amazing Joe Colombo Mino Kitchen, designed in 1963. "Cool" contains work from the 1980s and 1990s, including the Memphis Group's Tawaraya bed, Phillipe Starck's chair and the works of established Portuguese designers such as Tomás Tavira and Alvara Siza Vieria.

PADRÃO DOS DESCOBRIMENTOS AND AROUND

Map 7, E6. June–Sept Tues–Sun 9am–7pm; Nov–May Tues–Sun 9am–5pm; €2.

South of Praça do Império, and reached via an underpass beneath the Avenida da Índia and railway line, the

Padrão dos Descobrimentos (Monument to the Discoveries) is an angular slab of concrete erected in 1960 to commemorate the five-hundredth anniversary of the death of Henry the Navigator. An impressive statue of Henry appears on the prow along with that of Luís de Camões and other Portuguese heroes. Within the monument is a small exhibition space, with interesting temporary exhibits on the city's history – the entrance fee also includes a ride in the lift to the top for some fine views of the Tejo and the Torre de Belém. Just in front of the monument, the pavement is decorated with a map of the world charting the routes taken by Portuguese explorers, while the adjacent **Doca de Belém** shelters some up-market restaurants.

Heading west along the riverfront, you'll pass the **Museu de Arte Popular** (Map 7, D6; Tues–Sun 10am–12.30pm & 2–5pm; €1.75, free on Sun 10am–2pm), a province-by-province display of Portugal's diverse folk arts housed in a shed-like building on the waterfront. As well as farm implements there are regional costumes, pieces of furniture, bagpipes from northern Portugal and some beautiful ceramics. From here, you can continue west past another dockland development, the **Doca de Bom Sucesso**, to the Torre de Belém.

TORRE DE BELÉM

Map 7, A7. June–Sept Tues–Sun 10am–6.30pm; Oct–May Tues–Sun 10am–5pm; €3.

The **Torre de Belém**, still washed by the sea, is 500m west of the monastery, fronted by a little park with a café. Whimsical, multi-turreted and with a real hat-in-the-air exuberance, it was built over the last five years of Dom Manuel's reign (1515–20) to defend the mouth of the Tejo – before an earthquake shifted its course in 1777, it stood near the middle of the great river. As such, it is the one completely Manueline building in Portugal (the rest having been adaptations of earlier structures or completed in later years) and has become the favoured symbol used to promote Lisbon by the Portuguese Tourist Board.

Its architect, Francisco de Arruda, had previously worked on Portuguese fortifications in Morocco and a Moorish influence is clear in the delicately arched windows and balconies. Prominent also in the decoration are two great symbols of the age: Manuel's personal badge of an armillary sphere (representing the globe) and the cross of the military Order of Christ, once the Templars, who took a major role in all Portuguese conquests. The tower's interior is unremarkable except for the views from it and a "whispering gallery"; it was used into the nineteenth century as a prison, notoriously by Dom Miguel (1828–34), who kept political enemies in the waterlogged dungeons.

EAST TOWARDS ALCÂNTARA

Returning to Praça do Império and heading 500 metres east down Rua de Belém brings you to the second of the area's two main squares, **Praça Afonso de Albuquerque** (Map 7, H5).

On the northern side of the square is the **Museu dos Coches** (Map 7, H4; Tues–Sun 10am–6pm; €3), housed in the attractive former royal riding school. It was opened in 1905 on the initiative of the queen, Dona Amélia, and contains one of the largest collections of carriages and saddlery in the world, although the interminable line of royal coaches – Baroque, heavily gilded and sometimes beautifully painted – hardly explains the museum's claim to be one of the most visited tourist attractions in Lisbon.

Regular ferries depart from Belém's Estação Fluvial (Map 7,
I7; every 30min–1hr, Mon–Sat 6.30am–11.30pm, Sun
7.30–11.30pm) to Trafaria, which is a short bus ride from the
beaches of Caparica. Alternatively, get off at the first stop,
Porto Brandão, where there are some good fish restaurants
and views back to Belém.

Crossing over the railway footbridge to the riverside, past
the Belém ferry terminal, it is possible to walk the 2km
along the lawned riverside all the way from Belém to
Alcântara's Doca de Santo Amaro. Another option is to
cycle; in summer, the kiosk by the Belém ferry terminal
rents out bikes for around €5 an hour.

En route, around 1km east of Belém, is the extraordinary
redbrick **Museu da Electricidade** (Tues–Fri & Sun
10am–12.30pm & 2–5.30pm, Sat 10am–12.30pm &
2–8pm; €2), an industrial museum housed in an early
twentieth-century electricity generating station with cathedral-like windows. The highlights include a series of enormous generators, steam turbines and winches – resembling
a set from the science-fiction film *Brazil*. All in all, it is a
highly atmospheric place and hosts occasional art and technology exhibitions.

A further 500 metres east of the Museu da Electricidade,
a footbridge back over the railway line (next to the high-
tech Lisbon Congress Centre) leads on to the main Rua da
Junqueira. From here it is a short walk east (towards the city
centre) to the **Museu do Centro Científico e Cultural
de Macau** (Tues–Sun 10am–5pm, Sun noon–6pm, €2.50;
tram #15 from Belém or Cais do Sodré) at Rua da
Junqueira 30. The attractively laid-out museum is dedicated
to Portugal's trading links with the Orient and, specifically,
its former colony of Macau, which was handed back to
Chinese rule in 1999. There are model boats and audio

displays detailing early sea voyages, as well as various historic journals and artefacts including a seventeenth-century portable wooden altar, used by travelling clergymen. Upstairs, exhibitions of Chinese art from the sixteenth to the nineteenth centuries show off impressive collections of porcelain, statuary, silverware and applied art, most notably an impressive array of opium pipes and ivory boxes.

Avenida da Liberdade to the Gulbenkian

For a gradually rising view over the Baixa, head up the central strip of the grand, palm-lined **Avenida da Liberdade**, still much as Fernando Pessoa described it: "the finest artery in Lisbon . . . full of trees from beginning to end . . . small gardens, ponds, fountains, cascades and statues". The 1.5-kilometre-long avenue, together with its exclusive side streets, was once home to many of Lisbon's grandest figures, including **António Medeiros**, an art collector whose works are now displayed in a fine town-house museum. Also on the western side of the avenue, it's a short walk to two contrasting destinations: Lisbon's brashest modern building, the **Amoreiras** shopping centre; and the historic **Praça das Amoreiras**, a quiet square whose massive **aqueduct** arches tower over the beguiling artworks contained within the **Fundação Arpad Siznes-Viera da Silva**.

The avenue itself ends in a swirl of traffic at the landmark roundabout of **Praça Marquês de Pombal**, beyond which lies the city's principal park, **Parque Eduardo VII**. If you've strolled up the avenue, this is the place to rest and recharge the batteries, though art-lovers might be inspired to press on further east into the Saldanha district to view the paintings and *objets* in the **CasaMuseu Dr Anastácio Gonçalves**. Northwest of here, everyone should make the effort to visit the **Fundação Calouste Gulbenkian**, Portugal's premier cultural centre, which sits in its own extensive grounds. This combines one of Europe's richest art collections, on display in the **Museu Gulbenkian**, with Portuguese contemporary art shown in the **Centro de Arte Moderna**.

The area covered by this chapter is shown in detail on colour maps 8 and 9.

AVENIDA DA LIBERDADE

Map 8, G6–D2. Metros Restauradores, Avenida or Marquês de Pombal.

The southern end of **Avenida da Liberdade** is marked by the broad Praça dos Restauradores (see p.36). Heading north, you'll pass some of the city's nicest **outdoor cafés**, under the shade of trees that help cushion the roar of the passing traffic. Some of the nineteenth-century mansions have survived the wrecker's ball – no. 67 (Map 8, F6), a distinctive yellow building with triangular-faced windows, was the home of the artist **Carlos Botelho** (1899–1982), who specialized in Lisbon landscapes – though most have been replaced by modern buildings, with the upper end of the avenue, particularly, housing many of the city's grander hotels, designer shops, banks and airline offices. After dark, the avenue's leafy central strip is a favourite hangout for prostitutes, though there's rarely any hassle here.

A BACKSTREET STROLL

The following walk doesn't pass any particular sights, but does lead you down some of Lisbon's most characterful streets. It should take about an hour.

Starting at Praça Marquês de Pombal (Map 8, D2), head down the eastern side of Avenida da Liberdade and take the first left into Rua Alexander Herculano. The second turning on the right is the narrow **Rua de Santa Marta** (Map 8, F2), which passes the Hospital de Santa Marta before heading downhill. On this street you'll find an amazing collection of tiny shops selling port or antiques, as well as some of the city's cheapest lunchtime restaurants (see p.163). The road becomes Rua de São José as it descends past grand government buildings on the left, whose gardens spill down the slopes.

At **Largo da Anunciada**, just before Rua das Portas de Santo Antão, have a rest in the beautifully decorated **Pastelaria Anunciada** (Map 8, G6; see p.175). Directly opposite here is the **Elevador do Lavra** funicular (Mon–Sat 7am–10.45pm, Sun 9am–10.45pm), opened in 1882 and still Lisbon's least tourist-frequented *elevador*. Take a ride to the top of the precipitous Calçada do Lavra, where a brief detour to the left, on Travessa do Torel, takes you to **Jardim do Torel** (Map 8, G5), a tiny park offering exhilarating views over Lisbon. For a drink stop continue down Travessa do Torel, past some imposing mansions, to **Campo dos Mátires da Pátria** (Map 8, H4), a leafy square with a pond and attractive café.

Turning right instead at the top of the *elevador* along Rua Câmara Pestana, then turning right again, brings you to the long **Calçada de Santa Ana** (Map 8, H6). The top end of this road is dominated by the Hospital de São José, but heading downhill it becomes more residential; some of the city's most reasonably priced restaurants are at the foot of the road, as it bears to the left. Further on the road dips down again, becoming **Calçada de Garcia** (Map 8, I7) and ending at Largo São Domingos, next to Rossio.

AVENIDA DA LIBERADE

In summer, the avenida is closed to traffic on Sundays,
making it a delightful place for a stroll as well as the best
skateboarding slope in the city.

Just west of the avenue, philanthropist and art collector
António Medeiros maintained a home at Rua Rosa Araújo
41 until his death in 1986. This is now the **Fundação
Medeiros e Almeida** (Map 8, D3; Mon–Sat 1–5.30pm;
€5), which displays a priceless series of artefacts, including
2000-year old Chinese porcelain, an important collection of
sixteenth- to nineteenth-century watches, and English and
Portuguese silverware. Other highlights include a nineteenth-century pram, made in Portugal for the Duke of
Wellington's son; paintings by Thomas Gainsborough; glorious eighteenth-century azulejos in the Sala de Lago, a room
complete with full-sized water fountains; and a rare seventeenth-century night clock, made for Queen Catherine of
Bragança and mentioned by Samuel Pepys in his diary.

At the top of Avenida da Liberdade, traffic grinds around
the **Praça Marquês de Pombal** (Map 8, D1), also known
as Rotunda, a giant roundabout marked by a central statue
of the king's minister at the time of the Great Earthquake.
Beyond lie the sloping paths and plant-houses of the Parque
Eduardo VII, or it is just a short walk west from here to the
Amoreiras shopping centre.

For listings of the best restaurants on and around the
Avenida da Liberdade, see p.163.

AMOREIRAS

Map 2, C7. Metros Marquês de Pombal or Rato; bus #11 from
Rossio or Restauradores, or bus #58 from Cais do Sodré.
From Praça Marquês de Pombal, it's around ten minutes'

walk west (and uphill) along Rua Joaquim António de Aguiar to **Amoreiras** (daily 10am–midnight), Lisbon's eye-catching, post-modern shopping centre, visible on the city skyline from almost any approach. The complex, designed by Tomás Taveira, is Portugal's most adventurous – and most entertaining – modern building: a wild fantasy of pink and blue, sheltering ten cinemas, sixty cafés and restaurants, 370 shops and a hotel. Most of the shops here stay open until midnight, seven days a week; Sunday sees the heaviest human traffic, with entire families descending for an afternoon out.

AROUND PRAÇA DAS AMOREIRAS

Map 8, B3. Metro Rato.

From Amoreiras it is just five minutes' walk southeast to **Praça das Amoreiras**, one of Lisbon's most historic squares; head down the narrow Rua das Amoreiras (or take a short walk up the same road from metro Rato on Largo do Rato). The tranquil square, with a handy kiosk café (open Sun–Fri 9am–7pm) and kids' play area, is dominated on its western side by the final section of the **Aqueduto das Águas Livres,** the traditional source of Lisbon's water, with a chapel wedged into its arches. The "Free Waters Aqueduct" was opened in 1748, bringing reliable drinking water to the city for the first time, and the entire structure stretches some 60km, mostly underground (though sections of it can be seen on either side of the tracks on the train line to Sintra). Pessoa called it "a real national monument, and perhaps the most remarkable of its kind in Europe". Although the section visible from the square is impressive enough, you can see the highest section of the aqueduct (Map 2, C6) by catching bus #11 north from Amoreiras, which passes underneath it (any bus from Praça de Espanha to Caparica also provides good views). This towering section, like the rest of the structure, stood firm during the

1755 earthquake and later gained a more notorious reputation thanks to one Diogo Alves, a nineteenth-century serial killer who threw his victims off the top – a 70-metre drop.

For an unusual walk and some amazing views, you can stroll over the top of the aqueduct to Monsanto Park – for details of tours, call the Museu da Água ☎218 135 522.

On the south side of Praça das Amoreiras, the **Mãe d'Água** water cistern (Mon–Sat 10am–6pm; €1.80) marks the end of the line for the aqueduct. The interior holds a reservoir contained in a huge, cathedral-like stone building with Gothic lion heads along its square roof. Completed in 1843, the chunky, castellated structure nowadays holds a small water museum, which hosts occasional exhibitions.

Fundação Arpad Siznes-Viera da Silva

Map 8, B3. Mon & Wed–Sat noon–8pm, Sun 10am–6pm; €2.50. Metro Rato.

On the east side of Praça das Amoreiras, set in a former eighteenth-century silk factory, the **Fundação Arpad Siznes–Viera da Silva** is a gallery dedicated to the works of two painters and the artists who have been influenced by them. Arpad Siznes (1897–1985) was a Hungarian-born artist and friend of Henri Matisse and Pierre Bonnard, amongst others. In 1928, while working as a caricaturist in Paris, he met the Portuguese artist Maria Helena Viera da Silva (1908–1992), whose work was influenced by the surrealism of Joan Miró and Max Ernst, both of whom she knew. Siznes and Viera da Silva married in 1930 and, in 1936, both exhibited in Lisbon, where they briefly lived, before they eventually settled in France and took French nationality. The foundation shows the development of both the artists' works, with Viera da Silva's more abstract, subdued paintings contrasting with the more flamboyant Siznes, some of whose paintings show the clear influence of Miró.

PARQUE EDUARDO VII

Map 9, A6–C8. Metro Marquês de Pombal or Parque, or any bus to Marquês de Pombal (Rotunda).

At the northern end of Avenida da Liberdade is the steep, formally laid-out **Parque Eduardo VII**, named after Britain's Edward VII, who visited the city in 1903. The big attractions here are the two huge, rambling *estufas* (Map 9, A7; April–Sept daily 9am–5.30pm, Oct–March daily 9am–4.30pm; €1.10), filled with tropical plants, pools and endless varieties of palms and cacti. Of the two, the **Estufa Quente**, the hothouse, has the more exotic plants; the **Estufa Fria**, the coldhouse, hosts concerts and exhibitions.

Just south of the entrance to the *estufas*, below the duck pond, is the **Parque Infantil** (summer 9am–7pm, winter 9am–5.30pm), a play area for children built round a mock galleon and overlooked by a café. Across from the *estufas* on the eastern side of the park sits the ornately tiled **Pavilhão dos Desportos** (sports pavilion), which doubles as a venue for occasional concerts and cultural events. A good spot to aim for just north of here is the tranquil pond-side park café. Beyond here, two concrete poles mark a **viewing platform** with commanding views over Lisbon; on clear days, the view stretches to the hills south of the Tejo. Finally, the northern reaches of the park contain an appealing grassy hillock complete with its own olive grove and another shallow lake, which kids splash about in during the heat of the day; another pleasant café sits alongside it.

In summer, the top of the park is usually capped by a temporary ferris wheel offering dazzling views of the capital. At Easter, a huge wooden crucifix takes pride of place here.

CASA MUSEU DR ANASTÁCIO GONÇALVES

Map 9, E6. Tues 2–6pm, Wed–Sun 10am–6pm; €2. Metro Saldanha
or Picoas.

Around a kilometre northeast of Parque Eduardo VII, the
appealing Casa Malhoa, tucked away on Rua Pinheiro Chagas,
is now the **Casa Museu Dr Anastácio Gonçalves**. The
Neo-Romantic building with Art Nouveau touches – including a beautiful stained-glass window – was originally built for
the painter José Malhoa in 1904, but now holds the private
collection of ophthalmologist, Dr Anastácio Gonçalves, who
bought the house in the 1930s. Gonçalves was Calouste
Gulbenkian's doctor and, inspired by the Armenian's example
(see p.95), decided to collect art and applied art himself. When
he died in 1964, he left his collection of over 2000 works to
the state. Highlights include paintings by Portuguese landscape
artist João Vaz and by Malhoa himself, who specialized in historical paintings – his *Dream of Infante Henriques* is a typical
example. On the top floor you'll find Chinese porcelain from
the sixteenth-century Ming dynasty, along with furniture from
England, France, Holland and Spain dating from the seventeenth century. The downstairs rooms also host temporary
exhibits, from historical costume to contemporary art.

The museum is in the commercial Saldanha district, only
a few minutes' walk from the metro at Praça Duque de
Saldanha, at the southern end of the broad Avenida da
República. *Café Versailles* – one of Lisbon's grandest traditional cafés (see p.175) – lies on the avenue just north of the
square, a handy place to know about if you're looking for a
coffee after your museum visit.

FUNDAÇÃO CALOUSTE GULBENKIAN

Map 9, B4–C4. Ⓦwww.gulbenkian.pt. Tues 2pm–6pm; Wed–Sun
10am–6pm. Museu Calouste Gulbenkian: €3, free on Sun; Centro

de Arte Moderna: €3, free on Sun; combined ticket €5. Metro to Praça de Espanha or São Sebastião; bus #31 or #46 from Restauradores, or bus #51 from Belém (not weekends).

The **Fundação Calouste Gulbenkian** is the great cultural centre of Portugal – the wonder is that it's not better known internationally. Housed in a superb complex just north of Parque Eduardo VII, the foundation is set in its own park with a small lake, and features a museum whose collections seem to take in virtually every great phase of Eastern and Western art – from Ancient Egyptian scarabs to Art Nouveau jewellery. In a separate building across the park, a modern Portuguese art museum touches on most twentieth-century styles.

Astonishingly, all the main museum exhibits were acquired by just one man, the Armenian oil magnate **Calouste Gulbenkian** (1869–1955), whose legendary art-market coups included the acquisition of works from the Hermitage in St Petersburg following the Russian Revolution. In a scarcely less astute deal made during World War II, Gulbenkian auctioned himself and his collections to the European nations: Portugal bid security, an aristocratic palace home (a *marquês* was asked to move out) and tax exemption, acquiring in return one of the most important cultural patrons of the century.

Today the Gulbenkian Foundation has a multi-million dollar budget sufficient to run an orchestra, three concert halls and two galleries for temporary exhibitions in the capital alone. It also finances work in all spheres of Portuguese cultural life – there are Gulbenkian museums and libraries in even the smallest towns – and makes charitable grants to a vast range of projects.

Museu Calouste Gulbenkian

The **Museu Calouste Gulbenkian** (main entrance on Avenida de Berna) was completely renovated in 2001,

FUNDAÇÃO CALOUSTE GULBENKIAN

which has improved the layout and the labelling – now in English and Portuguese – as well as enlarging the exhibition space to allow viewing of items that were previously held in storage. The collections themselves aren't immense but each contains pieces of such individual interest and beauty that you need frequent unwinding sessions – well provided for by the basement **café-bar** and tranquil gardens.

Classical and Oriental art

It seems arbitrary to hint at highlights, but they must include the entire contents of the small **Egyptian room**, which covers almost every period of importance from the Old Kingdom (2700 BC) to the Roman period.

Particularly striking is the Head of Sestrostris III, a ruler of the XIIth dynasty (2026–1785 BC), and the remarkable bronze cats (664–525 BC), which look as if they were cast yesterday. Fine **Roman** statues, silver and glass, and intricate gold jewellery and coins from ancient **Greece**, follow. **Mesopotamia** produced the earliest forms of writing and two cylinder seals – one dating from before 2500 BC – are on display here, along with alabaster bas-reliefs from the Assyrian civilization. The **Islamic arts** are magnificently represented by a variety of ornamental texts, opulently woven carpets, glassware (such as the fourteenth-century mosque lamps from Syria) and Turkish azulejos. There is also some stunning fourteenth-century Syrian painted glass and intricate eighteenth-century silk coats from **Persia**. These are followed by a variety of remarkable illuminated manuscripts and ceramics from **Armenia**, porcelain from **China**, and beautiful **Japanese** prints and lacquer-work.

European art

European art includes work from all the major schools, beginning with a group of French medieval ivory diptychs (in particular, the six scenes depicting the *Life of the Virgin*) and a thirteenth-century manuscript of Saint John's prophetic *Apocalypse with the Commentary of Beregaudus*, produced in Kent and touched up in Italy. From fifteenth-century Flanders, there's a pair of panels by Rogier van der Weyden, and from the same period in Italy comes Domenico Ghirlandaio's *Portrait of a Young Woman*. The seventeenth-century collection yields two exceptional portraits – one by Peter Paul Rubens of his second wife, *Helena Fourment*, and Rembrandt's *Figure of an Old Man* – plus works by Anthony van Dyck and Jacob van Ruisdael. Featured eighteenth-century works include those by Jean Honoré Fragonard, Thomas Gainsborough – in particular the stunning *Portrait of Mrs Lowndes-Stone* – and Francesco

FUNDAÇÃO CALOUSTE GULBENKIAN

Guardi. Finally nineteenth- to twentieth-century France is represented by Jean Baptiste Camille Corot, Edouard Manet, Claude Monet, Edgar Degas and Auguste Renoir; Manet's *Boy With Cherries* and Renoir's *Portrait of Madame Claude Monet* are particularly worth seeking out.

Sculpture is poorly represented on the whole, though a fifteenth-century medallion of *Faith* by Luca della Robbia and a 1780 marble *Diana* by Jean-Antoine Houdon stand out. Elsewhere, you'll find **ceramics** from Spain and Italy; fifteenth-century Italian bronze **medals** (especially by Pisanello); **furniture** from the reigns of Louis XV and Louis XVI; eighteenth-century works from **French gold-smiths**; and assorted Italian tapestries and textiles, including a superb fifteenth-century red velvet parasol from Venice. The last room features a stunning **Art Nouveau** collection of 169 pieces of fantasy jewellery by René Lalique; look for the amazing bronze and ivory Medusa paperweight and the fantastical *Peitoral-libélula* (dragonfly breastpiece) brooch, half woman, half dragonfly, decorated with enamel work, gold, diamonds and moonstones.

Centro de Arte Moderna

To reach the **Centro de Arte Moderna** (main entrance on Rua Dr. Nicolau de Bettencourt) from the museum you can walk through the gardens, which are enlivened by some specially commissioned sculptures (including a Henry Moore). There are refreshments on hand in the popular self-service restaurant, adjacent to the centre.

The modern art centre features most of the big names on the twentieth-century Portuguese scene, including Almada Negreiros (1873–1970), the founder of *modernismo* (look out for his self-portrait, set in the café *A Brasileira*), Amadeu de Sousa Cardoso and Guilherme Santa-Rita (both of Futurist inclinations), and **Paula Rego** (one of Portugal's leading contemporary artists; see box below). Some international figures are also represented, including the American abstract-expressionist Arshile Gorky. Exhibits change regularly but it's worth watching out for works by rising Portuguese stars Pedro Cabrito Reis and Rui Chafes.

PAULA REGO

Paula Rego shot to international prominence in 1990 when she was appointed as the National Gallery Artist in Residence in London, and she is now considered one of the world's leading figurative painters. Although she has spent most of her life in England – she married English artist Vic Willing – her formative years were spent in Salazar's Lisbon, where she was born in 1935. Her sheltered childhood was passed in the confines of a wealthy family home and she still feels bitter about the way her mother became a "casualty" of a society that encouraged wealthy women to be idle, leaving work to their servants. Her women are portrayed as typical of the servants of her childhood: stocky and solid. Other adults are usually viewed with the unsentimental eye of a child, and she avoids graceful forms, preferring hairy, bony yet powerful female figures. Power and dominance are major themes of her work; she revives the military outfits of post-war Portugal for her men and dresses many of her women like dolls in national costume. Several of her pictures convey sexual opposition, the result perhaps of a background dominated by the regimes of the Roman Catholic Church and a military dictatorship. Her images are rarely beautiful, but are undoubtedly amusing, disturbing and powerful. Her work is often displayed at galleries and temporary exhibitions around Lisbon.

FUNDAÇÃO CALOUSTE GULBENKIAN

Outer Lisbon

ew visitors explore the bustling modern areas north of Parque Eduardo VII and the Gulbenkian. However, you may well travel in this way from the airport – most buses run through Campo Grande and past the bullring at Campo Pequeno – and, for anyone wanting to exhaust Lisbon's sights, there are a few diverting destinations in and around these neighbourhoods. **Campo Grande** features a small city fun fair, the **Feira Popular**, and a couple of minor museums, and there are two more low-key museums housed in an eighteenth-century palace in the suburb of **Lumiar**, 2km further to the north. It's on the city's western periphery, however, that the best attractions are sited: the city's zoo, the **Jardim Zoológico**, and the one must-see sight in outer Lisbon, the **Palácio dos Marquêses de Fronteira**, famed for its collection of azulejos.

The area covered by this chapter is shown in detail on colour map 2.

CAMPO GRANDE

Map 2, E3–E4.

Campo Grande (literally, "the big field") was once an

extensive park, although urban sprawl has severely diminished its extent and it's now one of Lisbon's main traffic arteries. Nonetheless the central grassy strip between the carriageways, sporting a lake and otherwise filled with trees, cafés and tennis courts, makes a surprisingly pleasant escape during the day (though you should take care here after dark). At the southern end of Campo Grande sits the **Feira Popular** (Map 2, E5; March–Oct Mon–Fri 7pm–1.30am, Sat & Sun 3pm–1.30am; Dec Tues–Fri 2.30–10pm, Sat & Sun 11am–10pm; closed Nov, Jan & Feb; €2, rides extra; metro Entrecampos), a fairground that is popular with the Portuguese youth and certainly makes a fun afternoon out for the kids. It neatly combines old-fashioned carousels with modern rollercoasters and white-knuckle rides. The cafés and restaurants are also pretty good and fairly inexpensive.

To the west of Campo Grande spreads the campus of the city's **university**, while at the top end are two museums, which you can reach on bus #1 from Cais do Sodré via Rossio, or by metro to Campo Grande. The **Museu da Cidade**, at Campo Grande 245 (Map 2, E3; Tues–Sun 10am–1pm & 2–6pm; €2, free on Sun) provides useful background on the city's history, tracing the development of Lisbon from the year dot to the present day. Installed in the eighteenth-century Palácio Pimenta on the western side of Campo Grande, its principal interest lies in an imaginatively displayed collection of prints and paintings, as well as an impressive model of pre-1755 Lisbon. Enjoyable, too, are various azulejo panels showing scenes of the city throughout history.

Another lovely mansion houses the **Museu Rafael Bordalo Pinheiro** (Map 2, E3; Tues–Sun 10am–1pm & 2–6pm; €1.40), seeing which involves a death-defying crossing of the road to Campo Grande 382. Pinheiro (1846–1905) was an architect, ceramicist and political caricaturist who ran a ceramics factory in Caldas da Rainha, north of Lisbon. Upstairs, exhibits include his amazing collection of ornate dishes crawling with ceramic crabs and lobsters, frogs and snakes. The paintings, cartoons and sketches downstairs are of less interest.

LUMIAR

Some 2km further north of the Museu da Cidade in the suburb of **Lumiar**, the eighteenth-century **Palácio do Monteiro-Mor** boasts some interesting period decor and also houses two specialist museums. The surrounding **park** (daily 9am until dusk) is at least as big an attraction – one of the most lush areas in the city, and featuring a good restaurant and café. To get there, take bus #1 from Restauradores or Campo Grande.

The **Museu do Traje** (Costume Museum; Map 2, E1; Tues–Sun 10am–6pm; joint ticket with Museu do Teatro €3, free on Sun 10am–2pm), has particularly extensive collections, which are drawn upon for temporary thematic exhibitions – excellent if costume is your subject, less gripping if you're not an aficionado of faded fabrics. The entrance is on Largo Júlio Castilho, Estrada do Paço do Lumiar. The small **Museu do Teatro** (Theatre Museum; Map 2, D1; Tues 2–6pm, Wed–Sun 10am–6pm; tickets as for Museu do Traje) is housed in another section of the palace, with its entrance on Estrada do Paço do Lumiar. This is of truly specialist interest, displaying photos of famous Portuguese actors, theatrical props and costumes.

JARDIM ZOOLÓGICO

Map 2, C4. ⓦwww.zoolisboa.pt. April–Sept daily 10am–8pm, Oct–March daily 10am–6pm; €10. Metro Jardim Zoológico or bus #31 or #46 from Restauradores.

Lisbon's zoo, the **Jardim Zoológico**, at Estrada da Benfica

158–160, has been given a facelift in recent years but, even so, remains one of the least inspiring of European zoos, exhibiting unhappy captives encouraged to perform demeaning tricks. On the other hand, it's really as much a rambling garden as anything else and its peculiarly Portuguese eruptions of kitsch (an extraordinary dogs' cemetery, for instance) make for an enjoyable afternoon's ramble. A small *teleferique* or **cable car** (daily from 11am until closing time; included in the price) transports you around the grounds in pods that resemble parrot cages. There's also a well-stocked reptile house (10am–noon & 1–6pm) and a boating lake as further diversions.

PALÁCIO DOS MARQUÊSES DE FRONTEIRA

Map 2, B5. Tours daily Mon–Sat: June–Sept at 10.30am, 11am, 11.30am and noon; Oct–May at 11am and noon; €5, gardens only €2.50; reservations advised ☏217 782 023. Bus #46 from Restauradores (or the zoo) passes nearby, or it's a 20min walk west from the zoo.

You certainly don't need to be a dyed-in-the-wool palace enthusiast to enjoy a visit to the **Palácio dos Marquêses de Fronteira**, a seventeenth-century former hunting lodge on the northeastern fringes of the Parque de Monsanto. Built in 1670 for the first Marquês de Fronteira, João de Mascarenhas, and still inhabited by descendents of the same family, the palace has been partly open to the public since 1989. With its entrance on Largo de São Domingos de Benfica, off Rua de São Domingos de Benfica, the small, pink country house stands out among the bland housing developments in this part of Lisbon. The formal gardens are particularly fine, complete with ornate topiary, statues and fountains, but it's the interior that impresses most, notably the stunning azulejos dating back to the seventeenth century. Some of the rooms are completely lined with them, including the **Sala das Batalhas** (Battle Room) whose tiles depict vivid scenes from the Restoration Wars with Spain. Guided tours of the interior last about an hour, after which you're free to wander in the gardens.

Parque das Nações

The **Parque das Nações** (Map 1, G5), or "Park of Nations", is the name given to the former site of Expo 98, which lies 5km to the east of the city centre. It's a huge attraction for Lisboetas, especially at weekends when it is packed (go during a weekday outside the summer and the park is far quieter). Its appeal is clear: the flat, wide, traffic-free walkways lined with fountains, palms, cafés and futuristic buildings are a complete contrast to the narrow, precipitous streets of old Lisbon. The main highlight is the **Oceanário de Lisboa**, the world's second-largest oceanarium and one of Lisbon's most impressive sights. The **Pavilhão de Realidade Virtual** (Virtual Reality Pavilion) is another popular draw, while the educational exhibits in the **Centro da Ciência Viva** (Centre of Live Science) are also rewarding. Other attractions here include water gardens, a cable car and viewing tower, and two of Lisbon's largest concert venues. In addition, there's a diverse array of shops, bars and restaurants, many with outdoor seating overlooking **Olivais dock** and the astonishing seventeen-kilometre-long Vasco da Gama bridge over the Tejo.

The easiest way to reach the Parque is by taking the metro to Oriente (red line from Alameda). See p.286 for details of ferry connections from Cacilhas.

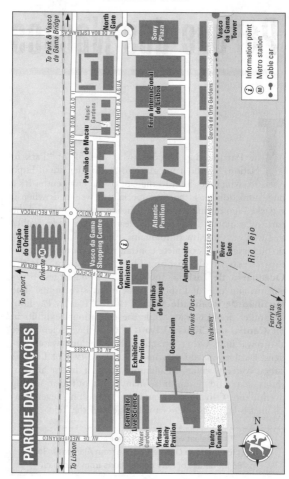

PARQUE DAS NAÇÕES

Key:
- *i* Information point
- Ⓜ Metro station
- ● Cable car

Labels on map:

To Park & Vasco da Gama Bridge
North Gate
AV. DE BOA ESPERANÇA
Sony Plaza
Vasco da Gama Tower
AVENIDA DOM JOÃO II
CAMINHO DA ÁGUA
Music Gardens
Pavilhão de Macau
Feira Internacional de Lisboa
Garcia de Orta Gardens
RUA DO BOJADOR
RUA DO INDICO
AV. DO INDICO
Atlantic Pavilion
Estação do Oriente
Vasco da Gama Shopping Centre
i
PASSEIO DAS TAGIDES
Rio Tejo
To airport
Oriente Ⓜ
AV. DE PACIFICO
AV. DE BERLIM
River Gate
Council of Ministers
RUA DO BOJADOR
Amphitheatre
Olivais Dock
Ferry to Cacilhas
RUA DOS ULISSES
AVENIDA DOM JOÃO II
Pavilhão de Portugal
Walkway
To Lisbon
CAMINHO DA ÁGUA
Exhibitions Pavilion
Oceanarium
Centre for Live Science
Water Garden
Virtual Reality Pavilion
Teatro Camões
AV. DE MEDITERRÂNEO
N

EXPO 98 AND AFTER

The **Expo 98 site** was built as a giant maritime-influenced theme park to coincide with the 500th anniversary of Vasco da Gama's arrival in India and the UN's "Year of the Oceans". The event was a huge success that placed Lisbon firmly in the international spotlight – for a year at least. But the funds raised for and generated by the event have also had a lasting impact on Lisbon as a whole, providing the impetus for a city-wide facelift. As well as revitalizing a derelict industrial area, virtually every city monument was touched up. Substantial improvements were carried out to the city's transport infrastructure, including a drastic expansion of the metro, a new rail line under the Ponte 25 de Abril, and a brand new bridge over the Tejo, the Ponte Vasco da Gama.

While the Parque das Nações is evolving into a thriving entertainment zone, it forms only part of a hugely ambitious urban regeneration project. An area of three square kilometres around the Parque is in the process of being transformed into a large-scale business and residential zone, with the aim of redirecting Lisbon's sprawling suburbs in a more planned fashion towards the east of the city; completion is due in the next ten years.

Arrival and information

Stepping off the metro, you arrive in the bowels of the **Estação do Oriente**, a stunning glass-and-concrete bus-and-train station designed by Spanish architect Santiago Calatrava. Leaving the station, it's easy to be drawn into the substantial Vasco da Gama shopping centre opposite (see p.226), but to reach the Parque, head right through the centre and you'll find the main **Posto de Informação** (information desk; daily 9.30am–8pm; @www.parquedasnacoes.pt), which has details of all the sights and events. If you want to visit everything, it is worth buying a **Cartão do Parque** from the desk. The "park card" (€11.50, or €28 for a family of four) allows free access to the main sights and discounts at other attractions.

It is not too taxing to walk to the principal attractions, especially if you take advantage of the cable car (see opposite) to jump between the Oceanário and the Torre Vasco da Gama. From the entrance, you can either turn right into the **southern** half of the Parque – where you'll find the Oceanário, Pavilhão da Realidade Virtual, and Centro da Ciência Viva – or left into the **northern** half, to the Torre Vasco da Gama, waterfront gardens and Sony Plaza. Alternatively, hop on the **toy train,** which trundles anti-clockwise around the whole Parque (every 20min, daily 10.30am–7pm; €1), starting and finishing in front of the Pavilhão Atlântico. You can also **rent bikes** from in front of Sony Plaza (from around €4 per hour; ID or a passport required as a deposit), a good way to get around the flat, traffic-free lanes.

PARQUE SOUTH

One of the most impressive of the many adventurous structures in the Parque is the **Pavilhão de Portugal** (Portugal Pavilion), the main building facing Olivais dock, featuring an enormous, sagging concrete canopy on its south side. Designed by Álvaro Siza Vieira, architect of the reconstructed Chiado district in the city, the building now holds Portugal's Council of Ministers (a forum for Portuguese Members of Parliament).

Cafés and restaurants line the calm waters of the **Olivais dock** (the best are reviewed on p.165) and heading south along here you'll pass the **Pavilhão das Exposições** (Exhibitions Pavilion) with temporary exhibitions on diverse themes, from the work of individual artists to the history of the tea trade. Next up is the **Centro da Ciência Viva** (Centre of Live Science; Tues–Fri 10am–6pm, Sat & Sun 11am–7pm, last entry an hour before closing; €4.50), run by Portugal's Ministry of Science and Technology (which shares the premises) and hosting changing exhibitions on subjects such as 3D animation and the latest computer technology. The permanent exhibits aimed at children – from flight simulators to holograms – are particularly good and there's also a cybercafé offering free internet access. Behind lies the **Jardim da Água** (Water Garden), crisscrossed by riverlets and ponds linked by stepping-stones, and with enough gushing fountains, water gadgets and pumps to keep children occupied for hours.

At the foot of the gardens stands the **Pavilhão da Realidade Virtual** (Virtual Reality Pavilion; daily noon–5.30pm; €8), inside which there's a fascinating recreation of Luís de Camões's sixteenth-century travels to the New World. The virtual experience starts slowly but culminates in a memorable ride on a caravel through a tempest and pirate attack.

On the riverfront side of the Virtual Reality Pavilion is the **Teatro Camões,** the Parque's main venue for theatre, classical music and opera. Beyond here, more cafés sprawl along the waterfront to the south, while to the north, a narrow walkway leads across Olivais dock, underneath the ski-lift-style **cable car** (daily 11am–7pm; €2.50 one way). This shuttles you to the northern side of the Parque, giving commanding views over the site on the way.

Oceanário de Lisboa

ⓦwww.oceanario.pt. Daily 10am–7pm, last entrance 6pm; €8.50.

Designed by Peter Chermaeff and looking like something off the set of a James Bond film, the **Oceanário de**

Lisboa (Lisbon Oceanarium), Europe's largest, contains some 25,000 fish and marine animals. Its main feature is the enormous central tank, the size of four Olympic-sized swimming pools, which you can look into from different levels for close-up, top-to-bottom views – of the sharks, which circle the main body of the water, down to the rays burying themselves into the sand on the sea bed. Almost more impressive, though, are the recreations of various ocean ecosystems, like the Antarctic tank, containing frolicking penguins, and the Pacific tank, where otters bob about and play in the rock pools. These areas are separated from the main tank by invisible acrylic sheets, giving the impression that all the marine creatures are swimming together in the same space. On the darkened lower level, smaller tanks contain shoals of brightly coloured tropical fish and other warm-water creatures. Find a window free of school parties and the whole experience becomes the closest you'll get to deep-sea diving without getting wet.

The Oceanarium attracts hefty queues, particularly at weekends; get there early or expect to wait up to an hour to get in.

PARQUE NORTH

The cable car from the Oceanarium takes you to the **Jardim Garcia de Orta**, (Garcia de Orta Garden), a leafy waterside strip displaying plant species collected from Portugal's former colonies. But the main draw on this side of the Parque is a lift ride to the top of the **Torre Vasco da Gama** (Vasco da Gama Tower; Mon–Thurs 10am–8pm, Fri & Sat 10am–10pm; €2.50). Once an integral part of an oil refinery, the viewing platform gives a 360° panorama over Lisbon, the Tejo and into the Alentejo to the south. The summit also holds a pricey restaurant (see p.166).

Opposite the tower is the **Sony Plaza**, Lisbon's largest purpose-built outdoor arena, which often hosts concerts and sports events. At other times, it's the site of **Adrenalina**, a small adventure park (Tues–Fri 2–7pm, Sat & Sun 11am–7pm; most rides/equipment €4) featuring skateboard ramps, climbing walls, trampolines and a "Skycoaster", a kind of bunjee swing suspended 35m up; there are also bouncy castles and inflatables for younger children. If all this isn't enough excitement, you can also rent bumper boats from here – little motorized pedaloes – for use on the stretch of water in Olivais dock, but these will set you back €4 for just ten minutes.

Opposite Sony Plaza, Lisbon's trade fair hall, the **Feira Internacional de Lisboa** (FIL), hosts various events including a handicrafts fair displaying ceramics and crafts from round the country (usually in July). This was the space formerly occupied by Expo 98's international pavilions and at the back of FIL is the only surviving exhibition, in the **Pavilhão de Macau** (Tues–Fri noon–6pm, Sat & Sun 3–8pm; €2). The former Portuguese colony of Macau was handed back to China in 1999 and the pavilion highlights various aspects of life in Hong Kong's much smaller neighbour. Behind the impressive mock-colonial facade, a cleverly laid out series of mirrors and winding corridors makes the pavilion feel a lot bigger than it really is. The sounds of Macau add an atmospheric backdrop to recreations of famous buildings, shop interiors and gambling halls, before a ten-minute film shows you images of the Chinese territory. You can sample tea in a typical *casa da cha* (tea house) before leaving via a typical Chinese garden, complete with a koi fish pond and basking terrapins.

Heading back towards the waterfront cafés and restaurants of Olivais dock you'll pass the bulk of the impressive

Pavilhão Atlântico (Atlantic Pavilion), officially Portugal's largest indoor arena and the venue for major visiting bands and sporting events.

LISTINGS

9	Accommodation	115
10	Eating	136
11	Cafés	167
12	Bars and clubs	176
13	Gay Lisbon	190
14	Live music	194
15	Cinema and theatre	205
16	Sport and outdoor activities	208
17	Shopping	216
18	Kids' Lisbon	228
19	Festivals	233
20	Directory	240

LISTINGS

Accommodation

Nearly every part of Lisbon offers comfortable accommodation, though if you're after affordable modern comforts you may need to move slightly away from the central Baixa grid. There are three basic types of accommodation: **pensions** (*pensões*; singular *pensão*), **guesthouses** (*residenciais*; singular *residencial*) and **hotels** – the only difference between the first two is that some *pensões* serve meals, while *residenciais* do not.

Pensions and guesthouses are officially graded from one to three stars, with the more basic ones having little more than a sink in the room, while three-star places may include en-suite bathroom facilities and a TV. One-star hotels are much the same as three-star *pensões,* but hotels with two stars are markedly better, while in three-star hotels and above you can expect **air conditioning** and mini-bars as standard. Where there's a TV in the room, channels in the cheaper hotels are likely to be Portuguese only. However, many three-star (and above) hotels can be counted on to have at least a few satellite or cable channels and even in-house video channels. All the pensions, guesthouses and hotels reviewed below have an **en-suite bath or shower** unless otherwise stated. Most guesthouses and hotels also include **breakfast**, comprising anything from bread, jam and coffee to a generous spread of rolls, cereals, croissants, cold meat, cheese and fruit.

There are scores of small, inexpensive pensions and guesthouses, often in tall tenement buildings in the central parts of the city. The most obvious – but also noisiest – accommodation area is at the **northern end of the Baixa** around Rossio, Praça dos Restauradores and Praça da Figueira. North of here, the streets parallel to **Avenida da Liberdade** (particularly Rua Portas de Santo Antão and the more seedy Rua da Glória) are where you're most likely to find a cheap bed at busy times of year, while the Avenida itself has some of the city's smartest hotels. The **central Baixa** has a fair selection of places, too, and there are a couple of more upmarket choices in the **Chiado** area. **Bairro Alto** is one of the more interesting parts of the city in which to stay, although rooms in its few pensions can be hard to come by and the noisy nightlife goes on late. For atmosphere, it is hard to beat the few attractive places on the periphery of **Alfama**, and up towards the castle. More upmarket hotels are located away from the city centre, either in the prosperous suburb of **Lapa**, around **Parque Eduardo VII**, or in the business area of **Saldanha**, near the Gulbenkian. Wherever you stay in central Lisbon, you're never much more than twenty or thirty minutes from the airport, so early flights shouldn't be a problem.

DISABLED ACCESS

Accommodation reviewed in this book with **disabled access** includes: Hotel Costa da Caparica (p.290); Hotel Fénix (p.132); Lapa Palace (p.128); Hotel Lisboa Plaza (p.130); Le Méridien Park Atlantic (p.132); Hotel Mundial (p.122); Hotel Veneza (p.130); Parque Municipal de Campismo (p.135); Pousada de Juventude de Lisboa (youth hostel) at Picoas (p.125); Pousada Dona Maria I, Queluz (p.269); Hotel Real Parque (p.133); Ritz Four Seasons (p.133); and Tivoli Lisboa (p.130).

Our listings are divided into the following areas: The Baixa
Grid (p.118); Rossio and around (p.119); Chiado (p.123);
Alfama and Castelo (p.123); Bairro Alto and around (p.126);
Lapa (p.127); Around Avenida da Liberdade (p.128); Parque
Eduardo VII and Saldanha (p.131).

There are four **youth hostels** (*pousadas de juventude*) in
and around Lisbon (see p.124), including one right in the
city centre, and another out at Sintra (see p.261). The city's
main **campsite** is in the hilltop Parque Florestal de
Monsanto, 6km out of the centre, and there are also some
decent campsites within commuting distance of Lisbon,
either near the Atlantic beaches of Costa da Caparica,
Guincho and Praia Grande, or near beaches south of the
Tejo; see p.134 for a complete listing.

The main tourist offices (see p.7 for details) can provide
accommodation lists, but won't reserve rooms for you. In
the summer months in particular, email, fax or telephone
a **reservation** at least a week in advance; most owners
understand English. It is also advisable to reconfirm any
booking a day or two in advance and, ideally, to get written confirmation, as some places have been known to
deny all knowledge of verbal reservations during busy
times. At Easter and in summer, **room availability** is
often stretched to the limit, with prices artificially inflated
(though August is often considered mid-season, as most
locals clear out of the city). At these times you should be
prepared to take anything vacant and, if need be, look
around the next day for somewhere better or cheaper.
Fortunately, during most of the year you should have little difficulty in finding a room and you can always try to
knock the price down at quieter times, especially if you
can summon a few good-natured phrases in Portuguese.

ACCOMMODATION

To phone Lisbon from abroad, dial the international access
code followed by 351, followed by the subscriber's nine-
figure number.

When doing the rounds, be warned that pensions tend
to occupy upper storeys of tall buildings – leaving one
person downstairs with all the bags is a good idea if you're
in company. **Addresses** are written in the form "Rua do
Crucifixo 50–4°", meaning the fourth storey of no. 50,
Rua do Crucifixo. The addition of e, d or r/c at the end
means the entrance is on the left (*esquerda*), right (*direita*)
or on the ground floor (*rés-do-chão*). Don't be unduly put
off by some fairly insalubrious staircases, but do be aware
that rooms facing onto the street can often be unbearably
noisy.

ACCOMMODATION PRICE CODES

Apart from information on youth hostels (when actual prices
are given), all the accommodation prices in this book have
been coded using the symbols below. The symbols represent
the price in euros of the **cheapest double room in high
season**.

❶ under €25	❹ €55–€75	❼ €125–€150
❷ €25–€35	❺ €75–€100	❽ €150–€200
❸ €35–€55	❻ €100–€125	❾ over €200

THE BAIXA GRID

Hotel Duas Nações
Map 3, G6. Rua da Vitória 41
☏ 213 460 710, ☏ 213 470
206

Classy, pleasantly faded nineteenth-century hotel with a
secure entrance and helpful,
English-speaking reception.
Surprisingly quiet for so cen-

tral a location. Rooms without private bathroom are priced a category lower. ❸

Residencial Insulana
Map 3, F6. Rua da Assunção 52 ⓣ & Ⓕ 213 427 625
Reached via a series of underwear shops, this is one of the more upmarket Baixa options, with carpeted entrance hall, smart rooms, English-speaking staff and its own bar overlooking a quiet pedestrianized street. ❸

Pensão Moderna
Map 3, E6. Rua dos Correeiros 205–4° ⓣ 213 460 818
Situated at the top of an offputting staircase, but once inside you'll find big, clean rooms crammed with elderly furniture. It could do with a lick of paint, but is fine for the bargain-basement price. Some rooms have (rickety) balconies overlooking the pedestrianized street. Shared bathrooms. ❷

Pensão Prata
Map 3, H5. Rua da Prata 71–3° ⓣ 213 468 908
You'll need mountaineering experience to climb the stairs to this pension, which has small rooms in a welcoming, family-run apartment – you pass to and fro via their TV lounge. Some rooms have their own showers (toilets are separate), while others share a clean bathroom. Book in advance as it's popular. ❷

ROSSIO AND AROUND

Pensão Arco da Bandeira
Map 3, E6. Rua dos Sapateiros 226–4° ⓣ 213 423 478
Basic but friendly *pensão* with half a dozen fading but comfortable rooms, some overlooking Rossio. The shared bathrooms are spotless. The entrance is just through the arch at the southern end of the square. Don't be put off by the dingy stairway, or by the fact it's opposite a porn cinema (actually Lisbon's oldest film house). ❸

Hotel Avenida Palace
Map 3, C7. Rua 1° Dezembro

123 Ⓣ213 460 151, Ⓕ213 422 884, Ⓦwww.hotel-avenida-palace.pt
Built at the end of the nineteenth century, this is one of Lisbon's most historic and grand hotels. Despite extensive modernization, the traditional feel has been maintained with stacks of chandeliers, period furniture, mirrors and marble throughout. There are eighty spacious rooms, each with high ceilings and colossal bathrooms. ❽

Pensão Beira Minho

Map 3, C5. Praça da Figueira 6–2° Ⓣ213 461 846
Very well situated on one of the main squares. Although rooms are small, some have fine views, especially on the upper floors, although the cheapest ones don't even have a window. The price includes breakfast. ❸

Pensão Coimbra e Madrid

Map 3, D6. Praça da Figueira 3–3° Ⓣ213 421 760, Ⓕ 213 423 264
Best choice on the square is this large, decently run (if faintly shabby) *pensão*, above the *Pastelaria Suíça*, with superb views of Rossio, Praça da Figueira and the castle beyond from (street-honkingly noisy) front-facing rooms. Some have their own shower or bath; there's a TV room, too, and breakfast is included in the price. ❹

Residencial Florescente

Map 3, A7. Rua das Portas de Santo Antão 99 Ⓣ213 426 609, Ⓕ213 427 733
One of the best-value establishments on this pedestrianized street. There's a large selection of rooms across four floors (some with TV and small bathroom) so if you don't like the look of the room you're shown – and some are very cramped – ask about alternatives. Be warned that street-facing rooms can be noisy. Breakfast is included. ❸

Pensão Residencial Gerês

Map 3, B5. Calçada da Garcia 6 Ⓣ218 810 497, Ⓕ218 882 006
Set on a steep side street just off Rossio, the beautifully tiled entrance hall and chunky wood doors set the tone for

one of the more characterful central options. The simple rooms of varying sizes are minimally furnished, though all have TVs; some, priced a category lower, share a bathroom. **④**

Pensão Ibérica

Map 3, D5. Praça da Figueira 10–2° ⊤ 218 865 781, Ⓕ 218 867 412

Boasts a central location and lots of rooms (most with TVs) but it's a bit ramshackle. The rooms overlooking the square have the best views and most light, but are very noisy. The price includes a generous breakfast and reception is open 24hr – useful for those planning a late night out. **③**

Pensão Imperial

Map 3, A7. Praça dos Restauradores 78–4° ⊤ & Ⓕ 213 420 166

In a sunny position at the bottom of Restauradores (by Rua Jardim Regedor), picked out by a fine blue-tiled facade. Enter through an optician's shop and climb to the top floor for small rooms, some with showers. The best have a view up Avenida da Liberdade. **②**

Hotel International

Map 3, D6. Rua da Betesga 3 ⊤ 213 461 913, Ⓕ 213 478 635

This is a smart central choice set in a traditional building and if you get one of the - albeit small - rooms with a balcony overlooking the city, you'll not be disappointed. There's also a bar and a friendly reception. **④**

Hotel Metrópole

Map 3, D7. Rossio 30 ⊤ 213 469 164, Ⓕ 213 469 166, Ⓦ www.almeidahotels.com

Very centrally located turn-of-the-century hotel, with an airy lounge bar – and most rooms – offering superb views over Rossio and the castle. The simply furnished but spacious rooms are comfortable, but you pay for the location and the square can be pretty noisy at night. **⑦**

Pensão Monumental

Map 8, F6. Rua da Glória 21 ⊤ 213 469 807, Ⓕ 213 430 213

A backpackers' favourite, with a mixed bag of rooms (some sleeping three) in a rambling old building. The hot water supply is a little erratic, but the

ROSSIO AND AROUND

pensão is in a good position close to the Portuguese Tourist Office and the *elevador* to the Bairro Alto. ③

Hotel Mundial

Map 3, C5. Rua Dom Duarte 4 ⓣ 218 842 000, ⓕ 218 842 110, ⓦ www.hotel-mundial.pt
Central four-star high-rise, with around three hundred rooms, at the southern edge of the broad Largo Martim Moniz. Although a little sterile, there's a Moorish-inspired rooftop terrace and great views from the eighth-floor restaurant. Rooms aren't always huge, but come with plush bathrooms. A large but poor-quality buffet breakfast is included. ⑥

Pensão Portuense

Map 3, A7. Rua das Portas de Santo Antão 151–153 ⓣ 213 464 197, ⓕ 213 424 239
Singles and doubles in a family-run place that takes good care of its guests – there's even internet access on request. The spacious bathrooms are kept meticulously clean, the water stays hot, and breakfast features crisp fresh bread and preserves. ③

Hotel Portugal

Map 3, C4. Rua João das Regras 4 ⓣ 218 877 581, ⓕ 218 867 343
Amazing old hotel that has suffered an appalling conversion, with its high decorative ceilings chopped up by wall partitions. Nevertheless, the rooms are comfortable and air conditioned, the bathrooms are marble-lined and there's an ornate TV room with period furniture. ④

Hotel Suíço Atlântico

Map 8, F6. Rua da Glória 3–19 ⓣ 213 461 713, ⓕ 213 469 013, ⓔ h.suisso.atlantico@mail .telepac.pt
Popular mid-range hotel in a good location, around the corner from the *elevador*, just off Restauradores. Rooms are fairly standard, though some come with balconies looking down on to seedy Rua da Glória. The bar's the best bit, an intriguing mock-baronial affair. ④

Residencial do Sul

Map 3, C7. Rossio 59 ⓣ 213 422 511, ⓕ 218 132 697
Entered through a small shop, this is very close to Rossio station and the National Theatre. It's a good first choice if you

want a view of Rossio from your room, but be prepared for the noise; there are some quieter back rooms, though some of these don't have windows. All rooms have TVs. ❸

CHIADO

Hotel Borges

Map 3, F9. Rua Garrett 108
☎ 213 461 951, ⓕ 213 426 617
In a prime spot on Chiado's main street, this traditional and elegantly furnished hotel is very popular. The rooms themselves are plain and aren't huge but are good value. Breakfast included. ❸

Hotel Lisboa Regency

Map 3, G7. Rua Nova do Almada 114 ☎ 213 256 100, ⓕ 213 256 161,
ⓦ www.regency-hotels -resort.com
For style and modern flare it would be hard to find a better central hotel. Designed by Álvaro Siza Viera – the architect responsible for the Chiado redevelopment – and with Oriental-inspired interior decor by the highly rated Portuguese designer Pedro Espírito Santo, the Lisboa Regency is spacious and uncluttered. Orange segment-shaped windows give glimpses of Chiado in one direction and the whole city in the other. The cheapest rooms lack much of an outlook, but the best ones have terraces with stunning views towards the castle – a view you get from the bar-terrace too. All rooms have fax points and modems. ❼

ALFAMA AND CASTELO

Palácio Belmonte

Map 4, C6. Pateo Dom Fradique 14 ☎ 218 862 582, ⓕ 218 862 592,
ⓔ office@palaciobelmonte.com
If you have over €500 a night to burn for a special occasion, check availability at this private club which rents out rooms when available. A highly atmospheric fifteenth-century palace, the property essentially retains its original decor apart from the odd designer bathroom. Dazzling eighteenth-century

azulejos, soaring ceilings and wood floors set the tone for the six individual suites, including one set in a tower with a 360° view of Alfama. There's also a small garden with plunge pool and terrace, and plans to open a café to the public. **9**

Pensão Ninho das Águias

Map 4, B3. Costa do Castelo 74 ℡218 854 070

Beautifully sited in its own view-laden terrace-garden, on the street looping around and below the castle, this is justifiably one of the most popular budget places in the city. Climb up the staircase and past the birdcages. Rooms are bright and white; some have en-suite facilities. Book in advance, though, as there are just fourteen rooms. **3**

YOUTH HOSTELS

The central booking office for Portugal's youth hostels (*pousadas de juventude*) is Movijovem, near metro Saldanha at Avda Duque de Ávila 137 ℡217 232 100, ℻213 596 002, Ⓦwww.pousadajuventude.pt. A youth hostel card is required for all Portuguese hostels, though if you don't have one, you can buy it on your first night's stay. For details of the youth hostel at Sintra, see p.261. Prices below are for high season.

Pousada de Juventude da Almada (Map 1, F7), Quinta do Bucelinho, Pragal, Almada ℡212 943 491, ℻212 943 497, Ⓔalmada@movijovem.pt. On the south side of the Tejo – with terrific views back over Lisbon – this is not particularly convenient for sightseeing in the city, but is within striking distance of the Caparica beaches. It has a games room, disabled access and internet

facilities. Over twenty four-bedded dorms at €12.50 per person, and thirteen twin-bedded rooms with their own toilets at €30 per room.

Pousada de Juventude de Catalazete (Map 1, D6), Estrada Marginal, Oeiras ℡214 430 638, ℻214 419 267, Ⓔcatalazete@movijovem.pt. Small, attractive hostel overlooking the beach at Oeiras, between Belém and

Pensão São João da Praça

Map 4, C9. Rua de São João da Praça 97–2° ☎218 862 591, ℻218 881 378
Attractively painted town house with street-facing wrought-iron balconies. It's a quiet and friendly choice immediately below the cathedral. Rooms are available with and without en-suite facilities, and meals can be provided. ❹

Sé Guest House

Map 4, C9. Rua de São João da Praça 97–1° ☎218 864 400, ℻263 271 612
Run by a welcoming family from Mozambique (who speak good English), this beautifully done-up town house features wooden floors and bright, airy rooms. Despite the communal bathrooms, it has a slightly more upmarket feel than the Pensão São João da Praça in

Cascais, with ten twin rooms and variously sized dorms. It is best reached by bus #44 from the airport, or take a train from Cais do Sodré to Oeiras station, then a taxi for the last 2km. Dorm rooms at €10.50 per person, twin rooms at €25.50.

Pousada de Juventude de Lisboa (Map 9, E7), Rua Andrade Corvo 46 ☎213 532 696, ℻213 537 541, ✉lisboa@movijovem.pt. This is the main city hostel, set in a rambling old building by metro Picoas, with a small bar (open 6pm to midnight), canteen (reserve meals in advance; served 1–2pm & 7–8pm), TV room and disabled access.

Thirty rooms sleeping four or six people (with shared bathrooms) for €15 per person; or better-value doubles with private shower for €33 per room. The price includes breakfast.

Lisboa Parque das Nações (Map, p.106), Rua de Moscavide 47–101, Parque das Nações ☎218 920 890, ℻218 920 891, ✉liboaparque@movijovem.pt. About five minutes' walk northeast of the Torre Vasco da Gama, towards the bridge, this modern youth hostel in Parque das Nações has a pool table and disabled access. Ten double rooms at €25.50 per room and 18 four-bedded dorms at €11 per person.

ALFAMA AND CASTELO

the same building. A substantial breakfast included in the price. ❹

Albergaria Senhora do Monte

Map 2, G8. Calçada do Monte 39 ☏ 218 866 002, ℱ 218 877 783, ℯ senhoradomonte @hotmail.com

Comfortable, modern hotel in a beautiful location with views of the castle and Graça convent from the south-facing rooms, some of which have terraces. Breakfast (included in the price) is taken on the fourth-floor terrace, and private parking is available. To get there, head north from Largo da Graça, taking the first left into Rua Damasceno Monteiro – Calçada do Monte is the first right. ❻

BAIRRO ALTO AND AROUND

Hotel Anjo Azul

Map 5, D3. Rua Luz Soriano 75 ☏ 213 478 069, ℯ anjoazul@mail.telepac.pt

The city's first gay hotel, the "Blue Angel" is set in a lovely blue-tiled town house right in the heart of the area's nightlife. There are just twelve simple but attractive rooms and very helpful staff. ❸

Residencial Camões

Map 5, E4. Trav. do Poço da Cidade 38–1° ☏ 213 467 510, ℱ 213 464 048

Small rooms, the best with balconies (others are somewhat gloomy), right in the heart of the Bairro Alto – so expect lots of noise, especially at weekends. A superb breakfast is provided (April–Oct only) in a pleasant dining room, and the English-speaking owners are very friendly. Rooms without bathroom are priced a category lower. ❸

Casa de São Mamede

Map 8, C5. Rua da Escola Politécnica 159 ☏ 213 963 166, ℱ 213 951 896

Slightly away from the Bairro Alto on a busy street north of Praça do Príncipe Real, this is a superb seventeenth-century town house with period fittings, bright breakfast room and even a grand stained-glass window. Rooms are rather ordinary, but all are equipped with TV. **5**

Pensão Duque
Map 5, G4. Calçada do Duque 53 ⊤ 213 463 444
Near São Roque church, down the steps off Largo T. Coelho, heading down to Rossio, so clear of the nightlife noise. It has basic but usually spotless rooms, with shared bathrooms. **2**

Pensão Globo
Map 5, F2. Rua do Teixeira 37 ⊤ 213 462 279
Attractive house in a relatively quiet street, bang in the middle of the Bairro Alto. Rooms are varied: all are simple and most are reasonably large, though those right at the top are a little cramped while a few don't have windows. Some rooms are en suite, priced a cate-

LAPA

As Janelas Verdes
Map 6, F5. Rua das Janelas Verdes 47 ⊤ 213 968 143, ⑤ 213 968 144, ⓦ www.heritage.pt

gory higher. **2**

Pensão Londres
Map 8, E7. Rua Dom Pedro V 53 ⊤ 213 462 203, ⑤ 213 465 682
Wonderful old building with high ceilings and pleasant enough rooms spread across a couple of floors. Some come with tiny bathrooms, though others without are priced a category lower, and breakfast is included. It has a reputation as a gay-friendly hotel, though not exclusively so. **3**

Pensão Luar
Map 5, F4. Rua das Gáveas 101–1° ⊤ 213 460 949
Polished interior and decently furnished rooms (with and without shower), which are comfortable but somewhat noisy. Some rooms are much larger than others, so ask to see first. **3**

Highly recommended, this discreet, eighteenth-century town house where Eça de Queirós wrote *Os Maios*, is just metres from the Museu de Arte Antiga. Well-propor-

LAPA

tioned rooms come with marble bathrooms, period furnishings and pictures, and breakfast is served in the delightful walled garden. Top-floor rooms command spectacular river views. Advance bookings recommended. **7**

Lapa Palace

Map 6, E5. Rua do Pau da Bandeira 4 ⓣ 213 949 494, Ⓕ 213 950 665, ⓦ www.orient.expresshotels.com

Justifiably considered Lisbon's top hotel, this stunning nineteenth-century mansion is set in its own lush gardens, with dramatic vistas over the Tejo. Rooms are luxurious, and those in the Palace Wing are each decorated in a different style, from Classical to Art Deco. In summer, grills are served by the outdoor pool. There's also a health club, disabled access and a list of facilities as long as your arm, from babysitting to banqueting. A double room costs well over €325 in high season. **9**

Residencial York House

Map 6, G5. Rua das Janelas Verdes 32 ⓣ 213 962 785, Ⓕ 213 972 793, Ⓔ yorkhouse@mail.telepac.pt

Located in a sixteenth-century convent (and hidden from the main street by high walls), rooms here come with rugs, tiles and four-poster beds. The best are grouped around a beautiful interior courtyard, where drinks and meals are served in summer, and there's a highly rated restaurant. Advance bookings recommended. **8**

AROUND AVENIDA DA LIBERDADE

Residencial 13° da Sorte

Map 2, E8. Rua do Salitre 13 ⓣ 213 531 851, Ⓕ 213 956 946

Its name translates roughly as "Lucky 13" and the owners are indeed fortunate with this good-value budget option set in a tall, traditional building. Spacious rooms are spread across five floors, each with a TV and mini-bar. **3**

Residencial Alegria

Map 8, F6. Praça da Alegria

12 ⓣ213 220 670, ⓕ213 347 8070, ⓔmail@alegrianet.com
Great position, facing the leafy Praça da Alegria ("Happy Square") and featuring spacious, spotless rooms with TVs. A few euros more get you a room with a bath rather than a shower. ❸

Hotel Altis

Map 8, D4. Rua Castilho 11 ⓣ213 106 000, ⓕ213 106 262, ⓦwww.hotel.altis.pt
Neat five-star a short walk from metro Avenida, with its own small third-floor swimming pool, sauna and fitness centre. The smart rooms all come with safes and TVs, while the twelfth-floor restaurant and bar has (slightly obscured) views over the city. ❼

Hotel Britania

Map 8, E3. Rua Rodrigues Sampaio 17 ⓣ213 155 016, ⓕ213 155 021, ⓦwww.heritage.pt
Designed in the 1940s by influential architect Cassiano Branco, this is a characterful option with good-sized rooms. It doesn't look much from the outside, but the marble-clad bathrooms and a classic Art Deco interior have been declared of national architectural importance. A superb buffet breakfast is included. ❽

Hotel Dom Carlos

Map 8, E1. Avenida Duque de Loulé 121 ⓣ213 512 590, ⓕ213 520 728, ⓔdcarlos@mail.telepac.pt
Decent three-star just off Praça Marquês de Pombal, with fair-sized rooms. Some overlook the neighbouring police and fire stations, which can add to the noise, but there's a downstairs bar and the price includes a good buffet breakfast. ❺

Residencial Dom Sancho I

Map 8, E3. Avenida da Liberdade 202 ⓣ213 548 648, ⓕ213 548 042, ⓔdsancho@iol.pt
One of the few inexpensive options right on the avenue and, what's more, set in a grand old mansion with high ceilings and decorative cornices – though, as you'd expect, the front rooms are noisy. The large, air-conditioned rooms come with TVs; breakfast (included in the price) is

served in a back room. ❹

Hotel Flamingo

Map 8, C2. Rua Castilho 41
ⓣ 213 841 200, ⓕ 213 841
208,
ⓔ hotelflamingo@netcabo.pt
Friendly, slightly faded hotel,
but with an appealing atmosphere, just west of the avenue.
Small rooms have cable TV
and mini-bars. The downstairs
bar looks like the setting for a
US sitcom. ❺

Hotel Lisboa Plaza

Map 8, F5. Trav. Salitre 7
ⓣ 213 218 218, ⓕ 213 471
630, ⓦ www.heritage.pt
Just off Avenida da Liberdade,
this bright, polished, four-star
hotel is a real treat – dried
flowers everywhere, marble
bathrooms, bar, restaurant
(good breakfast included), and
views of the botanical garden
from the rear rooms.
Recommended. ❽

Hotel Tivoli Jardim

Map 8, E4. Rua Júlio César
Machado 7–9 ⓣ 213 591 000,
ⓕ 213 591 243,
ⓦ www.tivolihotels.com
Related to the nearby Tivoli
Lisboa (whose pool and gardens you're allowed to use),
the four-star Tivoli Jardim is a
large modern building set back
in a quiet street. Most rooms
come with spacious balconies.
It's geared to business travellers, which means good
summer discounts. ❽

Tivoli Lisboa

Map 8, E4. Avda da Liberdade
185 ⓣ 213 198 900, ⓕ 213
198 950,
ⓦ www.tivolihotels.com
Flash five-star hotel with cavernous lobby-lounge, three
hundred sound-proofed
rooms, an outdoor pool, tennis
courts and garden. Breakfast is
included and there's a top-
floor grill-restaurant with
superb city views. ❽

Hotel Veneza

Map 8, E4. Avda da Liberdade
189 ⓣ 213 522 618, ⓕ 213
526 678,
ⓔ 3k.hoteis@mail.telepac.pt
Built in 1886, the distinguishing feature of this former town
house is an ornate staircase,
now flanked by modern
murals of Lisbon. The smallish
rooms are less individually
styled, with dull furnishings.
However, the price includes a
good buffet breakfast. ❼

SELF-CATERING APARTMENTS

Hotel Impala (Map 9, D6), Rua Filipe Folque 49 ☏ 213 148 914, Ⓕ 213 575 362. One of the few relatively inexpensive self-catering options, these small, simple apartments sleep up to four (though are better sized for two). Pension-standard bedrooms are attached to small kitchen-cum-living rooms with TVs. There are also laundry facilities. ⑤ per apartment.

VIP Orion Eden (Map 3, A8), Praça dos Restauradores 18–24 ☏ 213 216 600,

Ⓔ eden.lisboa@mail.telepac.pt. Stylish modern studios and apartments sleeping up to four people are available on the upper floors of the impressively converted Eden Theatre. Get a ninth-floor apartment with a balcony and you'll have the best views and be just below the breakfast bar and roof-top pool. All studios come with dishwashers, microwaves and satellite TV. Disabled access. ⑥ for studios and double apartments; ⑦ for larger apartments.

PARQUE EDUARDO VII AND SALDANHA

Residencial Avenida Alameda
Map 9, D8. Avda Sidónio Pais 4 ☏ 213 532 186, Ⓕ 213 526 703
Very pleasant three-star *residencial* with air-conditioned rooms, all with park views; breakfast included. ③

Residencial Canadá
Map 9, G5. Avda Defensores de Chaves 35 1–4° ☏ 213 513

480, Ⓕ 213 542 922
Close to the main bus station, this is excellent value for money, with biggish, airy rooms with TVs, kept immaculate by a bevy of charming ladies. There's also a sunny breakfast room and lounge area. Recommended. ④

Hotel Eduardo VII
Map 9, D8. Avda Fontes Pereira de Melo 5 ☏ 213 568

900, (F) 213 568 833,
(W) www.hoteleduardovii.pt
This renovated 1930s' hotel is
in an unattractive building on a
noisy road, but it is close to the
park and its small Art-Deco-
influenced rooms have mini-
bars and satellite TV. There's
also a rooftop bar and restaurant, and internet access. ⑤

Hotel Fénix

Map 8, D1. Praça Marquês de
Pombal 8 (T) 213 862 121,
(F) 213 860 131,
(E) h.fenix@ip.pt
Large four-star hotel facing
Lisbon's biggest traffic round-
about, with double-glazed
windows to keep out the
noise. The plush rooms, with

CAMPSITES

The Portuguese camping organization is **Orbitur**, Rua Diogo
do Couto 1–8 (T) 218 117 070, (W) www.orbitur.pt. Members get
a ten percent discount at their two campsites in the Lisbon
region. Check out (W) www.roteiro-campista.pt for details of
other campsites.

Campimeco (Map p.286),
Praia das Bicas, 2km northwest of Aldeio do Meco
(T) 219 747 669, (F) 219 748
728. A short walk to Praia
das Bicas, and with tennis
courts, restaurant, pool and
mini-market.

Camping Praia Grande
(Map 1, A4), Praia Grande
(T) 219 290 581, (F) 219 291
834, (E) wondertur@ip.pt.
Less than 1km from the
beach at Praia Grande, west
of Sintra. Bus #441 from
Sintra train station.

Fetais (Map p.286), Aldeio do
Meco (T) 212 682 978. Set
amongst pine trees, five
minutes' walk from town and
with a path to Praia do Meco.
Orbitur Guincho (Map 1,
A5), EN 247, Lugar da Areia,
Guincho (T) 214 870 450,
(F) 214 872 167,
(E) info@orbitur.pt. Close to
Guincho beach among the
pine trees, and served by
bus from Cascais. Has tennis
courts, mini-market and café,
and bungalows and caravans
for rent.

armchairs and TVs, overlook the square or the Parque Eduardo VII, while English newspapers are available in the lobby. There's also a restaurant and bar. ⑥

Le Méridien Park Atlantic
Map 9, A8. Rua Castilho 149

Ⓣ213 818 700, Ⓕ213 890 500, Ⓦwww.lemeridien-lisbon.com

A modern exterior shelters a superior luxury hotel (a short walk from Marquês de Pombal metro), with an impressive atrium, bright café-lounge and top-quality rooms. There's also a health club, music bar and

---

Orbitur Costa de Caparica (Map 1, E7), Avda Afonso de Albuquerque, Quinta de St António, Monte de Caparica Ⓣ212 901 366, Ⓕ212 900 661, Ⓔinfo@orbitur.pt. One of the few campsites in Caparica open to non-members, but it's not for those looking for solitude.

Outão Praia de Albarquel (Map p.286), 5km east of Pontinho da Arrábida Ⓣ265 238 318, Ⓕ265 228 098. Simple campsite set amongst trees, close to the small Praia de Albarquel.

Parque Municipal de Campismo (Map 2, A6), Estrada da Circunvalação, Parque Florestal de Monsanto Ⓣ217 623 100, Ⓕ217 623 106. The main city campsite – with a swimming pool and shops – is 6km west of Lisbon, with the entrance on the park's west side. Bus #43 from Praça da Figueira via Belém.

Parque O Repouso (Map p.286), Lagoa de Albufeira Ⓣ212 684 300; closed Oct–April. Simple campsite on scrubby ground, 1km back from the lagoon; it's a bit of a trek to the beach, but great if you like rural solitude.

Picheleiros (Map p.286), Vila Nogueira de Azeitão Ⓣ212 181 322. Just outside town, complete with mini-market, café and kids playground.

PARQUE EDUARDO VII AND SALDANHA

disabled access, and most of the spacious rooms have superb views over Parque Eduardo VII or the city. Guests can also use the tennis courts in the park. ⑧

Hotel Miraparque

Map 9, D8. Avda Sidónio Pais ⊤ 213 524 286, Ⓕ 213 578 920,
ⓔ miraparque@esoterica.pt
Housed in an attractive building overlooking Parque Eduardo VII, the *Miraparque* is pleasantly old-fashioned, though the reception staff can be a bit brusque. All rooms come with TV, and there's a decent bar and restaurant. ④

Residencial Pascoal de Melo

Map 2, F6. Rua Pascoal de Melo 127–131 ⊤ 213 577 639, Ⓕ 213 144 555
A spotless three-star *residencial* near Largo Dona Estefânia, with friendly staff and a azulejo-lined entry hall. Rooms are neat and come with TV and balcony. ③

Pensão Pátria

Map 9, F5. Avda Duque de Ávila 42 4–5° ⊤ 213 150 620, Ⓕ 213 578 310
Close to the main bus station and metro Saldanha, this cheerful establishment has plenty of spruce little rooms with wooden floors and clean bathrooms – some also come with rooftop views, others with glassed-in verandas – and there's also a sunny breakfast room. ②

Hotel Real Parque

Map 9, D6. Av. Luís Bívar 67 ⊤ 213 199 000, Ⓕ 213 570 750, ⓦ www.realparque.pt
Modern four-star in a quiet part of town, a short walk from Parque Eduardo VII and the Gulbenkian (and from Picoas and Parque metros), complete with its own restaurant, coffee shop and bar. Rooms are unimaginatively decorated but spacious. ⑧

Ritz Four Seasons

Map 9, A8. Rua Rodrigo da Fonseca 88 ⊤ 213 811 400, Ⓕ 213 831 783, ⓦ www.fourseasons.com
On the west side of Parque Eduardo VII, this vast building is one of the grandest – and most expensive – hotels in the city, with huge airy rooms, terraces overlooking the park,

and public areas replete with marble, antiques, old masters and overly attentive staff. There's also a fitness centre, highly rated restaurant and internet facilities, though expect to pay over €300 a night for a room. ⑨

Sana Classic Rex Hotel

Map 9, A8. Rua Castilho 169 ⓣ 213 882 161, ⓕ 213 887 581, ⓦ www.sanahotels.com
One of the less outrageously priced hotels in this neck of the woods, with an in-house restaurant and small but well-equipped rooms. The best are at the front, sporting large balconies overlooking Parque Eduardo VII. ⑥

Sheraton Lisboa Hotel & Towers

Map 9, E7. Rua Latino Coelho 1 ⓣ 213 120 000, ⓕ 213 547 164,
ⓦ www.sheraton.com/lisboa
One of Lisbon's first skyscrapers dominates this part of town, a bustling business and residential district. The upper rooms have unbeatable views, though you can get the view anyway from the top-floor Panorama Bar. All rooms have satellite TV and mini-bars and there are special floors for non-smokers. Other facilities include two restaurants, a swimming pool and health club. Metro Picoas is right outside. ⑨

PARQUE EDUARDO VII AND SALDANHA

●

Eating

Lisbon has some of the best-value **restaurants** of any European city, serving large portions of good Portuguese food at sensible prices. A set menu (*ementa turística*) at lunch or dinner will get you a three-course meal for €10–13 anywhere in the city, though you can eat for considerably less than this by sticking to the ample main dishes and choosing the daily specials.

At their finest, Portuguese dishes can be a revelation, made with fresh ingredients bursting with flavour. Grilled meats and fish tend to be the best bets, usually accompanied by chips or rice and salad. But unless you go upmarket, don't expect sophisticated sauces or delicate touches: stews, in particular, are not for the faint-hearted, offal features highly on most menus and even the ever-present bacalhau (dried salted cod) can be pretty heavy going if you choose the wrong variety (and there are reputedly 365). If you want to try **specialities from the Lisbon area**, go for *lulas fritas* (fried squid), *iscas* (marinated liver, often cooked with ham and potatoes) or *santola recheada* (stuffed spider crab). There's a helpful **menu reader** on p.328.

Unless you have a big appetite, you may find a *meia doce* (half portion) sufficient for a main course, or order one dish between two people. You will also usually be presented with starters of olives, cheeses, spreads and, sometimes, cold meats or seafood when you sit down. You'll be charged for anything you eat; if you don't take anything, make sure it's not put on your bill. If you do have room for dessert, don't expect a great variety: ice cream (*gelado*), fruit (*fruta*), crème caramel (*pudim flan*) and rice pudding (*arroz doce*) are fairly ubiquitous.

Our listings are divided into the following areas: Baixa (p.138); Rua das Portas de Santo Antão (p.141); Chiado (p.143); Cais do Sodré and Santos (p.145); Alfama and around (p.146); Santa Apolónia and Doca do Jardim do Tobaco (p.152); Bairro Alto and around (p.153); Lapa, Estrela and São Bento (p.160); Alcântara (p.161); Belém (p.162); Around Avenida da Liberdade (p.163); Parque Eduardo VII and Saldanha (p.164); Around Avenida Almirante Reis (p.165); Parque das Nações (p.165).

The city, naturally, features some of the country's best (and most expensive) restaurants, specializing for the most part in a hybrid French-Portuguese cuisine. It also has a rich vein of inexpensive foreign restaurants, particularly those featuring food from the former colonies, as well as an increasing number from Japan, Argentina, Mexico and Italy. Seafood is widely available, if generally more expensive than other dishes – an entire central street, **Rua das Portas de Santo Antão** (see p.141), specializes in it, as does an enclave of restaurants across the River Tejo at **Cacilhas** (see p.286). Several traditional restaurants also survive, most notably some beautifully tiled *cervejarias* (literally "beer halls"), where the emphasis is often as much on drinking as eating.

There are plenty of restaurants scattered around the **Baixa**, offering set lunches to office employees, and there are some good places in all the other areas in which you're likely to be sightseeing, especially in **Alfama** and **Belém**. By night the obvious place to be is the **Bairro Alto**, which hosts several of the city's trendiest restaurants, as well as some more basic,

RESTAURANT PRICES

The listings below have been coded into three categories: **inexpensive** (less than €15); **moderate** (€15–20); and **expensive** (above €20). These prices refer to the cost of a two-course meal including wine, but excluding tips. All the places listed accept major credit cards unless specifically stated.

value-for-money venues. More expensive are the various cafés and restaurants at the revitalized **riverside areas** of Doca de Santa Amaro (Alcântara), Doca do Jardim do Tobaco (Santo Apolónia), and Parque das Nações, where pricey international food and river views are the norm.

Note that many restaurants close for one day a week, often on **Sunday evenings** or **Mondays**, while on Saturday nights in midsummer you may need to book for the more popular places. **Telephone numbers** are given below for places where reservations are advised.

For the best vegetarian options see p.144; for a list of restaurants with great views see p. 145; for restaurants with the best outdoor seating see p. 150; for restaurants serving cuisines from Portugal's former colonies see p. 147.

BAIXA

A Berlenga

Map 3, C5. Rua Barros Queiroz 29.
Daily 8am–midnight.
Moderate to expensive.
A *cervejaria*-restaurant with a window stuffed full of crabs and seafood. Early evening snackers munch prawns at the bar, giving way later on to local diners who tend to eat meals chosen from the window displays, though there are also some meat dishes on the menu. The *ementa turística* offers the best value, otherwise expect to pay €18 and up.

BAIXA

If you'd prefer to make your own meals, see p.222 for details of the best places to buy food.

O Canastro

Map 3, B6. Calçada de Sant'Ana 7–9.

Daily 9am–11.30pm.

Inexpensive.

Well off the tourist circuit up a steep side street, this is a refreshingly unpretentious place with reliable Portuguese food. Fresh fish is particularly good value here.

Celeiro

Map 3, D7. Rua 1° de Dezembro 65.

Mon–Fri 9am–8pm. No credit cards. Inexpensive.

Just off Rossio, this self-service restaurant in the basement of a health-food supermarket offers tasty vegetarian spring rolls, quiches, pizza and the like. Go for the food, not the decor or ambience.

João do Grão

Map 3, E6. Rua dos Correeiros 220–228.

Daily noon–3.30pm & 6–11pm. Moderate.

One of the best of a row of restaurants on this pedestrianized street, whose appealing outdoor tables tempt you to sit down and sample the reasonably priced Portuguese favourites and interesting salads, though the marble- and azulejo-clad interior is just as attractive.

Leão d'Ouro

Map 3, C7. Rua 1° de Dezembro 105 ⓣ 213 426 195.

Daily noon–2pm & 7pm–midnight. Moderate to expensive.

Cool and attractive azulejo-covered restaurant, usually frequented more by tourists than Lisboetas. It specializes in seafood and grilled meats and prices are quite high, but then so is the quality. Dinner reservations are advised.

Martinho da Arcada

Map 3, J5. Praça do Comércio 3 ⓣ 218 879 259.

Mon–Sat noon–3pm & 7–11pm. Moderate.

Beautifully decorated restaurant tucked into the arcade around the square, with starched white tablecloths and attentive waiters, little changed

BAIXA

139

from the early 1900s, when it was frequented by writer Fernando Pessoa. Serves traditional Portuguese food, notably grilled meats, and things start to get expensive if you choose the seafood. Dinner reservations advised.

Restaurante Paris
Map 3, G6. Rua dos Sapateiros 126 ⓣ 213 469 797.
Daily 8am–10pm. Moderate.
One of the Baixa's longest-established restaurants, with delightful, traditional decor. The usual choices of fish, meat and salads are reliably well cooked; the swordfish is recommended. Reservations advised at dinner.

Refeições Naturais e Vegetarianos
Map 3, F6. Rua dos Correeiros 205, 2°.
Mon–Fri noon–7pm. No credit cards. Inexpensive.
Self-service canteen on the second floor of an old town house with a daily changing menu of inexpensive vegetarian hot and cold meals – usually crepes, rissoles and rice dishes.

Sol Posto
Map 3, B6. Calçada de Sant'Ana 11.
Daily 9am–11pm. No credit cards. Inexpensive.
Sol Posto is a popular spot for huge *arroz* (rice) dishes – *marisco* (seafood) and *pato* (duck) rice are two specialities – and fellow diners are more likely to be from the neighbourhood than a tour bus.

Terreiro do Paço
Map 3, J6. Praça do Comércio ⓣ 210 312 850.
Mon–Sat 12.30–3pm & 8pm–midnight; Sun 12.30–3pm. Expensive.
The Lisbon Welcome Centre's stylish restaurant serves high-quality meat and fish dishes accompanied by wine served in glasses the size of pumpkins. Downstairs tables are separated by wooden screens, though the nicest tables are in the cavernous, brick-vaulted upstairs room. Saturday lunch features a traditional serving of *cozido*, while Sunday brunch concentrates on Portuguese specialities – often including bacalhau. Reservations advised for Sunday brunch and for dinner.

BAIXA

RUA DAS PORTAS DE SANTO ANTÃO

Andorra
Map 3, A7. Rua das Portas de Santo Antão 82.
Daily noon–midnight.
Moderate to expensive.
Boasting an outdoor terrace on one of the broadest stretches of this street, this is the perfect place for people-watching and remains perenially popular with tourists. The Portuguese fish dishes and grills are good but slightly overpriced.

Bom Jardim/Rei dos Frangos
Map 3, A7. Trav. de Santo Antão 11–18.
Daily noon–11.30pm.
Inexpensive.
On both sides of an alleyway connecting Restauradores with Rua das Portas de Santo Antão, this is *the* place for spit-roast chicken, as long as you don't mind food with a high grease content. It's now so popular that it has spread into three buildings on either side of the road – if one is full, try another. Other dishes are also good value.

Casa do Alentejo
Map 3, A7. Rua das Portas de Santo Antão 58 ⓣ 213 469 231.
Daily noon–3pm & 7–11pm.
Moderate.
As much a centre dedicated to Alentejan culture as it is a restaurant, "Alentejo House" has an extravagantly decorated interior complete with stunning courtyard and seventeenth-century furniture. Various exhibitions are held here, adding a certain tone to the sound Portuguese food served in two upstairs dining rooms. Alentejo specialities include *sopa à alentejana* (garlic soup with egg) and *carne de porco à alentejana* (grilled pork with clams). Reservations advised.

Escorial
Map 3, A7. Rua das Portas de Santo Antão 47 ⓣ 213 464 429.
Daily 12.30pm–midnight.
Expensive.
Formal restaurant with a quality menu, offering dishes such as tiger prawns, steak, partridge and Spanish paella, not

to mention "selfish bisque" and "tarts of the house". The interior is rather dark, but there are a few outdoor tables, too. Reservations advised.

Gambrinus

Map 3, B7. Rua das Portas de Santo Antão 15 ☎213 421 466.

Daily noon–2am. Expensive.
Rated one of Lisbon's top seafood restaurants, with a smart, wood-panelled interior and crisp service. The menu features seasonal delights like broiled eel with bacon, or lobster, and there are crepes for dessert. Reservations advised.

Adega Santo Antão

Map 3, A7. Rua das Portas de Santo Antão 42.
Tues–Sun noon–11pm.
Inexpensive.
Very good value *adega* (wine cellar) with a bit of local character to it. There's a bustling bar area, and tables inside and out where you can tuck into great grilled meat and fish dishes; the grilled sardines are always superb.

Solar dos Presuntos

Map 8, G6. Rua das Portas de Santo Antão 150 ☎213 424 253.

Mon–Sat noon–3pm & 7–10.30pm. Expensive.
The "Manor House of Hams" is, not surprisingly, best-known for its smoked ham from the Minho in northern Portugal, served cold as a starter. There are also excellent rice and game dishes, not to mention a good wine list, though the service can be overly formal. It's right by the Elevador do Lavra. Reservations advised.

Solmar

Map 3, A7. Rua das Portas de Santo Antão 108.
Daily noon–3pm & 7–10pm. Expensive.
A vast and cavernous show-piece seafood restaurant, complete with fountain and marine mosaics, worth a visit as much for the experience as for the food, which can be hit or miss. Splash out on one of the lobsters trussed up in the bubbling tanks and you shouldn't leave disappointed.

CHIADO

1° de Maio
Map 5, D5. Rua da Atalaia 8
℡213 426 840.
Mon–Fri noon–3pm & 7–10.30
pm, Sat 7–10.30pm.
Moderate.
Traditional *adega* (wine cellar)
at the bottom end of Rua da
Atalaia, with a low, arched
ceiling, art on the walls and
pleasantly faded decor. There
are some excellent dishes of
the day and an array of sizzling grilled meat and fish
dishes. It fills up early, so
book ahead to be sure of a
table.

Associação Católica
Map 5, E8. Trav. Ferragial 1.
Mon–Fri noon–3pm. No credit
cards. Inexpensive.
There's no sign on the door
but look for no. 1 on this
small road just off Rua do
Ferragial and head to the top
floor for a self-service canteen offering a choice of different dishes – from grilled
fish to large salads - each day.
The chief attractions are the
low price and the rooftop
terrace with fine views over
the Tejo.

Belcanto
Map 5, F7. Largo de São
Carlos 10 ℡213 420 607.
Mon–Sat noon–2am.
Expensive.
Favoured by government
ministers and visitors to the
opera house opposite, this
intimate wood-panelled
restaurant exudes an air of
sophistication and tradition.
There's good bacalhau, a
range of international dishes
and an array of tempting
desserts. Reservations are
advised.

O Canteiro
Map 5, E8. Rua Vitor Cordon
8–10.
Mon–Fri 7.30am–8.30pm. No
credit cards. Inexpensive.
On a steep street served by
tram #28, the cool, azulejo-
covered interior harbours a
self-service counter feeding
local workers with a fine
range of dishes, like tuna and
black-eyed bean salad or
bacalhau rissoles, followed by
fresh strawberries. Particularly
busy at lunchtime, when you
may have to wait for a table.

L'Entrecôte

Map 5, E6. Rua do Alecrim
121 ⓣ 213 428 343.
Mon–Sat 12.30–3pm &
8pm–midnight, Sun 8–11pm.
Moderate to expensive.
This relaxing, wood-panelled
restaurant with soaring ceilings
has won awards for its
entrecôte, which is just as well
as that's all it serves. It is truly
delicious, served with a superb
creamy sauce. Dinner reservations advised.

Tágide

Map 5, F8. Largo Academia
das Belas Artes 18–20 ⓣ 213
420 720.
Mon–Fri 12.30–2.30pm &
7.30–10.30pm. Expensive.

One of Lisbon's priciest
restaurants, serving superb
Portuguese dishes such as partridge in port and octopus in
red wine. The light and airy
dining room has sweeping city
views that are hard to beat.
Book ahead, especially for a
window seat, and expect to
spend at least €30 per person.

Tavares Rico

Map 5, F5. Rua da
Misericórdia 35 ⓣ 213 421
112.
Mon–Fri 12.30–3pm &
7.30–11pm, Sun 7.30–11pm.
Expensive.
Gloriously ornate restaurant,
one of Lisbon's oldest, dating
from 1784, where you can
dine in splendour on richly

VEGETARIAN RESTAURANTS

All the following restaurants are reviewed in this chapter – not all of
them are purely vegetarian, but all offer good meat-free options.

Celeiro	Baixa, p.139
Centro de Arte Moderna	Saldanha, p.164
Centro de Alimentaçao e Saúde Natural	Avda da Liberdade, p.163
Espiral	Avda Almirante Reis, p.165
Farah's Tandoori	Lapa, p.160
Refeições Naturais	Baixa, p.140
Teatro Taborda	Castelo, p.149
Tibetanos	Avda da Liberdade, p.164

CHIADO

prepared lobster, duck and sole. Reservations are advised, except for the upstairs canteen, which is less ornate and offers cheaper self-service fare, such as chicken with rice.

CAIS DO SODRÉ AND SANTOS

Cais da Ribeira
Map 5, B9. Armazém A, Porta 2
T213 463 611 or 213 423 611.
Tues 7.30–11.30pm, Wed–Sat 7pm–2am, Sun noon–4pm & 7–11pm. Expensive.
On the riverfront next to Cais do Sodré station, this attractive converted warehouse with river views serves superior fish, meat and seafood straight from the market. Specialities include paella (for two people) and flambéed desserts. Reservations advised.

Marisqueira do Cais do Sodré
Map 5, A9. Cais do Sodré
T213 422 105.
Daily noon–3.30pm & 7.30–11.30pm; closed last week in Oct. Expensive.
Big seafood restaurant by the station, complete with bubbling fish tanks. Try the *caldeirada de tamboril* (monkfish stew), the *caril de gambas* (curried prawns) or the *parrilhada* (a seafood medley). Dinner reservations advised.

RESTAURANTS WITH VIEWS

Associação Católica	Chiado, p.143
Casa do Leão	Castelo, p.148
Casanova	Santa Apolónia, p.152
Cervejaria Farol	Cacilhas, p.288
Jardim do Marisco	Docado Jardim do Tobaco, p.152
La Paparrucha	Bairro Alto, p.156
Restaurante Panorâmico	Parque das Nações, p.166
Cervejaria Portugália	Avda Almirante Reis, p.165
Tágide	Chiado, p.144
Via Graça	Graça, p.151

CAIS DO SODRÉ AND SANTOS

Porto de Abrigo
Map 5, B8. Rua dos
Remolares 16–18.
Tues–Sun noon–3pm &
7–10.30pm. No credit cards.
Inexpensive.

It's worth delving into one of
Lisbon's grittier districts for a
meal at this old-style tavern-
restaurant, serving fresh fish
from the market at reasonable
prices. The *arroz de polvo* (octopus rice) is recommended.

ALFAMA AND AROUND

AROUND THE SÉ

Adega Triunfo
Map 3, I3. Rua dos
Bacalhoeiros 129.
Tues–Sun noon–midnight. No
credit cards. Inexpensive.
One of several no-frills, paper-
tablecloth café-restaurants
along this street, which you'll
find downhill from the Sé
towards the river. It has a
changing menu of meat and
fish dishes, pricier seafood and
cheap house wine. The *feijoada*
(bean stew) is a good bet.

Delhi Palace
Map 3, I3. Rua da Padaria
18–20.
Tues–Sun noon–3pm &
6.30pm–midnight. Moderate.
This bizarre combination of
Indian and Italian cuisine is all
the rage in Lisbon, and the

attractively tiled *Delhi Palace*
offers decent curries and pretty
passable pizzas and pastas.
Friendly, English-speaking
Indian owners.

Estrela da Sé
Map 3, I3. Largo S. António da
Sé 4.
Mon–Fri noon–3pm & 7–11pm.
Moderate.
Beautiful azulejo-covered
restaurant just uphill from the
Sé, serving inexpensive and
tasty dishes like *alheira* (chicken
sausage) and salmon. Its wood-
en booths – perfect for discreet
trysts – date from the nineteenth century.

Hua Ta Li
Map 3, I3. Rua dos
Bacalhoeiros 119 ⓣ 218 879
170.
Daily noon–3.30pm & 6–11pm.
Inexpensive.

PORTUGUESE COLONIAL FOOD

Portugal's former status as a great trading nation has had a great influence on world cuisine. Along with port, the Portuguese are credited with introducing foodstuffs such as marmalade (though Portuguese *marmelada* is made from quince), Japanese tempura and even Indian curries like vindaloo – indeed, the use of chillies in the East began only when the Portuguese started to import them from Mexico. Despite this global culinary influence, it is only relatively recently that Lisbon has embraced food with anything other than solid Portuguese ingredients (even when Portugal's empire was at its height, only the wealthy could afford to cook with the spices which fuelled the Portuguese economy). The ever-popular Chinese restaurants have now been joined by an increasing band of restaurants serving colonial cuisine. The following are some of the best around the city.

Águas do Bengo	Angolan/African, p.153
Algures na Mouraria	Angolan, p.148
Arco do Castelo	Goan, p.148
Atira-te ao Rio	Brazilian, p.287
Brasuca	Brazilian, p.154
Cantinho da Paz	Goan, p.160
Comida de Santo	Brazilian, p.158
Hua Ta Li	Macau/Chinese, p.146
Indo-Africa/Paz II	African/Indian, p.160
Real Fábrica	Brazilian, p.159
São Cristóvão	Cape Verdean/African, p.149
Zeno	Brazilian, p.162.

Very good Chinese restaurant, especially popular for Sunday lunch when it heaves with people (so it's best to book). Seafood scores highly; try the squid chop suey.

Retiro del Castilho
Map 3, I3. Rua da Padaria 34.

Daily 7am–midnight. No credit cards. Inexpensive.
Budget meals eaten off paper-topped tables in a subterranean vault off Rua de São Julião. A good lunchtime spot, especially if you like filling soups.

Rio Coura

Map 3, H1. Rua Augusto Rosa 30.
Daily 8am–midnight.
Inexpensive.
A couple of hundred metres up from the Sé, this popular place offers good-value meals (including rough house wine) for around €13, served in a traditional tiled dining room.

CASTELO AND MOURARIA

Algures na Mouraria

Map 3, D3. Rua das Farinhas 1.
Tues–Sun noon–3.30pm & 7.30–11.30pm. Inexpensive.
Buried in the earthy Mouraria district, this earthy restaurant offers excellent Angolan dishes such as *moamba de ginguba* (chicken with peanut sauce), *sarapatel* (kidney, liver and port), *frango à angolana* (chicken in ginger) and *caril de camarão* (prawn curry).

Arco do Castelo

Map 4, B6. Rua do Chão da Feira 25.
Mon–Sat noon–midnight.
Moderate.
Cheerful place just below the entrance to the castle, specializing in Goan dishes – choose from tempting shrimp curry, Indian sausage or spicy seafood.

Casa do Leão

Map 4, B4. Castelo de São Jorge ☎218 875 962.
Daily 12.30–3.30pm & 8–10pm. Expensive.
Couldn't be better sited, within the castle walls and providing a superb city view from its outside terrace and tiled interior. Service is slick and the top-rate traditional Portuguese food includes *caldeirão de cabrito* (goat stew). Prices are high but not outrageous, though there's a tourist menu at €28. Reservations advised.

Frei Pepinhas

Map 4, E4. Rua de São Tomé 13–21.
Mon–Sat 11am–3.30pm & 6pm–midnight. Inexpensive to moderate.

Despite its location near the castle, this long bar-restaurant with wrought-iron chairs and checked blue tablecloths is mainly the haunt of locals. Serves Portuguese staples – the *febras* (pork steaks) are always a good bet.

São Cristóvão

Map 3, E3. Rua de São Cristóvão 28–30 ⓣ 218 885 578.
Daily 10.30am–midnight.
Inexpensive.
Titchy Cape Verdean restaurant which crams in tables, a TV and live music on Friday to Sunday evenings, all overseen by motherly owner Mento. Dishes include *catchupa rica* (pork, chicken, maize and beans) and *galinha caboverdiana* (chicken with coconut milk). The restaurant is just off Largo de São Cristóvão. It's a good idea to reserve for dinner as there's not much room.

A Tasquinha

Map 4, D6. Largo do Contador Mor 5–7.
Mon–Sat 10am–11pm.
Moderate.
Considering its position, on the main route up to the castle,

this lovely *tasca* (dining room) has remained remarkably unaffected by tourism. The food – grilled fish and chicken – is good value, too, served either at the few tables in the traditionally decorated interior or on a fine outdoor terrace.

Teatro Taborda

Map 4, C3. Costa do Costelo 75.
Tues–Sun 2pm–midnight.
Moderate.
Fashionable theatre cafe-restaurant with fine views from the terrace. The menu offers fresh vegetarian dishes, including vegetable lasagne and Greek salad.

ALFAMA

Lautasco

Map 4, G7. Beco do Azinhal 7 ⓣ 218 860 173.
Mon–Sat 10am–3pm & 9–11.30pm; closed Dec.
Expensive.
Tucked just off the Largo do Chafariz de Dentro, in a picturesque Alfama courtyard: by day a shady retreat, by night a magical fairy-lit oasis. Multilingual menus and higher-than-usual prices suggest a largely

ALFAMA AND AROUND

149

RESTAURANTS WITH OUTDOOR SEATING

Adega do Teixeira	Bairro Alto, p.153
Bica do Sapato	Santa Apolónia, p.152
Casa da Comida	Around Avenida da Liberdade, p.159
Casa do Leão	Castelo, p.148
Cápsula	Belém. p.162
O Coreto	Around Avenida da Liberdade, p.163
Esplanada Santa Marta	Cascais, p.282
Lautasco	Alfama, p.149
Rouge	Bairro Alto, p.156
Santo António de Alfama	Alfama, p.150
A Tasquinha	Castelo, p.149
Cervejaria da Trindade	Bairro Alto, p.157
York House	Lapa, p.161

tourist clientele, but it's a great spot for *borrego* (lamb), *tamboril* (monkfish) and *cataplanas* (stews). Booking is advised.

Malmequer-Bemmequer
Map 4, E7. Rua de São Miguel 23–25.
Mon & Wed–Sat 12.30–3.30pm & 7–10.30pm, Tues 7pm–10.30pm; closed last week in Oct. Moderate to expensive.
Cheerily decorated place, overseen by a friendly owner. Grilled meat and fish dishes dominate the menu (try the *salmão no carvão* – charcoal-grilled salmon), or eat from the daily changing tourist menu for around €13.

Mestre André
Map 4, G7. Calçadinha de Santo Estevão 4–6.
Mon–Sat noon–2.30am. No credit cards. Moderate.
A fine tavern on the steps just off Rua dos Remédios, offering superb pork dishes and a good range of *churrasco* (grilled) dishes. There's an outdoor terrace, too, with seating in summer.

Santo António de Alfama
Map 4, F7. Beco de São Miguel 7 ⊤ 218 881 328 or 218 881 329.
Daily except Tues 8pm–1am.

Moderate to expensive.
With black-and-white photos of film stars on the wall and a lovely outdoor terrace shaded by vines, this is one of the nicest restaurant-bars in the Alfama; it's off Rua de São Miguel, and you should book to guarantee a table?. There's a very long list of expensive wines, but the food is more moderately priced – things like *carpaccio de carne* (meat carpaccio), Caesar salad and *bife com molho do mostarda* (beef with mustard sauce). For dessert, there's Haagen Dazs ice cream.

CAMPO DE SANTA CLARA AND GRAÇA

Haweli Tandoori
Map 2, G8. Trav. do Monte 14. Wed–Mon noon–3pm & 7–11.30pm. Inexpensive. Recommended, budget-priced Indian restaurant (with take-away service) near the Miradouro da Graça, serving a good range of curries, tandoori dishes and vegetarian options. It's on a small alley on the west side of Largo da Graça.

Mercado de Santa Clara
Map 4, I3. Mercado de Santa

Clara ⓣ 218 873 986. Tues–Fri 12.30pm–3pm & 8pm–midnight, Sat & Sun 12.30–3pm. Moderate to expensive.
Highly rated cuisine is served in the upstairs room of the old market building, with distant views of the Tejo. Come on Tuesday or Saturday lunchtime to be in the thick of the Feira da Ladra market bustle. The restaurant specializes in beef dishes, but also serves fish, while on Sunday *feijoada* is the dish of the day. Reservations are advised.

Via Graça
Map 4, E1. Rua Damasceno Monteiro 9b ⓣ 218 870 830. Mon–Fri 12.30–3.30pm & 7.30pm–midnight, Sat 7.30pm–midnight. Moderate to expensive.
Tucked away below the Miradouro da Graça (take a left after Largo da Graça becomes Rua da Graça), this smart restaurant in an unattractive modern building is a whole lot better on the inside, from where you can soak up the stunning panoramas of Lisbon. Specialities include *santola* (spider crab) and *pato com moscatel* (duck with moscatel).

ALFAMA AND AROUND

SANTA APOLÓNIA AND DOCA DO JARDIM DO TOBACO

Bica do Sapato

Map 4, L6. Avda Infante Dom Henrique, Armazém B, Cais da Pedra à Bica do Sapato. ℡218 810 320.
Mon 5pm–2am, Tues–Sat 9am–2am. Expensive.
Owned by actor John Malkovich, and attracting politicians and the glitterati, this very stylish but refreshingly informal warehouse conversion has mirrored walls to reflect the crisp Tejo vistas. There's an outside terrace too. The menu features a long list of international fish and meat dishes such as crab ravioli, as well as great *ciabatta* sandwiches, pasta, *carpaccio* and sushi. Reservations advised.

Casanova

Map 4, L6. Avda Infante Dom Henrique, Loja 7 Armazém B, Cais da Pedra à Bica do Sapato.
Tues 6pm–2am, Wed–Sun 12.30pm–2am. Moderate.
If *Bica do Sapato* (see above) is beyond your budget, the more modest *Casanova* next door

offers pizza, pasta and *crostini* accompanied by similar views from its outside terrace. It's phenomenally popular and you can't book, so turn up early.

Jardim do Marisco

Map 4, G9. Avda Infante Dom Henrique, Doca do Jardim do Tobaco Pavilhão AB. ℡218 824 240.
Daily 1–3.30pm & 8–11pm. Moderate to expensive.
Best-positioned of the row of warehouse restaurants in the Doca Jardim do Tobaco development. The counter by the main entrance groans under the weight of crabs, giant prawns and shellfish and, not surprisingly, seafood is the speciality – grilled, served in salads, or with pasta or *açorda* (a garlic and bread sauce). There's an upstairs terrace with great river views and an airy interior with high ceilings. Reservations advised.

Mesacais

Map 4, G9. Avda Infante Dom Henrique, Doca do Jardim do Tobaco Pavilhão AB ℡218 877 155.

Tues & Wed 8pm–midnight,
Thurs & Fri 8pm–2am, Sat
1–3pm & 8pm–2am, Sun 1–3pm
& 8pm–midnight. Expensive.
Classy, riverside haunt specializing in fondue dishes that
bubble at your table. The fish
and seafood is also superb and
includes *espetado de lulas com
camarão* (squid kebabs with
prawns). The starters – octopus
and runny cheeses – are delicious but add considerably to
the bill. Reservations advised.

BAIRRO ALTO AND AROUND

BAIRRO ALTO

Adega do Teixeira
Map 5, F2. Rua do Teixeira ??.
Mon–Sat 10am–midnight.
Moderate.
Down a quiet side street, this
makes a good choice if you
want a tranquil start to your
evening before hitting the
nearby bars. It has a smart
interior and a lovely leafy terrace, and offers largish meals
based around grilled fish, meat
and eggs.

Águas do Bengo
Map 5, F2. Rua do Teixeira 1
T 213 477 516.
Tues–Sat 7.30pm–midnight.
Moderate to expensive.
Owned by Angolan musician
Waldemar Bastos, this African
music bar-restaurant serves
tropically inspired dishes, from
grilled fish to chicken stewed
with palm oil. If Waldemar is
in town and in the mood, he'll
grab his guitar and play a tune
or two. Reservations advised.

Ali-a-Papa
Map 5, E4. Rua da Atalaia 95.
Mon & Wed–Sun
7.30pm–2am. Moderate.
One of Lisbon's few Moroccan
restaurants, with an attractive
interior and a fashionable
clientele. The couscous and
tajine dishes are pretty good
value and you can order a
refreshing mint tea.

Bota Alta
Map 5, F3. Trav. da Queimada
37 T 213 427 959.
Mon–Fri noon–4.30pm &
7–11pm, Sat 7pm–midnight.
Moderate.

Old tavern decorated with old boots (*botas*) and an eclectic picture collection. It attracts queues for its vast portions of traditional Portuguese food – *bacalhau com natas* (cod cooked in cream) among other things – and jugs of local wine. The tables are crammed in cheek-by-jowl and it's always packed; try to arrive before 8pm or book in advance.

Brasuca

Map 5, C2. Rua João Pereira da Rosa 7 ⓣ 213 220 740. Daily noon-3pm & 7-10.30pm; closed Mon from Nov to April. Moderate.

Well-established Brazilian restaurant in a great old building just down the hill from the Bairro Alto. Dishes include *feijoada moqueca* (chicken and bean stew), *picanha* (slices of garlicky beef) and lots of other meaty choices. Reservations advised, unless you don't mind waiting for a table.

Restaurante Calcuta

Map 5, E5. Rua do Norte 17 ⓣ 213 428 295. Mon–Sat noon-3pm & 6.30–11pm. Moderate.

Very popular Indian restaurant at the foot of the Bairro Alto,

attracting a youngish clientele. Lots of chicken, seafood and lamb curries, tandoori dishes, and good vegetarian options. Reservations advised.

O Cantinho do Bem Estar

Map 5, E5. Rua do Norte 46. Daily 7–11pm. Moderate.

The decor borders on the Portuguese kitsch, with ceramic chickens and over-the-top rural decor, but the "canteen of well-being" lives up to its name. Service is friendly and, from the menu, the rice dishes and generous salads are the best bet; the passable house wine is served in ceramic jugs.

Casa Trasmontana

Map 5, G4. Calç. do Duque 39 ⓣ 213 420 300. Daily noon–3pm & 7pm–2am. No credit cards. Inexpensive.

A different dish of the day – usually meat-orientated – is on offer in this tiny restaurant specializing in cuisine from the north of Portugal. It's a friendly little place, off Largo Trindade Coelho, on the steps that head down to Rossio station. Reservations are probably a good idea.

Consenso

Map 5, C2. Rua da Academia das Ciências 1–1a ☎ 213 468 611.
Mon–Fri 1–3pm & 7.30–11.30pm, Sat 7.30pm–12.30am, Sun 7.30–11.30pm. Moderate to expensive.
Set in the basement of the former house of the Marquês de Pombal, although – the bare stonework aside – everything about the restaurant is contemporary. Four themed rooms have decor influenced by the elements, while well-prepared international dishes include *gaspacho*, pasta, crepes, *picanha* (slices of garlicky beef) and Portuguese favourites. It's best to reserve in advance.

Estibordo

Map 5, G4. Trav. João de Deus 14.
Mon–Sat noon–midnight. Inexpensive.
Simple local restaurant with slightly gloomy nautical decor. Specialities include prawns or veal in breadcrumbs, served with a liberal dollop of mayonnaise - not for healthy eaters, but very good value. If you fancy something lighter,

grab a stool at the bar for a good range of *petiscos* (bar snacks).

Mamma Rosa

Map 5, F3. Rua do Grémio Lusitano 14 ☎ 213 465 350.
Daily 8pm–2am. Inexpensive.
Lively, intimate pizzeria, bustling with students, which dishes up uninspiring but inexpensive pasta, pizza and grilled meats. It's also a popular gay hangout and gets busy at the weekends, so you might want to book.

Novo Bonsai

Map 5, F1. Rua da Rosa 248 ☎ 213 462 515.
Tues–Fri & Sun noon–2pm & 7.30–10.30pm, Sat & Mon 7.30–10.30pm. Moderate to expensive.
Classy Japanese restaurant with low tables and silk screens. The long menu is not bad value and the fresh ingredients are prepared at an open kitchen. There's superb fresh sushi, or go for the tempura, deep-fried vegetables cooked in the style introduced to Japan by Portuguese explorers in the sixteenth century. Reservations advised.

BAIRRO ALTO AND AROUND

566

La Paparrucha

Map 5, F1. Rua Dom Pedro V
18-20 ☎ 213 425 333.
Daily 12.30pm–2am.
Expensive.
Formal Argentinian restaurant,
frequented mostly for the terrific panoramic views over
Lisbon, especially from its outdoor terrace. The food,
inevitably, is meat-orientated
with lots of beef on the menu,
and the price soon mounts up
once you add on vegetables and
salads. Reservations advised.

Pap'Açorda

Map 5, E4. Rua da Atalaia
57–59 ☎ 213 464 811.
Tues–Sat 12.30–2.30pm &
8–11pm. Expensive.
Renowned restaurant which
attracts Lisbon's fashionable
elite to its chandelier-hung
dining room, converted from
an old bakery. *Açorda* – a sort
of bread stew, seasoned with
fresh coriander and a raw egg
– is the house speciality, served
with seafood. Reservations
advised.

A Primavera do Jerónimo

Map 5, E4. Trav. da Espera 34
☎ 213 420 477.
Mon–Sat noon–3pm &

7–11pm. Inexpensive.
This tiny place neatly crams in
a couple of dozen diners, a bar
and kitchen area, overseen by
the owner and his daughter.
Azulejos inscribed with
Portuguese proverbs dot the
walls, while the home-cooked
Portuguese dishes are highly
rated (as newspaper reviews on
the walls testify). Portions
aren't huge by local standards,
but the crisp-like fried potatoes are a hit. Reservations
advised.

Rouge

Map 5, E4. Trav. dos Fiéis de
Deus 28 ☎ 213 426 372.
Tues–Sun 5pm–1am.
Moderate.
Fashionable clientele, Eastern-
inspired decor and an interesting mix of Thai and
Mediterranean cuisine, including decent Greek salads and
pasta dishes. The most appealing aspect is the outdoor seating – a rarity in the Bairro
Alto – on this stepped side
street. Reserve in advance if
you can.

Sabor e Arte

Map 5, E5. Trav. da Espera 29
☎ 213 471 846.
Daily noon–2am. Moderate.

Possibly the Bairro Alto's smallest restaurant, so not surprisingly it fills quickly. But come early or book ahead and you can choose from a good mix of moderately priced pastas, Portuguese cuisine and vegetarian dishes.

Sinal Vermelho
Map 5, F4. Rua das Gáveas 89 ⓣ 213 461 252.
Daily 12.30–3pm & 7.30–11.30pm; closed July.
Moderate.
Roomy, split-level *adega* (wine cellar) that's popular with Lisbon's moneyed young. Specialities include well-presented rabbit and liver dishes and there's an impressive wine list. You may have to wait in line if you don't book ahead.

Stasha
Map 5, F4. Rua das Gãveas 29–33.
Tues–Thurs 7.30pm–midnight, Fri–Sun 7.30pm–1am.
Moderate.
Very popular gay-friendly restaurant, which does decent Portuguese food with plenty of vegetarian options at moderate prices; it also hosts temporary art exhibitions from up-and-coming artists.

Sul
Map 5, E5. Rua do Norte 13 ⓣ 213 462 449.
Tues–Sun noon–2am.
Expensive.
Jazzy, split-level wine bar and restaurant. The upper level (weekend reservations advised) does interesting food from "o sul" (the south) – basically the Med and South America (from pasta to steaks) – while the lower level features a neat bar with classy wines and bar snacks.

Cervejaria da Trindade
Map 5, G5. Rua Nova da Trindade 20 ⓣ 213 423 506.
Daily 9am–2am. Inexpensive.
The city's oldest beer-hall dates from 1836. At busy times you'll be shown to your table; at others, avoid the dull modern extensions and find space in the original vaulted hall, decorated with some of the city's loveliest azulejos depicting the elements and seasons. Shellfish is the speciality, though the other fish and meat dishes are lighter on the wallet. There is also a patio garden and – a rarity – a children's menu; highchairs can be supplied.

Último Tango

Map 5, E4. Rua do Diário de
Notícias 62.
Mon–Sat 7.30–2am.
Moderate.
Welcoming Argentinian restaurant, with wooden tables and a
cosy interior. The large steaks
and huge mixed grills are what
most people come for and
they're rarely disappointed.

Vá e Volte

Map 5, F4. Rua do Diário de
Notícias 100.
Tues–Sun noon–midnight.
Inexpensive to moderate.
The small bar at the front
opens into a friendly little
family diner whose large plates
of fried or grilled fish and
meat, though nothing special,
are reliably cooked and filling.

PRAÇA DO
PRÍNCIPE REAL

Comida de Santo

Map 8, C6. Calçada
Engenheiro Miguel Pais 39
⊤ 213 963 339.
Daily 12.30–3.30pm &
7.30pm–1am. Expensive.
Rowdy, late-opening Brazilian
restaurant serving cocktails and

classic dishes such as *feijoada a
brasileira* (Brazilian bean stew).
It's off Rua da Escola
Politécnica, near the Science
and Natural History museums.
Reservations advised.

Conventual

Map 8, C7. Praça das Flores
⊤ 213 909 196.
Tues–Fri 12.30–3.30pm &
7.30–11pm, Sat & Sun
7.30–11pm. Expensive.
Set in a former convent, and
with an appropriately refined
atmosphere, *Conventual* produces a range of top-quality
dishes, starting with a flavour-
packed *gaspacho*, followed by
gambas em caril (prawn in curry
sauce), *crepes de camarão*
(shrimp crepes) or *perdiz estufa-
da* (baked partridge). This is a
good choice for a special night
and reservations are advised.

Taberna Espanhola

Map 8, C7. Praça das Flores
40 ⊤ 213 972 225.
Daily noon–1am. Moderate.
Lively Spanish restaurant with
an outdoor terrace facing the
leafy Praça das Flores. Tortilla
and paella are served, of
course, along with some typical Portuguese grills.
Reservations advised.

Faz Frio

Map 8, E7. Rua Dom Pedro V
96–98 ⊤ 213 461 860.
Daily 9am–midnight; usually
closed late August to late
September. Inexpensive.
A traditional restaurant,
replete with coloured tiles and
confessional-like cubicles.
Huge portions of bacalhau,
seafood paella, and prawns in
breadcrumbs are available, plus
a variety of dishes of the day,
though the service can be
patchy. Dinner reservations
advised, especially at the
weekend.

Tascardoso

Map 5, F1. Rua Dom Pedro V
137.
Mon–Fri noon–3pm & 7–10pm.
Inexpensive.
Go through the stand-up bar
and down the stairs to the tiny
eating area for excellent tapas-
style meats and cheeses and
good-value hot dishes.

RATO

- - - - - - - - - - - - - - - - - - - -

Casa da Comida

Map 8, B4. Trav. das
Amoreiras 1 ⊤ 213 885 376.
Mon–Fri 1–3pm & 8pm–mid-
night, Sat 8pm–midnight.

Expensive.
Just below one of Lisbon's
loveliest squares sits one of the
city's top restaurants, housed in
an old mansion and sporting
an outdoor patio. The menu is
particularly strong on fish –
*tamboril com molho de limão e
alho frances* (monkfish with
leeks and lemon sauce) and
crepes de camarão (shrimp
crepes) are highlights – or
there are meat choices like *pato
com azeitonas and perdiz* (duck
with olives and partidge).
Meals cost a good €30 and
upwards. Reservations advised.

Real Fábrica

Map 8, B5. Rua da Escola
Politécnica 275 ⊤ 213 852
090.
Daily 8am–2am. Expensive.
This former silk factory – with
stone walls and big mirrors - is
well-known for its beer, which
is brewed in huge barrels in a
corner. The curved wooden
bar downstairs offers inexpensive lunchtime snacks, while
the lovely upstairs dining room
(reservations advised) puts on a
colossal Brazilian buffet, which
includes beef, turkey with
bacon, fried bananas, pineap-
ple, and black beans and rice
for around €30 a head. There's
also an outdoor terrace.

BAIRRO ALTO AND AROUND

LAPA, ESTRELA AND SÃO BENTO

Cantinho da Paz

Map 6, I4. Rua da Paz 4, São Bento ⓣ 213 969 698.
Tues–Sun 12.30–2.30pm & 7.30–11pm. Moderate.
Simple Goan restaurant favoured by MPs from the parliament building; it's just off tram route #28, and reservations are advised since it's only small. There's shark soup, prawn curry and a few vegetarian options, served in a homely little dining room overseen by an enthusiastic owner who can guide you through the menu.

Farah's Tandoori

Map 6, F3. Rua de Santana à Lapa 73, Estrela.
Mon & Wed–Sun noon–3pm & 7–10.30pm. Inexpensive to moderate.
Between Lapa and Estrela, this is one of Lisbon's more reliable Indian restaurants and is especially good for vegetarians, who can choose from dishes like vegetable *tikka masala*, Bombay *alu* and *palak paneer*. Meat dishes are also fragrant and deli-

cious, and the owners speak English.

Flor da Estrela

Map 6, G3. Rua João de Deus 11, Estrela.
Mon–Sat 8am–midnight. Moderate.
Neighbourhood restaurant around the back of the Estrela basilica (there are a few outdoor tables), serving all the usual Portuguese dishes and cheap wine. Try the *feijoada de marisco* (bean stew with seafood).

Indo-Africa/Cantinho da Paz II

Map 6, I5. Rua do Poço dos Negros 64, São Bento ⓣ 213 908 638.
Daily except Tues 12.30–3.30pm & 7.30–11.30pm. Moderate.
This is the place to sample a range of Portuguese colonial cuisine under one roof: Goan, Cape Verdean and Angolan dishes, including highlights like *vitela com açafrão e amêndoa* (veal with saffron rice and almonds), *carne de vaca com molho de amendoim* (beef with

peanut sauce) and *feijoada Indiana* (Indian bean stew). There's live music at weekends, and it's best to book in advance.

Picanha

Map 6, G5. Rua das Janelas Verdes 47, Lapa ⓣ 213 975 401.
Mon–Fri 12.45–3pm & 7.45–11.30pm, Sat & Sun 7.45–11.30pm. Moderate.
Just up from the Museu de Arte Antiga, this ornately tiled restaurant specializes in *picanha* (thin slices of beef) accompanied by black-eyed beans, salad and potatoes. Great if this appeals to you, since for a

fixed-price of €13 you can eat as much of the stuff as you want; otherwise forget it, as it's all they do. Advance reservations advised.

York House

Map 6, G5. Rua das Janelas Verdes 47, Lapa ⓣ 213 968 143.
Daily 12.30–2.30pm & 7.30–9.30pm. Moderate to expensive.
Inside this sumptuous hotel is a surprisingly moderately priced restaurant serving delicious fish, meat, pasta and vegetarian options. In summer, you can dine in the tranquil courtyard. Reservations advised.

ALCÂNTARA

Alcântara Café

Map 6, B5. Rua Maria Luísa Holstein 15 ⓣ 213 637 176.
Daily 8pm–3am. Expensive.
Stunning designer bar-restaurant successfully blending industrial steel pillars with stylish decor. The food on offer includes prawns in lemon sauce, goat's cheese salad and an array of fish dishes. This is a place to be seen before moving on to the neighbouring

clubs, hence the high prices (and advised reservations).

Doca Peixe

Map 6, B7. Doca de Santo Amaro.
Tues–Sun 12.30pm–4am. Moderate.
Virtually under the bridge – and noisy when the trains rattle over – this modern place serves moderately priced fish and seafood, served grilled or

ALCÂNTARA

baked. Choosing lobster from the bubbling tanks pushes the price up a fair bit.

Espalha Brasas

Map 6, B7. Armazém 12, Doca de Santo Amaro.
Mon–Sat noon–2am.
Moderate.
Tapas and superb grilled meats can be enjoyed at outdoor riverside tables, or head for the bright upstairs room, which offers great views over the river.

Tertúlia do Tejo

Map 6, B7. Pavilhão 4, Doca de Santo Amaro ⓣ 213 955 552.
Daily 12.30–3pm & 7pm–midnight. Expensive.
Upmarket Portuguese restaurant, housed on three floors of a converted warehouse. There are evocative old photos of Portugal in the upstairs room and more intimate seating in the attic, plus fine river views throughout. The flavoured vodkas are a hit too. Reservations advised.

Zeno

Map 6, B7. Armazém 15, Doca de Santo Amaro ⓣ 213 973 948.
Mon–Sat 12.30pm–1.30am, Sun 8.30pm–1.30am.
Moderate to expensive.
Thriving Brazilian restaurant in a converted warehouse by the river, with live music most nights. The speciality is *feijoada à brasileira* (Brazilian bean stew), which you can follow with refreshing tropical desserts. You'll need to reserve ahead, especially at weekends.

BELÉM

Cápsula

Map 7, G5. Rua Vieira Portuense 74.
Mon noon–3pm, Wed–Sun noon–3pm & 7–11pm.
Moderate.
One of the many places in this pretty row of buildings facing the greenery of Praça do Império. This has a tiled interior, upstairs seating and outside tables catering for tourists tucking into tuna steaks, trout and the like at good-value prices.

Floresta Belém

Map 7, G5. Praça Afonso de Albuquerque 1.
Mon–Fri & Sun 9am–4pm & 6.30pm–midnight. Moderate.
On the corner with Rua Vieira Portuense, this is one of the best-value places on this stretch, attracting a largely Portuguese clientele, especially for lunch at the weekend. Great salads, grills and fresh fish, served inside or on a sunny outdoor terrace.

São Jerónimo

Map 7, F2. Rua dos Jerónimos 12 Ⓣ 213 648 797.
Mon–Fri & Sun 12.30–3pm & 7.30–10pm. Moderate.
Rustic-style dining by the side of the monastery. The fish is excellent, and the speciality is *migas*, a garlicky bread sauce from the Alentejo region served with meat or fish. This is tour-bus territory, so advance reservations are advised.

AROUND AVENIDA DA LIBERDADE

Centro de Alimentaçao e Saúde Natural

Map 8, D3. Rua Mouzinho da Silveira 25.
Mon–Fri 9am–2.30pm & 3.50–6pm. Inexpensive.
Self-service restaurant with light, bright upstairs dining rooms and a summer courtyard, offering good, inexpensive vegetarian food, like chickpea stew, pepper rice and natural fruit juices.

O Coreto

Map 8, H3. Jardim Campo dos Mátires da Pátria.
Mon–Fri 9am–11pm.

Inexpensive.
In a leafy square – part of the walk described on p.89 – this is very much a local café-restaurant, with a good-value menu and outdoor seating facing a little duck pond. Steak au poivre is the house speciality.

Restaurante Estrela

Map 8, F3. Rua Santa Marta 14a.
Mon–Fri 9am–midnight, Sat 9am–6pm. Inexpensive.
Tiny tiled tasca, just one of many remarkably inexpensive dining rooms on this street to the east of the Avenida da Liberdade, serving Portuguese

dishes like *arroz de pato* (duck rice). You'll find it on the walking route described on p.89.

Ribadouro

Map 8, F5. Avda da Liberdade 155 ☎ 213 549 411.
Daily noon–1am. Moderate.
The avenida's best *cervejaria*, serving a decent range of grilled meats and shellfish (but no fish). If you don't fancy a full meal, take a seat at the bar and order a beer with a plate of prawns. Best to book for the restaurant, especially at weekends.

Tibetanos

Map 8, D5. Rua do Salitre 117 ☎ 213 142 038.
Mon–Fri noon–2pm & 7.30–9.30pm. Inexpensive.
Run by a Buddhist Centre, this stripped-pine restaurant has superb and unusual veggie food, including vegetarian paella. It gets full at lunchtimes in particular, so get there early and grab a table or call ahead.

PARQUE EDUARDO VII AND SALDANHA

Botequim do Rei

Map 9, C7. Esplanade da Parque Eduardo VII.
Tues–Sun 10am–8pm. Moderate.
Fish and meat dishes are fairly average, but the setting, right in the park by a small lake, is particularly tranquil making this a good place to head for lunch. Take care here, though, after dark.

Centro de Arte Moderna

Map 9, C4. Rua Dr Bettencourt, Fundação Calouste Gulbenkian.
Tues–Sun 10am–5.45pm. No credit cards. Inexpensive.
Join the lunchtime queues at the museum restaurant for good-value hot and cold dishes. There's an excellent choice of salads for vegetarians, which you can eat overlooking the gardens. Get there early though before the smokers fume the place out.

Solar do Morais

Map 9, C6. Rua Augusto dos Santos 3.
Sun–Fri 9.30am–10.30pm. Inexpensive.

Very much a locals' joint, despite its position between the tourist draws of Parque Eduardo VII and the Gulbenkian, on a tiny road connecting Avenida António Augusto de Aguiar and Rua de São Sebastião da

Pedreira. The cool, arched interior has cabinets of fresh food, bottles lining the walls and a large ham on the bar. Trout and salmon dishes are always worth ordering, and there's a small outdoor terrace.

AROUND AVENIDA ALMIRANTE REIS

Cervejaria Portugália
Map 2, G6. Avda Almirante Reis 117 ☏ 218 851 024.
Daily 10am–1.30am.
Moderate.
The original *Portugália* – there are newer branches in Santos and Belém – and much the best, a busy beer-hall-restaurant near metro Arroios where you can either snack and drink at the bar or eat fine *mariscos* (shellfish) or steak in the dining room. It makes for a popular family outing and is always busy, so it's worth calling ahead if you want a table.

Espiral
Map 2, F6. Praça Ilha do Faial 14a.
Daily noon–9.30pm.
Inexpensive.
Self-service, macrobiotic restaurant downstairs (offering vegetarian, Chinese and fish dishes) with adjacent snack bar, plus upstairs bookshop and noticeboard with information on the city's alternative/green scene. The food isn't that great, but there's often live music at the weekend. Take the metro to either Picoas or Arroios stations; the restaurant is off Largo de Dona Estefânia.

PARQUE DAS NAÇÕES

Os Alentejanos
Cais dos Argonautas.
Daily 12.30–10pm. Moderate.

Great wooden barrels and hams dangling from the ceiling and waiters in broad-rimmed hats give a jolly feel to a restaurant specializing in regional food from the Alentejo – expect tapas (olives, cheeses, *presunto* ham), *açorda* with seafood and thick red wines, though genuine Alentejans would be horrified by the prices.

Chimarrão
Doca dos Olivais.
Daily noon–4pm & 7pm–midnight. Moderate to expensive.
In a prime position, with an outdoor terrace right on the waterside of Olivais docks, this Brazilian chain specializes in barbecued meats; if you have a

very large appetite, go for the set meals, which are vast. There's also a good salad bar for the less carnivorously inclined.

Oceanario Café
Armazém 204.
Mon–Thurs & Sun 10am–8pm, Fri & Sat 10am–1am.
Inexpensive.
Unpretentious self-service canteen and bar with outdoor tables near the Oceanarium; the buffet food is fresh and good value, with an extensive range of salads, hot dishes of the day and tasty desserts.

For a map of the Parque das Nações, see p.106.

Restaurante Panorâmico
Torre Vasco da Gama ☎ 218 939 550.
Tues–Sun noon–2pm & 8–10pm. Expensive.
The top of the old oil refinery tower is now an exclusive restaurant with fantastic views and some pretty decent Portuguese and international food at almost-as-high prices. Steamed sea bass, grilled tiger prawns and oven-baked duck are just some of the specialities. You'll need to reserve in advance.

Restaurante del Uruguay
Cais dos Argonautas.
Mon–Fri noon–4pm & 7–11.30pm, Sat & Sun noon–4.30pm & 7–11.30pm.
Moderate.
A chance to sample Uruguayan cuisine in a modern restaurant near the Water Gardens. The *picaña a la parrilla con papa paisana* (thin strips of beef with potatoes, garlic and salsa) is recommended.

PARQUE DAS NAÇÕES

Cafés

—

Lisbon has literally thousands of **cafés**, ranging from atmospheric turn-of-the-century artists' haunts and Art Deco wonders to those with minimalist interiors frequented by clubbers in designer clothing. Locals tend to head for a café or *pastelaria* (pastry shop) for a **breakfast** of a croissant or pastry of some kind washed down with a coffee. The latter is usually taken espresso-style (ask for *uma bica*), though the milky version (*um galão*), served in a glass, is also popular at breakfast time.

You'll often find a whole range of dishes served, but classic Portuguese **café snacks** include *rissóis de carne* (deep-fried meat patties), *pastéis de bacalhau* (cod fishcakes) and *prego no pão* (steak sandwich). Other cafés and some bars have signs advertising *petiscos* (bar snacks) usually consisting of plates of *camarões* (boiled prawns), *chouriço* (slices of smoked sausage) and *tremoços* (pickled lupin seeds). Among **sandwiches** (*sandes*) on offer, the most common fillings include *queijo* (cheese), *fiambre* (ham), *presunto* (smoked ham) and *chouriço* (smoked sausage). *Sandes mistas* are usually a combination of ham and cheese; grilled, they're called *tostas mistas*. Lisbon is also famous for its **cakes** (*bolos*) and **pastries**, particularly the *pastéis de nata* (custard-cream tarts).

Cafés with particularly good food have been listed in

"Eating" (p.136); those that are best for an alcoholic drink can be found in "Bars and clubs" (p.176). The following are recommended for a coffee, soft drink or snack.

Our listings are divided into the following areas: Baixa (p.168); Chiado (p.170); Cais do Sodré (p.171); Alfama and Graça (p.171); Bairro Alto (p.172); Lapa (p.173); Alcântara (p.173); Belém (p.174); Avenida da Liberdade (p.175); Parque Eduardo VII (p.175); Saldanha (p.175).

BAIXA

Atinel
Map 3, L4. Estação Fluvial, Praça do Comércio.
Mon–Fri 6am–9pm, Sat 6am–8.30pm.
A popular tourist spot, right by the ferry terminal. The riverside vista is unbeatable, even if the food is only average and you may find the sight of fish enjoying the effluent a little off-putting.

Beira Gare
Map 3, C7. Rua 1° de Dezembro 5.
Daily 6.30am–1am.
Well-established café-bar opposite Rossio station, serving stand-up Portuguese snacks, and cheap lunches and dinners. Constantly busy, which is recommendation enough.

Casa Chineza
Map 3, E7. Rua Aurea 274.
Mon–Fri 7am–8pm, Sat 7am–4pm.
Apart from the odd bit of neon lighting, this beautifully decorated old Baixa café hasn't changed for years and its tantalizing pastries and coffee attract a steady stream of local workers.

Casulo
Map 3, A7. Praça dos Restauradores.
Mon–Sat 6am–2am.
A fairly average café but in a great position, on the east side of the square. There are a few outdoor seats and it's a handy spot for breakfast.

Confeitaria Nacional
Map 3, D5. Praça da Figueira.
Daily 8am–8pm.
Opened in 1829 and little
changed since, with a stand-up
counter selling pastries and
sweets below a mirrored ceiling. There's a little side room
for sit-down coffees and
snacks.

Elevador de Santa Justa Café
Map 3, E7. Rua de Santa
Justa.
Daily 10am–7pm.
The drinks and snacks are
inevitably overpriced, but the
mark-up is justified by the
stunning views of the Baixa
from the breezy rooftop platform of this iron latticework
elevator, built in 1902.

Martinho da Arcada
Map 3, J5. Praça do Comércio
3.
Mon–Sat 7am–11pm.
One of Lisbon's oldest cafés,
first opened in 1782 and
declared a National
Monument as long ago as
1910. Over the years it has
been a gambling den, a meeting place for political dissidents
and, later, a more reputable

hangout for politicians, writers
and artists, including Fernando
Pessoa, Eça de Queirós and
Mário de Sá Carneiro. It is
now divided into a simple
stand-up café next to a considerably more expensive restaurant (see p.139). The outdoor
tables under the arches are the
perfect spot for a coffee and a
pastel de nata.

Nicola
Map 3, D7. Rossio 24.
Mon–Fri 9am–7.30pm, Sat
10am–1pm.
The only surviving Rossio
coffee house from the early
twentieth century is another
former haunt of some of
Lisbon's great literary figures.
Sited on the southwest side of
the square, the outdoor tables
overlooking the bustle of
Rossio are the café's best feature, though it has sacrificed
much of its period interior in
the name of modernization.

Suíça
Map 3, D6. Rossio
Daily 7am–10pm.
Famous for its cakes and pastries; you'll have a hard job
getting an outdoor table here,
though there's plenty of room
inside. The café stretches

BAIXA

through to Praça da Figueira, where you'll find the best alfresco seating.

Cafe do Teatro
Map 3, B7. Teatro Nacional de Dona Maria II, Rossio.
Mon–Fri 9am–7pm.

Lisbon's creative types frequent this theatre café, hidden among the imposing columns of Lisbon's main theatre. Moderately priced cakes, sandwiches and drinks come with views across to the Neo-Manueline Rossio station opposite.

For cafés with views, see p.172; for cafés with outdoor seating, see p.174.

CHIADO

Bernard
Map 5, F6. Rua Garrett 104.
Mon–Sat 8am–midnight.
Often overlooked because of its proximity to A *Brasileira*, this ornate café offers superb cakes, ice cream and coffees, and an outdoor terrace on Chiado's most fashionable street.

A Brasileira
Map 5, F6. Rua Garrett 120.
Daily 8am–2am.
Marked by an outdoor bronze statue of the poet Fernando Pessoa, this is the most famous of Lisbon's old-style coffee houses. The tables on the pedestrianized street get

snapped up by tourists, but the real appeal is in its traditional interior, where prices are considerably cheaper than at the outdoor esplanade, especially if you stand at the long bar. At night the clientele changes to a youthful brigade on the beer.

Café No Chiado
Map 5, F6. Largo do Picadeiro 11.
Mon–Sat 10pm–2am.
Café-restaurant at the top end of Rua Duque de Bragança, with outdoor tables in a picturesque square. There's internet access upstairs at *Ciber Chiado*.

CHIADO

CAIS DO SODRÉ

Wagons-Lit
Map 5, B9. Estação Fluvial.
Mon–Fri 7am–10pm, Sat &
Sun 7am–8.30pm.
A simple and tranquil spot
with outdoor tables facing the
river, offering inexpensive coffees, drinks and snacks; a great
place to while away a few
minutes if you have a ferry or
train to catch.

ALFAMA AND GRAÇA

O Café do Castelo
Map 4, B5. Castelo de São
Jorge.
Daily 9am–dusk.
Set within the castle walls, this
offers good-value buffet
lunches – all you can eat for
€6.50 – and drinks. Its outdoor tables are beautifully
positioned under shady trees,
facing a giant statue of a man
with a flowerpot for a head.

Cerca Moura
Map 4, E6. Largo das Portas
do Sol 4.
Mon–Sat 11am–2am, Sun
11am–8pm.
A good place to take a break
from climbing up and down
the hilly streets. However, the
main appeal is the stunning
view of Alfama from the
esplanade seats.

Esplanada da Graça
Map 4, E2. Largo da Graça.
Daily 10am–2am.
A tiny kiosk serving coffee,
drinks and snacks by the
Miradouro da Graça. It's not
cheap, but the seats have stunning views over the bridge and
the Baixa, particularly at sunset. After dark, it cranks up a
powerful music system to
change the atmosphere from
somnolent to decidedly lively.

Monasterium Café
Map 4, G4. Igreja São
Vicente de Fora, Calçada de
São Vicente.
Tues–Sun 10am–6pm.
The café in the São Vicente
monastery building boasts
comfortable indoor seating, a
tranquil patio and, best of all, a
small roof terrace with stupen-
dous views over Alfama and

CAFÉS WITH VIEWS

Atinel	Baixa, p.168
Cerca Moura	Alfama, p.171
Elevador de Santa Justa Café	Baixa, p.169
Esplanada da Graça	Graça, p.171
Monasterium Café	Alfama, p.171
Café Quadrante	Belém, p.174
Sítio do pica-pau	Lapa, p.173
Wagons-Lit	Cais do Sodré, p.171

the Tejo (including an aerial view of tram #28 squeezing through its narrowest street).

Pastelaria Estrela da Graça
Map 4, F1. Largo da Graça 98a.

Daily 7am–10pm.
Round the corner from the Miradouro da Graça on the main square, this local café serves superb home-made cakes and pastries, and inexpensive lunches. The toy fire engine outside keeps the kids happy.

BAIRRO ALTO

Académica
Map 3, E8. Largo do Carmo 1–3.
Daily 7am–midnight.
Outdoor tables on one of the city's nicest, quietest squares, outside the ruined Carmo church. Drinks and snacks aside, it also does light lunches; in summer, the grilled sardines are hard to beat.

O Outra Face da Lua
Map 5, F4. Rua do Norte 86.
Daily 3pm–midnight.
So *very* Bairro Alto – part shop, selling clothes by up-and-coming designers, part café, full of up-and-coming people sipping tea.

Pão de Canela
Map 8, C7. Praça das Flores 27–28.
Mon–Fri 7.30am–8pm, Sat & Sun 8am–8pm.

Tastefully modernized, tile-fronted café serving great pastries, soups and snacks. The outdoor terrace faces a children's play area on this lovely square.

Esplanada do Prínçipe Real
Map 8, D7. Praça do Prínçipe Real.
Daily 8am–midnight.
The outdoor tables set under the trees in this attractive square are its best feature, though the glass pavilion comes into its own when the weather turns. It's also a popular gay haunt.

Pastelaria São Roque
Map 8, F7. Rua Dom Pedro V 57c.
Daily 7am–7.30pm.
Relaxed corner café-cum-bakery with a wonderfully ornate ceiling, high enough to house a giraffe, where you can have coffee and croissants or buy fresh bread.

LAPA

O Chão da Lapa
Map 6, F5. Rua do Olival 10.
Daily 9am–8pm.
Sophisticated tea-rooms serving pastries and drinks to the good people of Lapa. It's just up the hill from the Museu de Arte Antiga.

Sítio do pica-pau
Map 6, G4. Rua dos Remédios à Lapa 61.
Mon–Fri 8am–8pm.
Tiny café right in the heart of Lapa, whose outdoor decking commands views over the rooftops and river.

ALCÂNTARA

Zonadoca
Map 6, B7. Pavilhão 7a, Doca de Santo Amaro.
Mon & Wed–Sun 12.30pm–3am.
Worth a visit for its ice cream alone, though you can also enjoy coffee or alcoholic drinks at this friendly, family-oriented café in a converted warehouse (with life-sized models of Laurel and Hardy for company). The outdoor seats are placed right underneath Ponte 25 de Abril.

CAFÉS WITH OUTDOOR SEATING

Académica	Bairro Alto, p.172
A Brasileira	Chiado, p.170
O Café do Castelo	Castelo, p.171
Café No Chiado	Chiado, p.170
Esplanada do Prínçipe Real	Bairro Alto, p.173
A Linha d'Água	Parque Eduardo VII, p.175
Martinho da Arcada	Baixa, p.169
Nicola	Baixa, p.169
Passeio d'Avenida	Avenida da Liberdade, p.175
Caffè Rosso	Chiado, p.179
Suíça	Baixa, p.169

BELÉM

Antiga Confeitaria de Belém
Map 7, G4. Rua de Belém 90.
Daily 8am–midnight.
No visit to Belém is complete without a coffee and hot *pastel de nata* (custard-cream tart) liberally sprinkled with *canela* (cinnamon) in this cavernous tiled pastry shop and café.

Café Quadrante
Map 7, D5. Centro Cultural de Belém.
Daily 10am–10pm.
Part of the Belém Cultural Centre, offering good-value self-service food. The best place to enjoy its coffee and snacks is on the outdoor terrace by the roof gardens, overlooking the bridge, river and Monument to the Discoveries. It's so popular with students that they are forbidden from studying here at mealtimes.

AVENIDA DA LIBERDADE

Bela Ipanema
Map 8, E4. Avda da Liberdade 169.
Mon–Sat 6am–2am.
Bustling café by the São Jorge cinema, where a steady stream of locals pops in for snacks, beers and coffees at the bar or in its small dining area; outdoor tables face the avenue.

Passeio d'Avenida
Map 8, G6. Praça Central, Avda da Liberdade.
Mon–Sat 9am–1am.

This glass-covered café-restaurant may be a tourist trap, but the outdoor seats on the leafy central swathe of the avenue are a great place for a coffee or a beer.

Pastelaria Anunciada
Map 8, G6. Largo da Anunciada.
Mon–Wed & Fri–Sun 8am–10pm.
Beautifully tiled *pastelaria*, at the foot of the Elevador do Lavra, its windows stuffed full of sweets and bottles of port.

PARQUE EDUARDO VII

A Linha d'Água
Map 9, B6. Parque Eduardo VII.
Daily 9am–6pm.
Glass-fronted café at the northern end of Lisbon's main park, facing a small lake where, in summer, kids splash about in the shallow waters. It's not a bad spot to down a coffee or beer, and decent buffet lunches are served too.

SALDANHA

Café Versailles
Map 9, F5. Avda da República 15a.
Daily 7.30am–10pm.
Traditional café full of busy waiters circling the starched tablecloths. It's liveliest at around 4pm, when Lisbon's elderly dames gather for a chat beneath the chandeliers.

Bars and clubs

You can get a drink of some sort, at almost any time of day or night, at one of Lisbon's innumerable **bars**. These vary from local places, where children scamper around family groups until midnight, to modern, designer spaces with happening sounds playing until the small hours. The **club scene** is more discreet, concentrated in select areas of the city, though to those in the know it's one of Europe's best-kept secrets, with the club *Lux* regularly featuring in the top ten of international newspapers and magazines.

At night, the best area to head for is the **Bairro Alto.** This hosts one of Europe's biggest parties, with up to fifty thousand people descending on the maze of streets, especially after 11pm or so from Thursday to Saturday. Really committed clubbers, drinkers and lowlife enthusiasts can also try one of a dozen places around **Cais do Sodré**, especially along **Rua Nova do Carvalho**, which range from the atmospheric to the downright seedy. A more popular early-hours destination for Lisbon's youth, however, is a little way west along **Avenida 24 de Julho**, around Santos station, to where much of the action moves around 2am or so. Further west still, the revitalized docks at **Alcântara** are full of tastefully done-up warehouse-style bars and clubs close to the river. This is the favoured hangout for moneyed Lisboetas, but the area also has a bit of a drugs problem. As a result, a very strict door policy is in operation at most clubs; it's best to dress smart (avoid jeans and sandals) if you want to get in. However, the current hot-spot is on the eastern side of the city centre, in the revamped dockside area around **Santa Apolónia** station. This, and most other nightlife areas are reasonably central, though to reach Alcântara you'll need to catch a train (until 2am) to Alcântara Mar station from Cais do Sodré, or hop in a taxi (around €8).

Drinks are uniformly expensive in all fashionable bars and clubs – from €4 for a beer – but the plus-side is that very few clubs charge **admission**. Instead, many places have a "minimum consumption" policy – designed to stop people dancing all night without buying a drink, which many Portuguese would happily do. Sometimes it's a set fee, though more often the price is at the whim of the door-man, who will reduce it if it's a quiet night or whack it up if it's busy or if he doesn't like the look of you. Generally, you can expect to pay anything from €10 to €20 (but sometimes as much as €50); keep hold of your ticket as drinks will be stamped on it to ensure you consume enough (otherwise you pay on exit). **Friday and Saturday nights** tend to be overcrowded and expensive everywhere, while on **Sunday**, especially in the Bairro Alto, places often close to recover from the weekend excesses.

Our listings are divided into the following areas: Baixa (p.178); Chiado (p.179); Cais do Sodré (p.179); Castelo (p.181); Santa Apolónia (p.181); Bairro Alto (p.182); Praça do Príncipe Real and São Bento (p.185); Alcântara (p.186); Alcântara Docks (p.187); Santos and Avenida 24 de Julho (p.189); Parque das Naçoes (p.189). For listings of gay and lesbian clubs and bars, see p.191.

BARS AND CLUBS

BAIXA

A Ginginha

Map 3, B6. Largo de São Domingos 8, Rossio.
Daily 9am–10.30pm.
Everyone should try *ginginha* – Portuguese cherry brandy – once. There's just about room in this microscopic joint to walk in, down a glassful and stagger outside to see the city in a new light.

Ginginha-Rubi

Map 3, B5. Rua B. Queiroz.
Daily 9am–10.30pm.
Worth a peer inside for its beautiful azulejos, this tiny watering-hole offers *ginginha* with or without the cherry stone (some argue that its presence enhances the alcoholic content).

A Licorista

Map 3, E6. Rua dos Sapateiros 218.
Mon–Fri 8am–8pm, Sat 8am–1pm.
This attractive tile-and-brick bar is a good local refreshment stop near the Baixa shops. At lunchtime, tables are laid for inexpensive meals.

PORTUGUESE DRINKS

Portugal is rightly famed for its excellent wines and, though the locals rarely drink it in bars, you can always get a decent glass of **vinho** (wine) or **porto** (port). Lisboetas are more likely to go for **cervejas** (beers) – the two most common brands are Sagres and Superbock, either in *garrafas* (bottles) or draught: a *caneca* is a pint, an *imperial* is a half. A *panaché* is a shandy. Local **spirits** are cheap and the measures more than generous. If you want to be more adventurous, the local brandy – *macieira* – is smooth on the palate (but rough on the head). Even more lethal are the local *aguardente* firewaters such as *Bagaço* and the cherry-based *ginginha*, which seem to fuel certain Lisboan workers from breakfast onwards.

O Pirata
Map 3, A8. Praça dos
Restauradores 15.
Mon–Sat 8am–midnight.
Tiny bar on the west side of
the *praça* for serious drinkers
who want to sample the
unique house drink, *Pirata*, a
spirit whose recipe is jealously
guarded. There are other
drinks for the less adventurous.

CHIADO

Bicaense
Map 5, C5. Rua da Bica
Duarte Belo 38–42.
Mon–Sat 12.30–3pm &
8pm–2am.
Small, fashionable bar on the
steep street used by the
Elevador da Bica, with jazz
and Latin sounds and a
moderately priced list of bar
food.

Caffè Rosso
Map 3, G8. Galerias Garrett,
Rua Ivens 53–61, entrance on
Rua Garrett.
Daily 10am–midnight.
Relaxed courtyard bar in the
shopping gallery, with seats
under huge square canopies. It
serves coffee and snacks too,
and there's a spacious downstairs room with modernist
seats and lighting.

CAIS DO SODRÉ

Absoluto
Map 5, A7. Rua D. Luís I 5.
Mon–Sat 8am–2am (club:
Thurs midnight–5am, Fri & Sat
midnight–6am).
Modern restaurant, bar and
disco complex playing everything from the latest hits to Júlio
Iglesias, bolstered by occasional
performances by live (usually
rock or pop) bands. There are
even a few outdoor tables.

British Bar
Map 5, C8. Rua Bernardino
Costa 52.
Mon–Sat noon–midnight.
Wonderful Anglo-Portuguese
hybrid stuck in a 1930s' time
warp, featuring ceiling fans,
marble counter and dark
wooden shelves stacked with

wines and spirits. There's also Guinness on tap and regulars who look as if they've been coming here since the day it opened.

Casa Cid

Map 5, B7. Rua de Ribeira Nova 32.
Daily 4am–9pm.
Something of an institution, serving food and drinks to early-rising market workers and down-at-heel nightlife stop-outs in one of Lisbon's most seedy, if atmospheric, streets.

Irish Pub O'Gilins

Map 5, C8. Rua dos Remolares 8–10.
Daily 11am–2am.
The oldest and best of Lisbon's Irish bars, with a pleasant, light, burnished wood interior. There's live music from Thursday to Saturday, and English-language pub quizzes (mostly aimed at expats) on Sunday.

Jamaica

Map 5, C8. Rua Nova do Carvalho 8.
Mon–Thurs 11pm–4am, Fri & Sat 11pm–6am.
Well-established club on a somewhat down-at-heel road full of tacky nightlife venues. This is definitely the best one, attracting a mixed bag of sailors, students, expats and trendies. Music is predominantly retro, with reggae on Tuesday nights.

Poisa Copos

Map 5, A9. Cais da Ribeira.
Tues–Sat 6am–4am.
Popular with students, this small bar by the river in a con-verted warehouse is just the spot for a pick-me-up at six in the morning.

Bar do Rio

Map 5, A9. Armazém 7, Cais do Sodré.
Mon–Sat 11pm–5am.
Former riverside warehouse now decked out as a hip esplanade-bar; a good place to join the young and beautiful, who end a night on the town here before the trains start running again.

CAIS DO SODRÉ

CASTELO

Costa do Castelo
Map 4, A5. Calç. do Marquês de Tancos 1b.
Tues–Sun 3pm–2am.
Beautifully positioned terrace-café with Baixa views, a long list of cocktails and a restaurant serving mid-price Mozambican dishes. There's live music (usually Brazilian or jazz) on Thursday and Friday nights, and poetry readings at other times.

Rêsto do Chapitô
Map 4, A5. Costa do Castelo 7.
Tues–Fri 7.30pm–1.30am, Sat & Sun noon–1.30am.
Multi-purpose venue incorporating a theatre, circus school, restaurant and tapas bar. The outdoor esplanade commands terrific views over Alfama. The restaurant (Tues–Sun 7.30pm–midnight) is in an upstairs dining room, reached via a spiral staircase, and serves moderately priced pastas, salads and one or two fish and meat dishes. But really, most people come here to drink and take in the view.

SANTA APOLÓNIA

Lux
Map 4, L6. Armazéns A, Cais da Pedra a Santa Apolónia.
Tues-Fri 6pm–6am, Sat & Sun 4pm–6am.
This converted former meat warehouse has become one of Europe's most fashionable spaces, attracting visiting stars like Prince and Cameron Diaz. Part-owned by actor John Malkovich, it was the first place to venture into the docks opposite Santa Apolónia station. There's a rooftop terrace with amazing views, various bars, projection screens, a frenzied downstairs dance floor, and music from pop and trance to jazz and dance. The club is also increasingly on the circuit for touring bands.

CASTELO • SANTA APOLÓNIA

BAIRRO ALTO

Arroz Doce

Map 5, E3. Rua da Atalaia
117–119.

Mon–Sat 6pm–4am.

Nice, unpretentious bar in the
middle of the frenetic Bairro
Alto nightlife, with friendly
owners; try "Auntie's" sangria,
poured from a jug the size of a
house.

Bar Ártis

Map 5, F3. Rua do Diário de
Notícias 95.

Tues–Fri 8.30pm–2am, Sat &
Sun 8.30pm–4am.

A laid-back jazz bar with arty
posters on the wall and marble
table tops. It's popular with
creative types, who usually
spend a night here in animated
conversation over a few bottles
of its excellent *vinho*. Also does
a fine range of snacks, like
chicken *tostas* (toasted sandwiches).

Catacumbas Jazz Bar

Map 5, E3. Trav. da Água da
Flor 43.

Mon–Sat 9pm-4am.

This is a pleasant spot for a
drink at any time, though it's
best and busiest on Thursday

nights when there's live jazz
(usually trad). At other times
anyone can play the piano,
which means lively entertainment most evenings.

Cena de Copos

Map 5, E4. Rua da Barroca
103–105.

Mon–Fri 9.30pm–2am, Sat &
Sun 10pm–4am.

Not a club to frequent unless
you're under 25 and bursting
with energy, though the cheap
cocktails may help you roll
back the years. Don't turn up
till after midnight for the full
experience. Usually plays the
latest dance sounds.

Di Vino

Map 5, E3. Rua da Atalaia 160.

Mon–Sat 9.30pm–1am.

Intimate Bairro Alto wine bar
with a warren of small rooms
at the back and tasty snacks
lined up on the main bar.
There's laid-back music, usually Latin or jazz.

Frágil

Map 5, E3. Rua da Atalaia 126.

Mon–Sat 11pm–4am.

Still a great club, after all these

years, particularly from Thursday to Saturday, though it doesn't really get going until after 1am. It's partly gay, definitely pretentious and has a strict door policy (it helps if you're young and beautiful; tatty jeans and sandals are a no go). Music is house and techno till late. You'll need to ring the bell to get in.

Harry's Bar
Map 5, F2. Rua de São Pedro de Alcântara 57–61.
Mon–Sat 10pm–4am.
A tiny front-room bar, featuring waiter service and some tasty bar snacks. It's frequented by an eclectic clientele, including slightly older luvvies from the nearby gay discos who pop in for late drinks. Ring the bell for admission.

Instituto do Vinho do Porto
Map 5, G2. Rua de São Pedro de Alcântara 45.
Mon–Sat 2pm–midnight.
Firmly on the tourist circuit, the *Instituto* lures in visitors with over three hundred types of port, starting at around €1 a glass and rising to nearly €25 for a glass of forty-year-old JW Burmester. Drinks are served at low tables in a comfortable old eighteenth-century mansion. The waiters are notoriously snooty and the cheaper ports never seem to be in stock, but it's still a good place to kick off an evening.

Keops
Map 5, E3. Rua da Rosa 157–159.
Mon–Sat 10pm–3.30am.
Friendly music bar, playing everything from Moby to Madonna. The doors are thrown open to the street, while the candlelit interior enhances the laid-back atmosphere.

Lisbona
Map 5, F2. Rua da Atalaia 196.
Mon–Sat 7pm–2am.
Earthy bar attracting its fair share of local characters and Bairro Alto trendies. Decor is basic - checkerboard tiles covered in soccer memorabilia, old film posters and graffiti – but there's catchy music (from U2 to Miles Davies) and good beer.

Portas Largas
Map 5, E3. Rua da Atalaia 105.
Daily 8pm–2am.
The bar's *portas largas* (big

BAIRRO ALTO

183

doors) are usually thrown wide open, inviting the neighbourhood into this friendly black-and-white-tiled *adega* (wine cellar). There are cheapish drinks, music from fado to pop, and a young, partly gay clientele, which spills onto the streets on warm evenings before hitting *Frágil*, just over the road.

São Martinho

Map 5, F2. Rua da Atalaia 156.
Tues–Sun noon–midnight.
A rare, authentically crusty bar in this part of town, which has avoided its neighbours' pretensions. Grab a low stool and enjoy cheapish beer in a bar tiled like a public toilet; a games room is attached.

O Tacão Grande

Map 5, F2. Trav. da Cara 3.
Daily midnight–4am.
For those into raw rock, free peanuts, inexpensive beer and lots of youthful company, this barn-like place is the one for you.

Café Targus

Map 5, E4. Rua do Diário de Notícias 40.
Mon–Fri noon–2am, Sat & Sun 8pm–4am.
A popular designer watering hole - the bar separated from the seats by rectangular pillars covered in gold mosaics - that attracts architects, journalists and arty professionals. By day, people come to admire the temporary art exhibitions; otherwise, people flood in at midnight before moving on to the clubs. Sounds usually include a good mix of soul, Latin and jazz.

A Tasca Tequila Bar

Map 5, F3. Trav. da Queimada 13–15.
Daily 11.30pm–2am.
Colourful Mexican bar which often opens up way before its official opening time to cater to a good-time crowd downing tequilas, margaritas and Brazilian *caipirinhas*.

Tertúlia

Map 5, E4. Rua do Diário de Notícias 60.
Mon–Thurs 8.30pm–3am, Fri & Sat 8.30pm–4am.
Relaxed café-bar with inexpensive drinks, newspapers to browse, background jazz and varied art exhibitions that change every couple of weeks. There's a piano for customers

BAIRRO ALTO

too, if you've the urge to play.

Os Três Pastorinhos

Map 5, E4. Rua da Barroca 111.
Mon–Sat 9pm–4am.

Welcoming music bar with
great dance sounds (soul, reggae and Latin). It attracts a
slightly oddball crowd and gets
very busy at weekends.

PRAÇA DO PRÍNCIPE REAL AND SÃO BENTO

Enoteca

Map 8, E6. Chafariz da Mãe
de Agua, Rua Mãe Agua.
Tues-Sun 6pm-2am.
This extraordinary wine bar is
set in the bowels of a nineteenth-century bathhouse
whose underground tunnels
once piped water into Lisbon.
Inside, cool stone rooms are
laid out with tables. The bar
offers a long list of Portuguese
wines, which you can enjoy
with regional breads and
assorted *petiscos* (snacks). It gets
busy at weekends so it's best to
reserve if you want to eat
(☎ 213 422 079), though you
can always squeeze in for a
drink or sit at one of the outside tables. It's at the foot of
the steps on the road leading
down from Príncipe Real.

Foxtrot

Map 6, I3. Trav. de Santa Teresa.
Mon–Thurs 6pm–2am, Fri–Sat

6.30pm–2am, Sun 9pm–2am.
Relaxed bar on the São Bento
side of the Bairro Alto, with
comfortable sofas and snooker
tables, plus an outdoor patio,
snacks and a long list of cocktails. From Praça do Príncipe
Real, head down Rua Jasmine
and Trav. da Palmeira and bear
right into Trav. de Santa Teresa.

Incógnito

Map 6, I4. Rua dos Poiais de
São Bento 37.
Wed–Sat 11pm–4am.
Appropriately named – the
only giveaway from the outside is a pair of large metallic
doors. Once within, you'll
find the low-lit dance floor
booming with retro sounds,
though Wednesday nights are
more cutting-edge.

Pavilhão Chinês

Map 5, G1. Rua Dom Pedro V
89.

Mon–Sat 6pm–2am, Sun 9pm–2am.

Once a nineteenth-century tea and coffee merchants, this is now a quirky bar, completely lined with mirrored cabinets containing ludicrous and bizarre tableaux of artefacts from around the world, including a cabinet of model trams. There is waiter service and the usual drinks are supplemented by a long list of exotic cocktails.

Snob

Map 5, D1. Rua do Século 178.

Daily 4.30pm–3am.

Upmarket bar-restaurant on the way from Bairro Alto to Praça do Prínçipe Real, full of media types enjoying cocktails in a smart pub-like atmosphere. It's a good late-night eating option for inexpensive steaks or light snacks.

ALCÂNTARA

Kasino

Map 6, B5. Rua Cozinha Económica 11.

Wed–Sat 11pm–6am.

Big, glitzy spot for house and techno, in half of what was the famous Alcântara-Mar club. Less brash than its neighbour *W* (see below), but good if you just want a place to dance the night away.

LX

Map 6, B5. Rua Maria Luisa Holstein.

Wed–Sun 11.30pm–4am.

Popular African music club. Its name is a play on the clothes label for Extra Large and larg-er-than-life characters certainly appear in abundance dancing to the latest African sounds.

Paradise Garage

Map 6 C4. Rua João de Oliveira Miguens 48.

Thurs–Sat 11.30pm–4am.

Large, ultra-fashionable club on a tiny side road off Rua da Cruz à Alcântara, offering various sounds from disco to garage. It is also becoming a major venue for visiting bands.

Pillon

Map 6, B4. Rua do Alvito 10.

Daily 10pm–4am.

Rhythmic Cape Verdean and

African disco sounds for a relaxed crowd. The liveliest night is usually Tuesday.

W
Map 6, B5. Rua Maria Luisa Holstein.

Wed–Saturday, 11pm–6am. Recently revamped and renamed club with a laid-back atmosphere and a healthy mix of people out for a fun night. Wednesday is "Ladies' Night", with free drinks for women.

ALCÂNTARA DOCKS

Blues Café
Map 6, D6. Rua da Cintura do Porto de Lisboa.
Mon–Thurs 8.30pm–3am, Fri 8.30pm–4.30am, Sat 8.30pm–5am.
Lisbon's only blues club occupies a converted dockside warehouse. There's Cajun food served in the restaurant (until 12.30am), live music on Mondays and Thursdays, and club nights with the latest dance sounds on Fridays and Saturdays from 2.30am. As with the other clubs along this stretch, the clientele is largely thirty-something with money to burn.

The docks are best reached by train from Cais do Sodré to Alcântara Mar station. Trains run until around 2am, after which a taxi back to town will cost approximately €8.

Doca 6
Map 6, B7. Doca de Santo Amaro.
Daily 12.30pm–2am; closed Mon from Nov to April.
Rated one of the best bars in the docks, with a lively atmosphere and good if pricey food like bouillabaisse and other French-influenced dishes. Most people grab a drink from the bar and people-watch from the river-facing terrace.

Doca de Santo
Map 6, B6. Doca de Santo Amaro.
Daily 12.30pm–4am.
The first prominent building

you come across approaching from Alcântara Mar station, this palm-fringed club, bar and restaurant was one of the earliest places in the docks to attract – and then keep – a late-night clientele. The cocktail bar on the esplanade is the latest enticement.

Docks Club

Map 6, D6. Doca de Alcântara. Mon–Sat 10pm–6am.

A thriving warehouse conversion funded by nightclub mogul Pedro Luz; most nights it's a dance temple for Lisbon's moneyed set, with sounds from Madonna to trance. Tuesday night is "Ladies' Night" with free drinks for women; Thursday night features Latin music.

Havana

Map 6, B7. Armazéns 5, Doca de Santo Amaro.

Mon–Wed & Sun noon–3am, Thurs–Sat noon–4am.

Cuban-themed bar-restaurant with wicker chairs, Latin sounds and salsa lessons on request, usually undertaken in the bar area.

Queens

Map 6, D6. Rua Cintura do Porto de Lisboa, Armázem H Naves A–B.

Wed–Sat 10pm–6am.

Pedro Luz launched this club as a "high-tech gay disco", but it has since successfully attracted a large following of beautiful people of all sexual persuasions. It's a huge, pulsating place – there's an excellent sound system – which can hold 2500 people. Tuesday night is "Ladies' Night" involving a male strip show; there are visiting DJs on other nights.

Salsa Latina

Map 6, B7. Gare Marítima de Alcântara, Doca de Santo Amaro.

Mon–Sat: restaurant 8pm–midnight; club 8pm–6am.

A bar-restaurant and club, lying just outside the docks, housed in a 1940s' maritime station. There's salsa from Tuesday to Saturday (with lessons on Tuesday and Thursday) and music from a live band at the weekends. Alternatively, just come and admire the views from the terrace.

SANTOS AND AVENIDA 24 DE JULHO

Kapital

Map 6, G6. Avda 24 de Julho 68.
Mon & Sun
10.30pm–4am, Tues–Sat
10.30pm–6am.
Long-established venue, with
three sleekly designed floors
full of bright young things
buying expensive drinks and
dancing to techno, but it's hard
work getting past the style
police on the door. There's a
great rooftop terrace.
Wednesday night is rock night.

Kremlin

Map 6, G6. Escadinhas da
Praia 5.
Tues–Thurs midnight–7am, Fri
& Sat midnight–9am.
Its tough door policy, based on
its reputation as one of the
city's most fashionable
nightspots, has put off many
good-time clubbers, though
it's still packed with flash,
young, raving Lisboetas. Best
to come after 2am.

PARQUE DAS NAÇÕES

Bugix

Rua D. Fuas Roupinho.
Tues–Sun noon–5am.
The in spot in the Parque at
present, with live music at
midnight and pulsating techno
from 2–5am, Thursdays to
Saturdays. The rest of the
week, Bugix is a relatively
quiet restaurant serving moderately priced Portuguese
food. Diners pay half the €10
club entry fee.

Gay Lisbon

Lisbon's gay and lesbian scene is becoming more open in a city that was, until quite recently, fairly conservative. The **Centro Comunitário Gay e Lèsbica de Lisboa** (Lisbon Gay and Lesbian Community Centre), at Rua de São Lazaro 88, Martim Moniz (Map 8, I5; Mon–Sat 4–8pm; ☎218 873 918, ⓦwww.ilga-portugal.org), organizes gay events and can help with information and medical advice – their comprehensive website (in English and Portuguese) is useful and the centre also has a bar and internet café. The organization **Opus Gay**, Rua Ilha Terceira 34-2° (Map 2, F6; Mon–Sat 4–8pm; ☎213 151 396, ⓦwww.opusgayassociation.com) is also a good source of advice and information.

Nightlife focuses on the Bairro Alto and Praça do Prínçipe Real, where a group of generally laid-back clubs and bars attracts gay people of all ages. As at other clubs, the best nights are from Thursday to Saturday, with the action kicking off at 9pm and ending well after sunrise. Hangovers are eased on gay **beaches** such as the one south of Caparica at mini-railway stop #18 (see p.289), or further south at Praia do Meco. One of the main annual events is the **Gay Film Festival** (see p.237), held at various city cinemas in September. June sees an increasingly well-attended **Gay Pride** event (Arraial Pride), though the gathering has recently been moved from outside the City Hall to the Torre de Belém by the conservative council; more details can be found on Ⓦ www.ilga-portugal.org.

The following bars and clubs are pretty much gay and lesbian only. Places that attract a mixed gay and straight crowd are included in Chapter 12, "Bars and clubs".

For details of Lisbon's gay-friendly hotel, the Blue Angel in Bairro Alto, see p.126.

BARS AND CLUBS

106
Map 8, D7. Rua São Marçal 106, Príncipe Real.
Daily 9pm–2am.
Ring on the doorbell and you'll be given a quick look-over before being allowed into this friendly if sparse bar, which makes a good place to start the evening.

Água no Bico
Map 8, D7. Rua de São Marçal 170, Príncipe Real.
Daily 9pm–2am.
Welcoming gay bar with tables packed in cheek-by-jowl to promote intimate conversation.

Baliza
Map 5, C5. Rua da Bica de Duarte Belo 51a, Bica.

Mon–Fri 1pm–2am, Sat 4pm–2am.
Small, friendly café-bar at the top of the Elevador da Bica. Gays and locals from this traditional district come together to enjoy the music, from jazz to Latin, retro to dance.

Bric-a-Bar
Map 8, D7. Rua Cecílio de Sousa 82–84, Príncipe Real.
Daily 9pm–4am.
On a steep road beyond Praça do Príncipe Real, this cruisy disco has a large dance floor, "dark room" and various bars.

Finalmente
Map 8, D7. Rua da Palmeira 38, Príncipe Real.
Daily 10.30pm–4.30am.

A well-known and very busy place, with a first-class disco and lashings of kitsch. Weekend drag shows (2am) feature skimpily dressed young *senhoritas* camping it up to high-tech sounds. Entry's free, but there's a minimum drinks consumption of around €6.

Katedral

Map 8, C7. Rua de Manuel Bernardes 22, Príncipe Real. Mon–Thurs & Sun 7pm–2am; Fri & Sat 8pm–4am. Intimate, relaxed snooker bar attracting a lesbian crowd; one of the city's better places for gay women.

Mania's Bar

Map 5, D1. Rua do Século 127, Bairro Alto. Mon–Thurs 8pm–2am, Fri –Sun 8pm–3am. There are few lesbian-only bars in Lisbon, so this friendly place is a welcome addition to the scene.

Memorial

Map 8, D6. Rua Gustavo Matos Sequeira 42, Príncipe Real. Tues–Sat 11pm–4am, Sun 4pm–8pm. A lesbian club with floor

shows some nights. Otherwise it's low key, with disco and "romantic" sounds.

MF (Mistura Fina)

Map 5, F4. Rua das Gáveas 15–17, Bairro Alto. Daily 4pm–2am. Popular cocktail bar right in the middle of the Bairro Alto. It's a bit pretentious but can be fun in a campy kind of way.

Purex

Map 5, E5. Rua das Salgadeiras 28, Bairro Alto. Tues–Sun 11pm–4am. This small and friendly dance bar, popular with lesbians but not exclusively so, offers ambient music on Tuesdays and Wednesdays, and more upbeat sounds - guaranteed to fill the small dance floor - on Thursday to Sunday nights.

Sétimo Ceu

Map 5, E5. Trav. da Espera 54, Bairro Alto. Mon–Sat 10pm–2am. A real success story of recent years; now an obligatory stop for gays and lesbians, who imbibe beers and *caipirinhas* served by the Brazilian owner. The great atmosphere spills out onto the street.

Stasha is a gay-run restaurant in the Bairro Alto worth
seeking out, see p.157.

Trumps

Map 8, C6. Rua da Imprensa
Nacional 104b, Príncipe Real.
Daily 10pm–6am.
Popular gay disco with a reasonably relaxed door policy.
It's a bit cruisy during the
middle of the week, and gets
packed from Thursday to
Saturday, when there's also a
good lesbian turnout. Drag
shows are held on Wednesdays
and Sundays. Admission is
free, though there's sometimes
a minimum consumption of
€10 if the doorman has the
hump.

Live music

Although tourist brochures tend to suggest that **live music** in Lisbon begins and ends with **fado**, the city's traditional music, there's no reason to miss out on other forms. **Brazilian** and **African** music from the former colonies are very popular, while Portuguese **jazz** can be good (and there are big international jazz festivals in the summer: see p.236). The **rock and pop** scene throws the occasional surprise, and **classical music** also has a keen following, with performances in churches, historic buildings and cultural centres throughout the city. In addition, many of Lisbon's **festivals** feature performances of fado, classical and jazz music – see Chapter 19 for full festival listings.

It's worth checking the listings magazines (see p.9) and posters around the city to see what's on. **Admission charges** at most music clubs run from €2 to €15 or more, depending on the performer and the venue; this usually covers your first drink, and most clubs stay open until around 4am or later. In addition, top American and British rock bands, as well as visiting Brazilian singers, play at the major venues listed on p.204. You can usually get advance tickets for concerts (usually in the region of €20–40), and ticket and programme details for all the city's cinemas and theatres, from the **Agencia de Bilhetes para**

Espectaculos Publicos (ABEP) kiosk (Map 3, B7; daily 9am–9.30pm) on the southeast corner of Praça dos Restauradores, near the post office. Concert tickets can also be purchased from FNAC (see p.219) or online at Ⓦwww.ondaticket.com.

Our music listings are divided as follows: fado and folk (p.195); African and Brazilian (p.199); rock and pop (p.202); jazz (p.203); classical (p.203).

FADO AND FOLK

Along with Coimbra (which has its own distinct tradition), Lisbon is still the best place to hear fado. There are thirty or so fado clubs in the Bairro Alto, Alfama and elsewhere, usually called either a *casa de fado* or an *adega típica*. There's no real distinction between the two: all are small and all serve food (though you don't always have to eat). Doors usually open around 8pm, performances kick off at around 9pm and get going towards midnight, and the clubs stay open until 2 or 3am. In the more formal clubs you'll be expected to remain quiet during performances, though emotions let rip once the artists have finished.

The drawbacks of fado clubs are the inflated minimum charges – these days rarely below €15 per person – and, in the more touristy places, extreme tackiness. Uniformed bouncers are fast becoming the norm, as are warm-up singers crooning folk songs and photographers snapping at the table of bewildered-looking coach parties. We've selected only the most authentic places.

You can find out more about fado in the Casa do Fado museum, see p.47.

FADO AND FOLK

FADO: THE PORTUGUESE BLUES

Fado songs inevitably evoke the characteristically Portuguese emotion of *saudade*, a yearning for something lost or missed: popular fado themes are love, death, destiny, bullfighting and fate itself. Its origins are believed to be a fusion of rural folk quatrains with the lascivious song and dance – *fofa* and *lundum* – popular with the African and Brazilian immigrants who settled in Alfama in the early nineteenth century.

One of the first known fado stars was **Maria Severa**, an Alfama singer whose tumultuous relationship with the Count of Vimiosa scandalized Lisbon society in the 1830s. The first recorded example of fado was performed by **Isabel Costa** in 1904 and by the 1930s it was considered relatively highbrow entertainment, often performed in theatres. The 1930s also saw the establishment of the first **casas do fado** (fado houses), though all of the singers' lyrics had to be approved by Salazar's paranoid dictatorial government. Singers often found a way around the censorship by performing an official version when it seemed wise to do so, and an unofficial one at other times. In this way the *fadistas* could quietly criticize the government, and fado quickly caught the popular imagination.

Fado became truly commercial after World War II when it featured in just about every Portuguese film made right up until the 1970s. The main voice of fado in the cinema was **Amália Rodrigues**, the daughter of an Alfama orange-seller, whose voice and stunning looks made her one of the country's most successful artists. Her death in 1999, which set off three days of national mourning, seemed to mark the end of the Golden Age of fado – no one has managed to evoke so much passion since, though Mísia's modern take on fado has won her many international admirers. Other **contemporary singers** to look out for are Camané, Helder Moutinho, Carlos do Carmo, Maria da Fé and Cristina Branco, though you may find the most entertaining fado of all is performed spontaneously by amateurs, in bars and restaurants.

FADO AND FOLK

ALFAMA

Clube do Fado

Map 4, C9. Rua de São João
da Praça 92–94 ☎ 218 852
704.

Daily 8.30pm–2am.
Intimate and homely place
with stone pillars, an old well
as a decorative feature, and a
mainly local clientele. It
attracts small-time performers,
up-and-coming talent and the
occasional big name.
Minimum charge around €10.

A Parreirinha de Alfama

Map 4, G7. Beco do Espírito
Santo 1 ☎ 218 868 209.
Daily 8pm–2am.
One of the best fado venues,
just off Largo do Chafariz de
Dentro, which often attracts
leading stars and an enthusiastic local clientele. Reservations
are advised when the big
names appear. Minimum
charge around €13, or up to
around €30 with food.

Taverna do Embuçado

Map 4, F8. Beco dos
Cortumes 10 ☎ 218 865 088.
Mon–Sat 8.30pm–2.30am.
First opened in 1966, this

Alfama *adega* rarely gets too
packed, even when the big-
name artists are in town. The
food is great too, though you
can expect to pay a minimum
of €18, more like €40 with
food.

A Taverna do Julião

Map 4, F6. Largo do Peneireiro
5 ☎ 218 872 271.
Wed–Sun 9pm–2am.
An authentic option in the
heart of Alfama. The house
singer, Argentina Santos, is
well worth catching.
Minimum charge around €10.

BAIRRO ALTO

Adega Machado

Map 5, F4. Rua do Norte 91
☎ 213 224 640.
Tues–Sun 8.30pm–3am.
One of the longest-established
Bairro Alto joints, as the faded
photos on the wall attest, presenting fado from both Lisbon
and Coimbra. A minimum
charge of €15 builds to at least
€20 a head if you sample the
fine Portuguese cooking.

Adega Mesquita

Map 5, F3. Rua do Diário de

FADO AND FOLK

●

197

Notícias 107 ⓣ 213 219 280.
Daily 8pm–1.30am.
Another of the big Bairro Alto names, featuring better-than-average music and traditional dancing and singing. It packs in the tourists, although the food here is poor. Minimum consumption €15.

Adega do Ribatejo

Map 5, F3. Rua do Diário de Notícias 23 ⓣ 213 468 343.
Mon–Sat 7.30pm–12.30am.
Great little *adega*, still popular with the locals, who describe the fado here as "pure emotion". The singers include a couple of professionals, the manager and – best of all – the cooks. Also has one of the lowest minimum charges (around €10) and enjoyable food.

Restaurante Luso

Map 5, F3. Trav. da Queimada 10 ⓣ 213 422 281.
Mon–Sat 9.30pm–2am.
A rather dark restaurant that packs in its customers for decent food (served until midnight) and some interesting sounds. Portuguese folk dancing kicks things off at around 9pm, with fado from 11pm. Minimum consumption of around €16.

NôNô

Map 5, E5. Rua do Norte 47–49 ⓣ 218 342 9989.
Daily 8pm–2.30am.
Small, attractively tiled restaurant, where the *fado* gets going at 9.15pm. Prices are moderate, with a minimum consumption of around €18.

A Severa

Map 5, F5. Rua das Gáveas 51–61 ⓣ 213 428 314.
Mon–Wed & Fri–Sun 9.30pm–1am.
A city institution, named after the nineteenth-century singer Maria Severa. The club attracts big fado names and equally big prices. Minimum consumption €18, more like €23 with food (served until midnight).

CAIS DO SODRÉ

Mercado da Ribeira

Map 5, A7. Avda 24 de Julho.
Fri & Sat 10pm–1am.
The revamped market (see p.224) forms the backdrop to free weekend music sessions which often feature fado and Portuguese folk. Acoustics aren't great and don't expect top performers, but it's an enjoyable place to catch some music. The

market restaurant, *Comida da Ribeira*, next door to the stage, has a changing daily menu.

LAPA

O Senhor Vinho
Map 6, G4. Rua do Meio à Lapa 18 ☎ 213 972 681.
Mon–Sat 8.30pm–2.30am.
Famous club with a relaxed atmosphere, sporting some of the best singers in Portugal, which makes the €20 minimum charge (rising to around

€40 after a meal) pretty reasonable. Reservations are advised.

ALCÂNTARA

Timpanas
Map 6, C5. Rua Gilberto Rola 24 ☎ 213 906 655.
Mon, Tues & Thurs–Sun 8.30pm–2am.
A bit out of the way, though this is one of Lisbon's most authentic fado clubs, with decent food and a minimum charge of €10.

AFRICAN AND BRAZILIAN

In recent years, Lisboetas have embraced the musical styles of the former colonies with vigour, perhaps because the lively **African and Brazilian** beats are in such complete contrast to the nostalgic tradition of fado. Musicians from Brazil, Cape Verde, Guinea-Bissau, Angola and Mozambique all play regular gigs in the city: the big Cape Verdean star to listen out for is Cesária Evora, a world-famous ballad (*morna*) singer, who performs barefoot; while Waldemar Bastos, who owns a restaurant in Bairro Alto (see p.153), is one of the catchiest Angolan performers.

ALFAMA

Chafarica
Map 4, G4. Calçada de São

Vicente 81 ☎ 218 867 449.
Mon–Thurs & Sun 10pm–3am, Fri & Sat 10pm–4am.
Long-established Brazilian bar with live music every night.

Best after midnight, especially after a few *caipirinhas*, the lethal Brazilian concoction of rum, lime, sugar and ice.

Pé Sujo

Map 4, C8. Largo de São Martinho 6–7 ⊤ 218 866 144. Tues–Sun 11pm–3am.
The "Dirty Foot" is five minutes' walk from the Sé, at the point where Rua A. Rosa becomes Rua do Limoeiro; there's a large wooden terrace outside. Hit a good night and there'll be massive audience participation and table-banging samba sessions in the tiny room, though it's less lively if the house band isn't up to scratch.

BAIRRO ALTO AND AROUND

Pintaí

Map 5, F3. Largo Trindade Coelho 22 ⊤ 213 424 802. Tues–Sat 10pm–4am.
Small, popular "tropical" bar across the road from São Roque church, with live Brazilian music most nights and the party atmosphere fuelled by a long list of cocktails.

Ritz Club

Map 8, F6. Rua da Glória 57 ⊤ 213 425 140.
Tues–Sat 10.30pm–4am.
Lisbon's largest African club occupies the premises of an old brothel-cum-music hall, and it should re-open shortly after extensive renovation. It's a great place, with a restaurant (8pm–3am), a resident Cape Verdean band, plus occasional big-name performers. If you fancy a break from the music there are quiet rooms with wicker chairs for a drink and a chat.

SÃO BENTO AND SANTOS

B.leza

Map 6, I5. Largo do Conde Barão 50, Santos ⊤ 213 963 735.
Mon–Sat 11.30pm–4am.
Live African music most nights in this wonderful sixteenth-century building, with space to dance in, tables to relax at, and Cape Verdean food too.

Lontra

Map 6, I3. Rua de São Bento 157, São Bento ⊤ 213 691 083.

AFRICAN AND BRAZILIAN

Tues–Sun 11pm–4am.
You'll be hard pushed not to join in the dancing at this intimate African club, which has live music most nights; come after midnight.

ALCÂNTARA

Kussunguila
Map 6, B4. Rua dos Lusíadas 5 ⓣ 213 633 590.
Daily 11pm–6am.
Over-the-top African club with live bands on Monday and Thursday nights, plus discos, African karaoke and other extravaganzas the rest of the time.

Luanda
Map 6, B5. Trav. Teixeira Júnior 6 ⓣ 213 633 959.
Mon, Wed, Thurs & Sun 10.30pm–4am, Fri & Sat 10.30pm–6am; Oct–April closed Mon–Wed.
With a smart chrome-and-wood interior, this is one of the biggest and most popular of Lisbon's African clubs. It's big with the Bairro Alto

crowd, who like ending a night here.

Salsa Latina
Map 6, B7. Gare Marítima de Alcântara ⓣ 213 950 555.
Daily 12.30pm–3am.
Set in the 1940s' maritime station by Doca de Santa Amaro, this is part bar-restaurant, part salsa club, with riotous dancing to live bands serving up Brazilian rhythms, jazz, Dixieland and other infectious sounds.

CAMPO PEQUENO

Bipi-Bipi
Map 2, F5. Rua Oliveira Martins 6 ⓣ 217 978 924.
Sun–Thurs 10.30pm–2am, Fri & Sat 10.30pm–6am.
Uptown venue for Brazilian bands, exotic cocktails and dirty dancing. It's particularly riotous at weekends after midnight. To get here, take the metro to Campo Pequeno, then head along Avda João XXI – Rua Oliveira Martins is the third on the left.

AFRICAN AND BRAZILIAN

ROCK AND POP

Lisbon's clubs and bars are quick to catch on to the latest international rock and pop sounds, though in recent years there's been a boom in the popularity of local bands. Pedro Abrunhosa's jazzy rap sounds are still very popular while mainstream pop bands Delfins, Rio Grande and Santos e Pecadores are also big. Madredeus are long-established giants who fuse folk with haunting lyrics. More contemporary rock bands include Silence 4 and Clã. The three places listed below can be relied upon for live bands most nights, while there are also regular gigs at clubs like *Lux* (Santa Apolónia), *Bugix* (Parque das Nações) and *Paradise Garage* (Alcântara)– see Chapter 12 for more details of those.

Álcool Puro

Map 6, H5. Avda Dom Carlos I 59, Santos ⓣ 213 967 467.
Mon–Sat 11pm–4am.
Different bands every night in this fashionable rock bar whose name translates as "pure alcohol". It's a good place to check out up-and-coming Portuguese rock bands.

Anos Sessenta

Map 4, C1. Largo do Terreirinho 21, Mouraria ⓣ 218 873 444.
Daily 10pm–4am.
This small club, "the Sixties", has rock bands playing every Friday and Saturday, and different sounds on other nights;
the music is predominantly retro, as its name suggests. It's a few minutes' walk uphill from Largo Martim Moniz, near the castle.

Sua Excelência O Marquês

Map 4, C9. Largo Marquês do Lavradio 1, Alfama ⓣ 218 850 786.
Mon–Sat 10pm–4am.
Dark rock bar with live music most nights, hidden away in a little square behind the Sé (from the Sé it's on the right-hand side going down Rua de São João da Praça). It's a surprisingly noisy place for this neck of the woods.

JAZZ

Jazz has a loyal and committed following in Lisbon – you'll hear it in many bars, and it also features prominently in several of Lisbon's summer festivals – so it's somewhat surprising that there are so few clubs specifically dedicated to it. Touring jazz acts sometimes play at the following venues, and also appear at the large music venues listed in the box on p.204.

Hot Clube de Portugal

Map 8, F6. Praça da Alegria 39, metro Avenida ⓣ 213 621 740.

Tues–Sat 10pm–2am.

The city's best jazz venue, in a tiny basement club hosting local and visiting artists. It's appropriately named, as it can get very steamy in summer, but there's a tiny courtyard to escape to if things get too hot.

Café Puro

Map 3, J7. Rua do Arsenal 21, Baixa ⓣ 210 312 700.

Mon–Sat 10pm–2am.

The Lisbon Welcome Centre's otherwise sterile café hosts lively music nights, often jazz but also world music and fado. The performers are non-professional but pretty good, and are appreciated by an enthusiastic audience most nights.

Speakeasy

Map 6, F7. Armazém 115, Cais das Oficinas, Doca de Alcântara ⓣ 213 957 308.

Mon–Sat 10pm–4am.

Docklands jazz bar and restaurant presenting a mixture of big and up-and-coming names, usually Tuesday to Thursday after 11pm.

CLASSICAL

Classical music has an avid following in Lisbon. The Gulbenkian has its own respected orchestra, while visiting orchestras, musicians and opera stars frequently appear at the main venues listed in the box on p.204.

There are three concert halls at the **Fundação Calouste Gulbenkian** (Map 9, C3; ⓣ 217 823 000, ⓦ www.gul-

JAZZ • CLASSICAL

benkian.pt), including a beautifully positioned open-air amphitheatre, which features alfresco classical and jazz performances in the summer. It's also worth checking out performances at the auditoriums at the **Centro Cultural de Belém** (Map 7, D5; ☎213 612 400, ⓦwww.ccb.pt), and in the **Culturgest** arts complex at Avenida João XXI 63 (Map 2, F5; ☎217 905 155, ⓦwww.cgd.pt), near metro Campo Pequeno. All three arts centres publish full seasonal programmes, which are available from the centres themselves, or from large hotels and tourist offices.

LARGE MUSIC VENUES

Aula Magna (Map 2, E4), Reitoria da Universidade de Lisboa, Alamada da Universidade ☎217 967 624. Right opposite metro Cidade Universitária, this student-union venue attracts some big names, but it's all seated, which can detract from the atmosphere.

Coliseu dos Recreios (Map 8, H6), Rua das Portas de Santo Antão 96, Baixa ☎213 240 580. A lovely old domed building, originally built as a circus ring, now the city centre's main indoor music venue.

Estádio José Alvalade (Map 2, E2), Alvalade ☎217 140 000. The Sporting Lisbon soccer stadium stages concerts by huge international stars. Highly atmospheric when it's full, though things may change when the soccer team moves into a new stadium next door in 2003.

Pavilhão Atlântico (Map, p.106), Parque das Nações ☎218 918 440. Portugal's largest indoor venue holds up to 17,000 spectators and hosts big-name stars.

Sony Plaza (Map, p.106), Parque das Nações ☎218 919 000. The Parque's main outdoor venue holds up to 10,000 people for summer concerts and New Year's Eve extravaganzas.

CLASSICAL

Cinema and theatre

Lisbon and its environs have dozens of **cinemas**, virtually all of them showing original-language films with Portuguese subtitles, and ticket prices are low (around €4–5; cheaper on Mondays). The tourist offices should be able to tell you what's on, or consult the listings outside the ABEP kiosk on the southeast corner of Restauradores (though remember that film titles are often totally different in Portuguese and may not be direct translations). Most cinemas are open from around midday, with last performances at around 11pm. Sadly, most of the city's Art Nouveau and Art Deco film palaces have given way to multiplex centres, though there are still several surviving old **theatres**, which present a diverse range of plays from experimental contemporary works to Shakespeare and the Greek classics.

CINEMAS

Among the most interesting art-house venues is **Quarteto**, Rua das Flores Lima 1 (Map 2, F4; ☎217 971 378; metro Entre Campos), off Avenida Estados Unidos, with four screens. Every June, it acts as the Lisbon venue for the Troia International Film Festival, which showcases movies (subtitled in Portuguese) from countries that produce fewer than 21 films per year. The **Instituto da Cinemateca**

Portuguesa, Rua Barata Salgueiro (Map 8, D4; ☎213 546
279; metro Avenida), the national film theatre, has twice-
daily shows, ranging from contemporary Portuguese films
to silent classics.

Mainstream movies are shown at various **multiplexes**
around the city. The best and most central is the São Jorge,
Avenida da Liberdade 175 (Map 8, E4; ☎213 103 400),
with just three large screens. At the Amoreiras complex
(Map 2, D7; ☎213 831 275) there are no fewer than eleven
screens, though all are modest in size. Other multiplexes
include the larger eight screens in the Edifício
Monumental, Avenida Praia da Vitória 71, Saldanha (Map
9, G6; ☎213 142 223); the eleven screens at the top floor
of the Vasco da Gama shopping centre in Parque das
Nações (☎218 922 280); and the eleven screens at the vast
Centro Colombo shopping centre, Avenida Lusíada Letras
(Map 2, B3; ☎217 113 200; metro Colégio Militar-Luz).

Just **out of the city**, Carcavelos has the two-screen
Carcavelos Atlátida Cine, right by the train station (☎214
565 653); Caparica has the small Movicine on the main
Praça da Liberdade (Map 1, E7; ☎212 913 759); while if
you're in Cascais on a rainy day, you can escape to the
seven-screen Warner-Lusomundo at the massive and well-
signposted shopping mall, Cascais Shopping (☎214 600
420), on the EN9.

THEATRES

You could try the performances of Portuguese and foreign
plays – usually in Portuguese, but occasionally in English –
at the **Teatro Nacional de Dona Maria II** on Rossio
(Map 3, B7; ☎213 472 246; see also p.34). You may also
want to check out performances by **The Lisbon Players**,
an amateur English-speaking theatrical group consisting
largely of expat actors. Performances and readings – which

THEATRES

can be of very good quality – take place at Rua da Estrela 10, Lapa (Map 6, G2; ⓣ213 961 946). Finally, the **Centro Cultural de Belém** (Map 7, D5; ⓣ213 612 400, ⓦwww.ccb.pt) stages various plays throughout the year, often adventurous performances by international touring groups, sometimes in English.

THEATRES

Sport and outdoor activities

Portugal's national game is **football**, and during the football season from September to June Lisbon men who aren't at the game tend to have radios clamped to their ears on match days. Despite this football mania, matches in Lisbon are surprisingly family orientated and relaxed, and it's definitely worth a trip to those held at either of Lisbon's giants: Benfica and Sporting.

Another sport with a loyal (if smaller) following is **bull-fighting**, and summer spectacles in Lisbon and Cascais are undeniably impressive. The influence of the Atlantic gives Lisbon an ideal climate for **golf** and some of the country's top courses are in the Lisbon area. The hefty Atlantic breakers also attract **surfers** to Lisbon's beaches, while the greater city area has good facilities for those into sailing, tennis or horse-riding. Annual spectator events to look out for include the world **windsurfing** championships and the Lisbon **marathon**. Estoril used to host a **Formula One Grand Prix**, but the Autodromo do Estoril at Alcabideche (on the EN9 from Estoril to Sintra) has fallen into disrepute, since races were cancelled in the late 1990s because the course was considered to be too potholed to run races in safety.

KILLING ME SOFTLY

The Portuguese **tourada** (bullfight) is neither as commonplace nor as famous as its Spanish counterpart, but as a spectacle it's marginally preferable. In Portugal the bull isn't killed in the ring, but instead is wrestled to the ground in a genuinely elegant, colourful and skilled display. After the fight, however, the bull is usually injured and it is always slaughtered later in any case. A small but growing band of Portuguese bullfight fans want to follow the Spanish model and Pedrito, a leading Portuguese bullfighter, recently pushed the boundaries by killing a bull in the ring at Moita, near Lisbon. He became a *cause célèbre* when the police threatened to arrest him for the act, which currently carries the risk of imprisonment or a €400,000 fine.

A tourada opens with the bull, its horns padded or sheared flat, facing a mounted **toureiro** in elaborate eighteenth-century costume. His job is to provoke and exhaust the bull and to plant the dart-like **farpas** (or *bandarilhas*) in its back, while avoiding the charge – a demonstration of incredible riding prowess. Once the beast is tired, the *moços-de-forcado*, or simply **forcados**, move in, an eight-man team which tries finally to immobilize the bull. It appears a totally suicidal task – they line up behind each other across the ring from the bull and persuade it to charge them, the front man leaping between the horns while the rest grab hold and try to subdue it. It's as absurd as it is courageous, and often takes two or three attempts, the first tries often resulting with one or more of the *forcados* being tossed spectacularly into the air.

BULLFIGHTING

The great Portuguese bullfight centre is Ribatejo, just northwest of Lisbon, where the animals are bred, and regular bullfights take place in the small towns around here. In

BULLFIGHTING

Lisbon itself, from Easter Sunday to the end of September, bullfights take place most Thursday evenings at the **Praça de Touros do Campo Pequeno** (Map 9, G2; ☎ 217 932 093; metro Campo Pequeno), an impressive Moorish-style bullring built in 1892 and seating 9000 spectators. Tickets cost between €15 and €60, depending on where you sit, and performances start at 10pm. There are less frequent fights at Cascais in summer (see p.278); look out for posters round town or contact the Cascais tourist board for details.

FOOTBALL

Football is easily the biggest game in the city and Lisbon boasts two European giants, Benfica and Sporting, and one other First Division team, Belenenses of Belém. Regular **league fixtures** take place on Sunday afternoons, or Friday, Sunday or Monday evenings for big televised matches. The daily soccer tabloid *Bola,* available from any newsagent or newspaper kiosk, has fixtures, match reports and news, as do the websites Ⓦ www.portuguesesoccer.com and Ⓦ www.infodesporto.pt/futebal. To buy advance tickets for big games – which cost between €3 and €30 – go to the ABEP kiosk in Praça dos Restauradores (for a small commission), or at kiosks (not the turnstiles) at the grounds on the night. Obtaining tickets isn't usually a problem unless it's a big European tie or a championship crunch game involving Sporting, Benfica or Porto.

    Benfica (officially called Sport Lisboa e Benfica), Lisbon's most famous football team, have a glorious past. They have won both the Portuguese championship and the Portuguese cup over twenty times, and were European champions in 1961–62, beating Real Madrid 5–3 in a classic final in which the great Eusébio was the hero. They were European Cup finalists again in 1968 (when they lost another classic to Manchester United), and runners-up in 1988 and 1990.

However, recent years have been difficult, with the club rocked by financial irregularities and an alarming loss of form, which has continued despite new management and the adoption of virtually an entire new team. The team's famous **Estádio da Luz**, Avenida Gen. Norton Matos, metro Colégio Militar-Luz (Map 2, B3; ℡ 217 266 129, Ⓦ www.slbenfica.pt), north of the city centre, is being rebuilt in preparation for the 2004 European Championships, to be held in Portugal, for which it will be the main venue. In the meantime, Benfica's temporary home is the **Estádio National**, Praça da Maratona, Cruz Quebrada (℡ 214 197 212; bus #6 from Algés or train to Cruz Quebrada from Cais do Sodré). This stadium holds up to 55,000 and currently hosts international games and the annual Portuguese Cup Final, but is pretty run-down and soulless – it's not among the eight stadiums selected as venues for 2004.

Benfica's traditional rivals, Sporting Club de Portugal – usually known as **Sporting Lisbon** – play at the 75,000-capacity **Estádio José Alvalade**, Rua Francisco Stromp (Map 2, E2; ℡ 217 514 098 or 217 514 000, Ⓦ www.sporting.pt; metro Campo Grande or bus #1 or #36). They are due to move to a new state-of-the-art stadium next door in 2003 (which will be Lisbon's other venue for the 2004 European Championships). Sporting won the championship in 2000, breaking some two decades of domination by Benfica and Porto, and were successful again in 2002 (when they also won the Portuguese cup), establishing themselves as Lisbon's leading team of the new millennium.

Belenenses are comparative lightweights, having won just one league title, back in 1946. Their attractively sited **Estádio do Restelo** (Map 9, E1; ℡ 213 010 461; tram #15 from Praça da Figueira), round the back of Belém's Mosteiro dos Jerónimos, offers such picturesque views over the river that the soccer action is almost insignificant; nevertheless, top teams frequently visit.

FOOTBALL

●

EUROPEAN FOOTBALL CHAMPIONSHIPS 2004

There has been a surge in interest in Portuguese football after it was announced that the country will host the **European Football Championships** in 2004. Despite crashing out of the 2002 World Cup, Portugal's national team Is still considered one of Europe's top sides, based around the so-called "Golden Generation" of players who have progressed together from the Portuguese youth team. Until the blip of World Cup 2002 (when they lost to the USA and South Korea), the Portuguese team had been on a good run – one of the strongest teams in the 1998 World Cup, and losing semi-finalists in the European Football Championships of 2000 (after a controversial golden goal penalty to eventual winners France). Portugal's most famous player is Luís Figo, who for a time was the world's most expensive player when he moved to Real Madrid in 2000; in late 2001 he was crowned World Footballer of the Year. However, there is concern that most of the Golden Generation Is on the wane: not only Luís Figo but also Rui Jorge, João Pinto, Fernando Couto and Rui Costa will all be well into their thirties by 2004. There is a crop of promising younger players, though, like Nuno Gomes and Hugo Viana, on whose shoulders Portuguese hopes rest.

GOLF

Portugal is famous for its **golf courses**, and there are twelve highly rated examples in the Lisbon area. Many of the best ones are between Estoril and Sintra, and many of the better local hotels (like *Lawrence's Hotel*, Sintra, see p.260) can organize golfing packages on request. Larger hotels and the golf courses themselves can supply golf passes, at around €200 for five rounds. This works out cheaper than paying for individual rounds, which start at around €50, though if you play during the week or late afternoon prices are often reduced. Late October or early November welcomes golfers to Estoril's major courses for its **International Golf Week**. For more golfing information, see the excellent Ⓦ www.portugalgolf.pt.

Perhaps the most famous course is at the upmarket **Penha Longa Golf Club**, Estrada da Lagoa Azul-Linhó, off the EN9 from Estoril to Sintra (Map 1, B5; ℗219 249 031), in a former monastic estate, designed by Robert Trent Jones and which has hosted the Portuguese Open. The **Estoril Golf Club**, Avenida da República (Map 1, B6; ℗214 680 176), right on the A5 motorway from Lisbon to Cascais, has 27 holes designed by McKenzie Ross. This also hosts the Portuguese Open and international competitions. **Quinta de Marinha**, just outside Cascais on the Guincho road (Map 1, A6; ℗214 860 100), was also designed by Robert Trent Jones and is part of a holiday complex, which also features a driving range, six tennis courts and a hotel. Another option is **Campo de Golfe de Belas**, Alameda do Aqueduto, Belas (Map 1, E5; ℗219 626 640), near Queluz-Belas train station, a Championship-standard golf course designed by William Rocky Roquemore.

HORSE-RIDING

There are several riding schools that can arrange riding lessons, especially in the Sintra and Cascais area. The **Quinta da Marinha Riding School** near Cascais (Map 1, A6; ℗214 869 282) charges around €20 per hour and also arranges various riding events throughout the year. Horse treks are available around Sintra with the **Centro Hípico de Seteais**, *Palácio de Seteais* (see p.261; ℗219 240 868 or 918 627 062). Two-hour treks to Monserrate and Capuchos with a guide cost €40; they also offer lessons from €15. The tourist office in Cascais (see p.276) can give details of other stables in the area. In June, look out for the Equestrian Jumping Competition at **Campo Grande Hippodrome** (Map 2, E3; ℗217 817 410).

HORSE-RIDING

MARATHON RUNNING

Portugal has produced some world-class long-distance runners in recent years, including marathon runner Rosa Mota – who in 1988 became the first Portuguese woman to win an Olympic gold medal – and António Pinto, who has won the London Marathon on three occasions. Top names can often be seen performing at the **Discoveries Marathon** in November, which usually starts at the Ponte 25 de Abril and finishes at Belém's Mosteiro dos Jerónimos, though routes are altered every few years. There's also a half-marathon in the city in March.

SURFING AND WINDSURFING

If you want to **surf**, head for Caparica (see p.289) or Praia Grande (see p.266), though be careful not to get in the way of the local surfers, who have very strict codes of conduct. Ericeira is another good base, an hour's bus ride north of Lisbon or Sintra; you can rent surfing equipment for around €30 a day from Ultimar at Rua 5 de Outubro 37 (☏261 862 371).

Windsurfing is best in the calmer waters round Cascais, where you can rent equipment from the *John Davies* bar on Praia da Duquesa (May to September only; ☏214 830 455), the next bay round from Praia da Conceição. Carcavelos also has a windsurfing school, Mistral, at the *Windsurf Café*, Avenida Marginal 2775 (☏214 578 965), though be warned that the sea here is even dirtier than at Cascais, itself badly polluted. Sections of the **World Windsurfing Championships** are usually held at Praia da Ribeira d'Ilhas, a small resort 3km north of Ericeira. Praia do Guincho (see p.278), north of Cascais, also holds Windsurfing and Surfing Championships, usually in August.

SWIMMING

The best **beaches** close to Lisbon are found along the Cascais train line (though the water quality along this coast is poor), with fine stretches at Carcavelos (the most polluted), Estoril (the least polluted) and Cascais itself. Far cleaner water is to be found at Guincho (see p.278) and Caparica (see p.289); at the last two, watch out for dangerous currents. In Lisbon, the most central **swimming pool** is in the Atheneum club on Rua das Portas de Santo Antão, next to the Coliseu dos Recreios (Mon–Fri 3.30–4.30pm & 9–10pm, Sat 3.30–7pm; €3.20) – head through the cavernous union building and upstairs to the pool, once open air but now sadly glassed in.

TENNIS

As well as relatively inexpensive municipal courts at Jardim do Campo Grande (Map 2, E3; metro Campo Grande), you can also find private courts at the Clube VII, Parque Eduardo VII (Map 9, A8; ☎213 865 818); Quinta do Junqueiro, Carcavelos (Map 1, D6; ☎214 563 668); Estoril Tennis Club, Avenida Conde de Barcelona, Estoril (Map 1, C6; ☎214 662 7700); and Quinta da Marinha, Cascais (Map 1, A6; ☎214 860 180). Courts must be reserved in advance, and non-club members have to pay through the nose for the privilege (around €5–8 per player for an hour), but facilities are first rate.

The best place to catch international tennis stars is at the **Estoril Open**, held at the Estádio Nacional in Cruz Quebrada (also the venue for the football Cup Final, see "Football", above), usually in early April.

Shopping

Lisbon may not be the first city that springs to mind for those with the shop-till-you drop mentality, but if you are used to the characterless shopping malls of most European city centres you'll find the **Baixa**'s traditional and specialist shops a pleasurable experience. For more cutting-edge outlets, head to the **Bairro Alto**, fast becoming a centre for offbeat designer clothes and furniture, while the top end of **Avenida da Liberdade** is home to the big international designer names. Lisbon also boasts its own array of shopping centres, including **Amoreiras** in the city centre and **Colombo**, out in the northwest suburbs, the latter being the largest shopping centre in Iberia.

Traditional local crafts, **azulejos** (tiles), **ceramics** and **textiles**, can be found at various outlets around the city; we've listed those shops that offer the best value or quality. Other than these, perhaps the most Portuguese of items to take home is a bottle of **wine** or **port**: check out the vintages at the *Instituto do Vinho do Porto* (see p.183), and then buy from one of the specialist shops listed, or from any deli or supermarket. You may also be inspired to buy some **fado music** on CD or cassette: a couple of specialist shops can oblige or check the racks in the large book-and-music stores FNAC and Valentim de Carvalho, which are also among the best places to track down **English-language books**.

Traditionally, **shopping hours** are Monday to Friday 9am to 1pm and 3pm to 7pm or 8pm, Saturday 9am to 1am, though many of the larger chain stores stay open until late on Saturday and some open on Sunday. Many of the Bairro Alto shops are open afternoons and evenings only, usually 2pm to 9pm, while shops in the big shopping centres often stay open from 9am until midnight (11pm on Sundays). **Credit cards** are widely accepted. Most shops are **closed on public holidays**, and all are closed on Christmas Day.

ARTS, CRAFTS, ANTIQUES AND SOUVENIRS

Cheapish **arts and crafts** shops are concentrated along Rua do Alecrim in Chiado, while more exclusive **antique shops** are to be found along Rua Dom Pedro V in the Bairro Alto and Rua de São Bento between São Bento and Rato. Other interesting shops include the following.

Casa do Governador
Map 4, B5. Castelo.
Daily 10am–1pm & 2–6pm.
Right by the castle entrance – so aimed at passing tourists – the former Governor of Lisbon's house is now a shop with a motley collection of art books, black-and-white postcards of old Lisbon, fado and world music CDs, and some tasteful ceramics.

Casa do Turista
Map 8, F5. Avda da Liberdade 159, metro Avenida.
Daily 9am–7pm.
Crammed with regional arts, crafts, ceramics and T-shirts. It's not too pricey and there's some good stuff amongst the tack, including some fine toy trams.

Espaço Oikos,

Map 3, H1. Rua Augusta Rosa 40, Alfama.

Mon–Fri 11am–7.30pm.

Housed in the stables of a former Archbishop's Palace, this atmospheric stone-floored space has frequent exhibitions, usually connected to the developing world; exhibits are displayed in huge stone troughs. It also sells stylish antiques, craftwork and CDs.

Fábrica Sant'ana

Map 5, E6. Rua do Alecrim 95, Chiado.

Mon–Fri 9.30am–7pm, Sat 10am–2pm.

If you're interested in Portuguese azulejos, check out this factory shop, founded in 1741, which sells copies of traditional designs and a great range of pots and ceramics.

Fábrica Viúva Lamego

Map 2, F8. Largo do Intendente 25, Intendente.

Mon–Fri 9am–1pm & 3–7pm, Sat 9am–1pm; closed Sat July & Aug.

Highly rated azulejo factory shop near metro Intendente producing made-to-order hand-painted designs. You can also order reproduction antiques.

Loja de Artesenato

Map 5, A7. Mercado da Ribeira, Avda 24 de Julho.

Mon–Sat 10am–10pm.

In the upper level of Lisbon's main market (see p.224), this craft shop specializes in art and crafts from Lisbon and the Tejo valley, and doubles as an exhibition space.

Loja do Mar

Map, p.106. Oceanariário de Lisboa, Esplanada Dom Carlos I, Parque das Nações.

Daily 10am–7pm.

The Oceanarium shop sells an imaginative range of toys, books, clothes and beauty products, all connected to the sea in some way; a good place for souvenir-shopping.

Madeira House

Map 3, G6. Rua Augusta 133, Baixa.

Mon–Sat 9am–7pm.

Along with a scattering of tacky souvenirs you'll find some attractively crafted azulejos, lace tablecloths and pottery, mostly from Madeira.

Palácio da Independência
Map 3, B6. Largo de São Domingos 11, Baixa.
Daily 10am–8pm.
Space for temporary exhibitions specializing in Portuguese regional arts and crafts, usually books, ceramics, baskets and embroidery, which range from the tasteful to tacky.

Ratton Cerâmicas.
Map 5, B2. Rua da Academia das Ciências 2c, São Bento.
Mon–Fri 10am–1pm & 3–7.30pm.

Art gallery that also displays and sells ceramics and tiles by some of the country's leading designers; prices, accordingly, are high.

Santos Ofícios
Map 3. I4. Rua da Madalena 87, Baixa.
Mon–Sat 10am–8pm.
Small shop stuffed with a somewhat touristy collection of regional crafts, but including some attractive ceramics, rugs, embroidery, baskets and toys. There's another branch at the Lisbon Welcome Centre (entrance on Rua do Arsenal; daily 10am–8pm).

BOOKS

FNAC
Map 3, F7. Rua do Crucifixo 103, Chiado.
Daily 10am–8pm.
Branch of the international chain, offering a good range of English-language books, along with extensive music and computer departments; also has desk selling tickets to major events (see p.195). There's another branch at Loja 103a, Centro Colombo (see p.226).

Livraria Bertrand
Map 3, G7. Rua Garrett 73, Chiado.
Mon–Thurs 9am–8pm, Fri & Sat 9am–10pm, Sun 2–7pm.
One of Lisbon's oldest and best-known general bookshops, with novels in English and a range of foreign magazines. It's a good place to find English translations of Portuguese writers like Fernando Pessoa.

BOOKS

Livraria Britânica
Map 8, D6. Rua de S. Marçal 83, Bairro Alto.
Mon–Fri 9.30am–7pm, Sat 9.30am–1pm.
Big, exclusively English-language bookshop, which caters mainly for the nearby British Council – pricey but well stocked.

Livraria Buchholz
Map 8, D2. Rua Duque de Palmela 4, Avda da Liberdade.
Mon–Fri 9am–6pm, Sat 9am–1pm.

Just off the top end of Avenida da Liberdade, this has a good range of English-language novels and books on Portugal, plus helpful and efficient staff.

Livraria Portugal
Map 3, F7. Rua do Carmo 70–74, Chiado.
Mon–Fri 9am–12.30pm & 2.30–7pm, Sat 9am–1pm.
Well laid-out bookshop, with a good range of novels and non-fiction in Portuguese and English. It sells many of the books listed on pp.316–323.

CLOTHES AND ACCESSORIES

International **designers** have outlets at the northern end of Avenida da Liberdade, while Portuguese designers' shops can be found in Amoreiras shopping centre and in various fashionable stores in Chiado and the Bairro Alto. More prosaic **chain store** clothes shops are generally located in the modern city, from metro Roma down Avenida de Roma to Praça de Londres (Map 2, F4–F5). Despite its reputation for good **shoes**, Lisbon's shoe shops tend to have limited styles and very small sizes.

Ana Salazar
Map 3, F7. Rua do Carmo 87, Chiado.
Mon–Sat 10am–7pm.
One of Lisbon's best-known names for designer clothes,

though her reputation is based more on style than on the materials used. There's another branch at Avda da Roma 16.

Azevedo Rua
Map 3, C6. Rossio 73, Baixa.

Mon–Fri 9am–7pm, Sat
9am–1pm.
Long-established, traditional
shop selling good, old-fashioned hats and umbrellas; the
latter in particular can be useful outside the summer
months.

Eldorado

Map 5, E5. Rua do Norte
23–25, Bairro Alto.
Mon–Fri 1–9pm, Sat 3–9pm.
An interesting mixture of
club-wear and second-hand
cast-offs (plus old records and
CDs) aimed at Lisbon's young
groovers. A good place to
head for if you need a new
wardrobe for a night out
without breaking the bank.

José António Tenente

Map 5, G5. Trav. do Carmo 8,
Bairro Alto.
Mon–Sat 10.30am–7.30pm.
Famous – and currently very
popular – designer clothes for
men and women, particularly
good for stylish suits, shirts and
accessories.

Lena Ayres

Map 5, E3. Rua da Atalaia 96,
Bairro Alto.
Mon–Wed 2–8pm, Thurs & Fri
2–10pm, Sat 5–10pm.

This shop offers wacky dresses
and other imaginative clothes
for women.

Luvaria Ulisses

Map 3, F7. Rua do Carmo
87a, Chiado.
Mon–Sat 9.30am–7pm.
The superb ornate doorway
leads you into a minuscule
glove shop with hand-wear to
suit all tastes tucked into rows
of boxes; even if it's boiling
outside, think ahead and consider getting next winter's
gloves here.

Mala Miss

Map 3, C5. Rua B. Queiroz 5,
Baixa.
Mon–Fri 9.30pm–7pm, Sat
9.30am–1.30pm.
Aptly translates as "Miss Bag",
sporting a wide range of inexpensive leather handbags, brief-
cases and belts – there are lots
of other shops selling shoes and
leather goods on this road too.

Moda Lisboa Design

Map 3, J7. Lisbon Welcome
Centre, Rua do Arsenal, Baixa.
Tues–Sun 11am–8pm.
The Lisbon Welcome Centre's
shop-cum-showcase for the
city's leading designers, with
clothes from established names

CLOTHES AND ACCESSORIES

221

such as Luis Buchíno, Paulo Cravo e Nuno, Manuel Gonçalves, and Baltazar. Look out for adventurous clothes from rising star Alexandra Moura.

Zara
Map 3, H6. Rua Augusta 71, Baixa.
Mon–Sat 10am–8pm.
Stylish Spanish store selling a wide range of inexpensive but colourful, summery clothing for men, women and children. It's nearly always packed. There's another branch in the Chiado at Rua Garrett 1–9.

FOOD AND DRINK

Casa Pereira da Conceição
Map 3, H6. Rua Augusta 102–104, Baixa.
Mon–Fri 9.40am–1pm & 3–7pm, Sat 9.40am–1pm.
Fine Art Deco shop on the Baixa's main pedestrianized street, selling tempting coffee beans, teas, chocolates, cafetieres, fans and china. The aroma alone makes it worth a visit.

Confeitaria Nacional
Map 3, D6. Praça da Figueira 18, Baixa.
Mon–Sat 8am–8pm.
On the corner with Rua dos Correeiros, this traditional nineteenth-century confec-tioner's offers a superb range of pastries, cakes and sweets.

Conserveira de Lisboa
Map 4, A9. Rua dos Bacalhoeiras 34, Baixa.
Mon–Fri 9am–1.30pm & 2.30–7pm, Sat 9am–1pm.
Wall-to-wall tin cans make this colourful shop a bizarre but intriguing place to stock up on tinned sardines, squid, salmon, mussels and just about any other sea beastie you can think of.

For general food supplies, see "Supermarkets" (p.227). A couple of the markets listed on p.223 are also good places to stock up on provisions.

Ferreira & Silva

Map 4, C9. Rua de São João da Praça 118, Alfama.
Mon–Fri 9am–1pm & 3–7pm; Sat 9am–1pm.
Geared to tourists, though it does stock a good range of wines and ports, with knowledgeable English-speaking staff to advise; prices are on the high side.

Manuel Tavares

Map 3, D5. Rua da Betesga 1a, Baixa.
Mon–Fri 9.30am–7.30pm, Sat 9am–1pm; July–Sept also open Sat 9am–7pm.
Small, century-old treasure trove with a great selection of nuts, chocolate and national cheeses, and a basement stuffed with vintage wines and ports, some dating from the early 1900s.

Napoleão

Map 3, H4. Rua dos

Fanqueiros 70, Baixa.
Mon–Sat 9am–8pm.
This stocks a great range of quality port and wine, and has enthusiastic, English-speaking staff to help you with your choices. It's at the junction with Rua da Conceição.

Torres and Brinkmann

Map 5, F5. Rua Nova da Trindade 1b, Chiado.
Mon 2.30–7pm, Tues–Fri 9.30am–7pm, Sat 9.30am–1.30pm & 3–7pm.
The best place in the city to buy cookery equipment to rustle up that Portuguese recipe; stylish, high-quality pots, pans and utensils, including coffee-making gear and griddles. There's another branch just up the road at Trav. da Trindade 18–22 specializing in porcelain, glass and silverware.

MARKETS

Feira da Ladra

Map 4, I3–K3. Campo de Santa Clara, Alfama.
Tues & Sat 7am–6pm.
Lisbon's twice-weekly

"Thieves' Market", on the eastern edge of Alfama, is the place to browse for old colonial objects and memorabilia, pseudo-antiques and complete junk.

See p.278 for details of the Wednesday market in Cascais,
and p.273 for the Thursday market in Carcavelos.

Feira Numismática

Map 3, J5. Praça do
Comércio, Baixa.
Sun 9am–noon.
A good Sunday outing if
you're interested in the country's past, selling old coins and
notes from Portugal and the
former colonies, from stalls
spilling out under the arches of
the arcades.

Mercado 31 de Janeiro

Map 9, F7. Rua Eng. Vieira de
Silva, Saldanha.
Mon–Sat 7am–2pm.
Once an outdoor affair, this is
now housed in a smart new
building on two floors, which
feature everything from fresh
fish and flowers to traditional
arts and crafts.

Mercado da Ribeira

Map 5, A7. Avda 24 de Julho,
Cais do Sodré.
Mon–Sat: food market
5am–2pm; flower market
3pm–7pm; collector's market
9am–1pm.
One of Lisbon's most atmospheric covered markets, just a
short walk from Cais do
Sodré; the fish hall in particular is fascinating, revealing
some of the Atlantic's huge
diversity of creatures. The collector's market throws up an
array of coins and stamps,
many from Portugal's former
colonies.

Parque das Nações

Map, p.106. Estação do
Oriente, Level 2.
Sun 10am–7pm.
Changing markets take place
weekly, on Sundays, above the
metro station. The first Sunday
of the month sees a stamp,
coin and collectables fair; the
second features handicrafts; the
third antiques; and the fourth
decorative arts.

Praça de Espanha

Map 9, A3. Praça de Espanha.
Mon–Sat 9am–6pm.
Downmarket affair near the
Gulbenkian, with stalls selling
African music CDs, cheap
clothes and general bric-a-
brac.

MARKETS

MUSIC

Casa do Fado e da Guitarra Portuguesa
Map 4, G7. Largo do Chafariz de Dentro 1, Alfama.
Daily 10am–1pm & 2–5pm.
The museum shop contains an excellent selection of fado CDs and cassettes, and the staff is generally available to give expert advice.

Discoteca Amália
Map 3, E7. Rua Aurea 272, Baixa.
Mon–Fri 9.30am–2pm &

3–7pm, Sat 9.30am–1pm.
A small but well-stocked shop with a good collection of the latest sounds. If you're looking for a fado recommendation, the staff are usually happy to help.

Valentim de Carvalho
Map 3, F7. Rua do Carmo 28, Chiado.
Mon–Sat 10am–8pm.
Huge department store in the old Grandela building, specializing in CDs and books.

SHOPPING CENTRES

Amoreiras
Map 2, D7. Avda Engenheiro Duarte Pacheco, Amoreiras.
Daily 10am–midnight.
The first of Lisbon's modern shopping centres. Along with its ten cinemas and array of fast-food cafés and restaurants, there are countless shops, mostly international chain stores, selling everything from Portuguese football team strips to children's toys, women's underwear to kitchen equipment.

Armazéns do Chiado
Map 3, F7. Rua do Carmo 2, Chiado.
Daily 10am–midnight.
This well-designed shopping centre sits on six floors above metro Baixa-Chiado in a structure that has risen from the ashes of the Chiado fire. It retains its traditional facade, while a glass roof throws light down a central well, with escalators linking various shops including branches of FNAC, Benetton, Lego and Massimo

MUSIC • SHOPPING CENTRES

Duti. The top floor has a series of cafés and restaurants, most offering great views.

Centro Colombo

Map 2, B3. Avda Colégio Militar-Luz, Luz.
Mon–Sat 10am–midnight, Sun 9am–1pm.

A vast complex sited above metro Colégio Militar-Luz which boasts 420 shops, 65 restaurants, 11 cinema screens, plus endless palm-filled atriums and water features. Major stores include FNAC, C&A, Zara, Habitat and Toys R Us, while the top floor has the usual fast-food outlets along with a sit-down dining area in the jungle-draped "Cidade Perdida" (Lost City). There is also a "Fun Centre" complete with rides, roundabouts, bumper cars, ten-pin bowling and even a roller-coaster which whizzes overhead. An outdoor area boasts a go-cart track, toy car and boat rides, and mini-bunjee jumps.

Centro Comércial Mouraria

Map 3, B3. Largo Martim Moniz, Mouraria.
Mon–Sat 10am–9pm.
Lisbon's tackiest and most run-down shopping centre is sufficiently atmospheric to warrant a look around its six levels (three of them underground). Hundreds of small, family-run stores selling Indian fabrics, and Oriental and African produce, as well as an aromatic collection of cafés on Level 3 – it's a real insight into Lisbon's ethnic communities.

Centro Vasco da Gama

Map, p.106. Avda D. João II, Parque das Nações.
Daily 10am–midnight.

Three floors of local and international stores under a glass roof permanently washed by running water; includes branches of Celeiro, Hugo Boss, Pierre Cardin, Mango and C&A, with top-floor restaurants including Pizza Hut and McDonalds. There are also ten cinema screens, children's areas and disabled access.

Tivoli Forum

Map 8, F4. Avda da Liberdade, metro Avenida.
Mon–Sat 9am–9pm.
Flash marble-fronted shopping emporium sheltering the likes of DKNY, French Connection and Adolfo Dominguez. Also has a supermarket, cafés and a juice bar.

SHOPPING CENTRES

SUPERMARKETS

For general supplies, there's a huge **Pão d'Açúcar** super-market in the Amoreiras shopping centre (daily 9am–midnight); this Brazilian chain has other branches throughout the city – most stay open until around 8pm. On a smaller scale, try the more central **Mercado da Figueira**, Praça da Figueira 10 (Map 3, D5; Mon–Fri 8.30am–8pm, Sat 8.30am–7pm), or the branches of **Pingo Doce** that are dotted around the city such as in Tivoli Forum (Map 8, F4; Avda da Liberdade; daily 8.30am–9pm) and at Rua 1 Dezembro 123 (Map 3, D7; Mon–Sat 10am–8pm).

Kids' Lisbon

There are plenty of activities to keep kids entertained in the Lisbon area. The tourist office and the city's listings magazines (see p.9) can provide **information** about events specifically for children – *Agenda Cultural*, in particular, has a good section on child-friendly events.

Most **hotels and pensions** will happily provide extra beds or cots for children if notified in advance. There is usually no charge for children under six who share their parents' room, while discounts of up to fifty percent on accommodation for six- to eight-year-olds are not uncommon. Cots can be arranged on request, often free of charge. On **public transport**, under-fives go free while five- to eleven-year-olds travel half price on trains but pay full fare on metros and buses.

Should you hit a spell of bad weather, your best bet is to head for the various attractions at Parque das Nações or Belém, both of which have several attractions suitable for older children.

Parents with **prams and pushchairs** will find Lisbon's steep streets hard work, with pavements notoriously potholed and often blocked by parked cars. Cars are the main worry for parents: always keep a look-out for vehicles which cut corners and don't observe pedestrian crossings. Finally, **changing facilities** in restaurants, cafés and public toilets are non-existent, and when you do find them – such as in larger shopping centres – they are usually located only in women's toilets.

CAFÉS AND RESTAURANTS

Children will be welcomed in most **cafés and restaurants** at any time of the day. Indeed, waiters often go out of their way to spend a few minutes entertaining restless children; toddlers may even find themselves being carried off for a quick tour of the kitchens while parents finish their meals in peace. **High-chairs and menus** specifically for children are scarce – though restaurants happily do half portions (ask for *uma meia dose*). Restaurants rarely open much before 8pm, so kids will need to adjust to Portuguese hours; local children are still up at midnight.

Fresh milk is sold in larger shops and supermarkets; smaller shops and cafés usually stock UHT milk only. Nappies are widely available in supermarkets and pharmacies; the latter also sell formula milk, babies' bottles and jars of baby food.

MUSEUMS AND ATTRACTIONS

The Parque das Nações (see Chapter 8) has a whole range of children's attractions, of which the **Centro da Ciência Viva** (Centre for Live Science), the **Pavilhão da Realidade Virtual** (Virtual Reality Pavilion) and the giant **Oceanário de Lisboa** (Lisbon Oceanarium) are particularly good for children.

In Belém (Chapter 5), the **Museu de Arte Popular**

(Folk Art Museum), the **Museu dos Coches** (Coach Museum) and the **Museu da Marinha** (Maritime Museum) are all good bets for older children; the latter even has its own children's section, the **Museu das Crianças**, with interactive and hands-on displays designed to raise children's awareness of other children's feelings. There's also a rather underwhelming planetarium, the **Planetário Calouste Gulbenkian**, Praça do Império, Belém (℡213 620 002; Sat and Sun only at 3.30pm in Portuguese & 5pm in English; €3); Finally, in Sintra (Chapter 21), the **Museu do Brinquedo** is a well-laid-out toy museum, and nearby there's also a small virtual reality cinema, the **Teatro Virtual**.

PARKS, PLAY AREAS AND ACTIVITIES

Lisbon has several parks and squares with children's play areas, though loose bolts on some of the equipment can be alarming. **Parque Eduardo VII** contains an impressive mock-galleon in a play area just south of the *estufas*, and there are small children's playgrounds in **Praça Príncipe Real** and the **Jardim da Estrela** (Estrela Gardens). The gardens at the Fundação Calouste Gulbenkian are often awash with uniformed children from the local crèche, the **Centro Artístico Infantil** (entrance just off Rua Marquês de Sá da Bandeira). The centre is well-stocked with toys and offers free childcare sessions for four- to twelve-year-olds between 9.30am and 5.30pm, which means you can leave your kids there while you look around the museum.

At **Parque das Nações** there are various areas dedicated to children, including the **Jardim da Água** (water garden), near the Oceanarium, and the **music gardens** (next to the Pavilhão de Macau, with gongs, humming stones and the like. The **Parque de Gil** next to the Teatro Camões (Mon–Fri 2.30–7.30pm, Sat & Sun 10am–8pm; under 6s free, €1.80 for 6–12s) has ball parks, inflatables and soft play areas, while older kids can enjoy the **Radical Zone** in Sony Plaza (Tues–Fri 2–7pm, Sat & Sun 11am–7pm; €4), with more inflatables, slides, skating and trampolines. Nearby, there's also ten-pin bowling at the **Bowling Internacional de Lisboa**, Caminho da Água (Mon–Thurs noon–2am, Fri noon–4am, Sat 11am–4am, Sun 11am–2am; €4.50).

Even if you don't approve of the caged animals, Lisbon's zoo (see p.102) is set in a lovely park, and there's an enjoyable cable-car ride too.

In **Sintra**, the Castelo dos Mouros, the gardens around the Palácio da Pena, and the gardens of Monserrate, are all great places for kids to let off steam, while in **Cascais**, along with the beaches there's a lovely park, Parque Municipal da Gandarinha, with duck ponds and play equipment.

PUPPETS AND PUPPET SHOWS

The **Museu da Marioneta** (Puppet Museum), Rua da Esperança 146, Santos (Map 6, H5; Wed–Sun 10am–1pm & 2–6pm; €2.50, children €1.50; tram #25 from Praça do Comércio), set in a former convent ten minutes' walk east of the Museu de Arte Antiga, displays shadow puppets, paper marionettes and Spitting Image-style models in a well-laid-out museum with its own café. There are occasional entertaining demonstrations of puppetry, but otherwise the glass display cases are a bit dull for smaller children. **Puppet shows** – in Portuguese – are held more regularly at the **Teatro Taborda**, Costa do Castelo 75, Mouraria (Map 4, C3; ☎5218 854 190), on Fridays, Saturdays and Sundays; call for details or look in *Agenda Cultural* under *Crianças* (children).

SWIMMING AND BEACHES

Sea-swimming can be dangerous in the Lisbon area; the beaches at **Cascais** are relatively calm but pollution levels are questionable. The safest waters are in the sheltered **Arrábida peninsula** south of Lisbon. Clean, blue-flag water at **Sesimbra** and **Caparica** can be accompanied by dangerous undertows. However, Caparica has supervised areas and the waves are superb for older kids into boogie-boarding or body-surfing, while the toy train up the beach is always a big hit for kids of all ages.

TRANSPORT AND FUN RIDES

Taking rides on Lisbon's **trams, elevadores and ferries** can provide hours of endless fun; see p.17 for details of tram, bus and ferry tours. In summer, a series of tourist **toy trains** shuttles tourists around several of the main sites, including Belém, Cascais and Parque das Nações – the latter also has a cable-car ride. There is also a quaint fairground offering fun rides at the **Feira Popular**, by Entrecampos metro.

In Sintra you can take a pricey **horse and carriage ride** around town, or a tram from nearby Ribeira da Sintra to the beach at Praia das Maçãs. The **Centro Colombo** shopping centre, by metro Colégio Militar-Luz, contains whole zones set aside to keep restless kids happy while their parents shop; there's even a roller-coaster ride.

Festivals

The Portuguese have a reputation for being somewhat reserved, at least in comparison with their Spanish neighbours, but they know how to have a good time when it comes to **festivals**. This is especially so during the celebrations for the **Santos Populares** (Popular Saints), when parts of Lisbon become one big street party. Music and the arts are also highly valued in Lisbon and the year is punctuated by a series of **cultural events** that present concerts and exhibitions at venues across the city and its surroundings, many of them free.

SPRING

Fado/Harbour Festival
February Innovative music festival combining fado with music from other port cities from around the world. New Orleans' jazz and rebetika from Athens have featured in recent years.

Carnaval
Late February or early March Muted city carnival, though the council has tried to revive it recently with Brazilian-style parades and costumes, especially at Parque das Nações. Parades and events are also held at Estoril, Cascais, and Sesimbra.

Super Bock Rock Festival
March Two weeks of rock held at major venues

PUBLIC HOLIDAYS

Lisbon has a generous helping of public holidays when most of the city shuts down; don't attempt to travel in or out of the city at either end of these holidays. The fixed dates below fall on different days each year. If they fall on a Sunday, the holiday is lost; if the holiday falls on a Thursday or Tuesday, many people don't bother working on the Friday or Monday.

Official holidays are: January 1 (New Year's Day); February/March (Carnival); Good Friday; April 25 (celebrating the 1974 revolution); May 1 (Labour Day); June 10 (Portugal Day and Camões Day); June 13 (Santo António); August 15 (Feast of the Assumption); October 5 (Republic Day); November 1 (All Saints' Day); December 1 (Independence Day, celebrating independence from Spain in 1640); December 8 (Immaculate Conception); December 24–25 (Christmas).

throughout the city, with big international names being joined by local bands.

Moda Lisboa (Lisbon Fashion)

March/April The luvvies of the fashion world come to Lisbon's biannual fashion show (the other one is usually in November), when mainly Portuguese designers get the chance to parade their clothes on the catwalk.

SUMMER

Santos Populares (Popular Saints)

June Lisbon's main popular festivals, featuring fireworks, fairground rides and street-partying to celebrate the *Santos Populares* – saints António (June 13), João (June 24) and Pedro (June 29). Celebrations for each begin on the evening before the actual day. The festival of Santo António is the largest and the whole city is decked out in coloured ribbons, with pots of lucky basil on every window sill. On 12 June, the mayor sponsors free weddings at the Igreja de Santo António (Anthony was credited as being able to solve tricky relationships) and there are festivals in each district on that evening, with a main parade down Avenida da Liberdade. The best street party is in Alfama, with food and drinks stalls taking over just about every square. In Sintra, the main *festa* is for São Pedro, starting on 28 June.

Festas da Lisboa

June A series of city-sponsored cultural and other events, many promoted by the Fundação Calouste Gulbenkian, including free concerts, exhibitions and culinary contests at various venues round the city. There's also an increasingly popular Gay Pride event.

Sintra Music Festival

Late June, July and August Adventurous performances by international orchestras, musicians and dance groups in and around Sintra, Estoril and Cascais. Concerts are held in parks, gardens and palaces, including the fantastic Palácio de Queluz. An offshoot of the festival are the "Noites de Bailado" held in the gardens of the *Palácio de Seteais* during July and August – a series of ballet, dance and operatic performances, again with top international names. Tickets and programmes for all performances are available from the Gabinete do Sintra-Festival, Praça da República 23, Sintra ⓣ 219 243 518, ⓦ www.cm -sintra.pt. You can also buy tickets from the main agencies in Lisbon (see p.194) or online from ⓦ www.ondaticket.com.

SUMMER

For details of Lisbon's major sporting events,
see p.208.

Jazz Numa Noite de Verão

July or August Big annual "jazz on a summer night" festival at the Gulbenkian; the events in the open-air amphitheatre are particularly attractive, and there are usually appearances by international bands and performers. Similar events also take place in Estoril.

Feira Internacional Artesanato (Handicrafts Fair)

July State-run handicrafts fair, with live folk music, held in Estoril on the Avenida de Portugal, near the Casino. A similar event occurs during the same period at FIL, the main exhibition hall at the Parque das Nações, when international and Portuguese regional crafts are displayed (and offered for sale). There are also craft and cookery demonstrations.

Baixanima

July to September During the summer, Saturdays and Sunday afternoons see free street entertainment in the Baixa, consisting of music, dance, theatre and circus acts. The main venues are Praça do Município, Praça do Comércio, Praça da Figueira, Rua Augusta and Largo do Chiado.

Festival dos Oceanos (Oceans Festival)

August Celebrates Lisbon's links with the sea with a series of free events throughout the city, including street parades, music, fireworks and laser displays. There are also literary tours, children's events, art exhibitions, sailing regattas and special film screenings.

SUMMER

World Press Photograph Exhibition

August Annual display of entries for the World Press Photography Award at the Centro Cultural de Belém.

Festival da Música dos Capuchos (Capuchos Music Festival)

August and September Innovative performances of classical music, opera and ballet as well as some pop and jazz at the Convento dos Capuchos, just outside Caparica (not to be confused with the one near Sintra), as well as at other venues along the coast.

AUTUMN

Festa das Vindimas (Wine Harvest Festival)

First or second weekend of September Held in the hilltop town of Palmela – around an hour by bus from Praça de Espanha – in the heart of some fine vineyards, this event includes the chance to taste the local produce and enjoy parades, bull-running, folk music and fireworks.

Festival de Cinema Gay e Lésbico (Gay and Lesbian Film Festival)

September Increasingly respected gay and lesbian film festival with screenings of radical and mainstream movies, plus talks by directors, usually held at the Instituto da Cinemateca Portuguesa (see p.205) and other venues.

Encontros ACARTE

September Culmination of a cultural programme organized by – and partly held at – the Fundação Calouste Gulbenkian, promoting up-and-coming local and international talent, with shows around the city featuring music, art, the performing arts and animation.

AUTUMN

Seixal Jazz
October and early November The industrial suburb of Seixal (a short ferry ride over the Tejo from Estação Fluvial by Praça de Comércio) hosts big names from the Portuguese and international jazz world at the Fórum Cultural do Seixal (information on ☎212 226 413).

WINTER

Todos Santos (All Saints' Day) and São Martinho
November 1 and 11 Candles are lit for the dead on All Saints' Day (Nov 1), while November 11 sees the more earthy festival of São Martinho, when the saint's day is traditionally celebrated by eating chestnuts and drinking *agua pé* – literally "foot water" – the first of the year's wine harvest.

Festival do Vinho
November Launched to promote the region's wines, this usually coincides with São Martinho, and combines a formal series of tastings with a cultural programme.

Dança na Cidade (Dance in the City Festival)
November Cultural festival, with a series of classical and contemporary dance events held at the Centro Cultural de Belém and other venues.

Christmas
December The build-up to December 25 begins in early December with lights decorating central shopping streets and a huge Christmas tree filling the centre of Praça da Figueira. The bullring at Campo Pequeno usually hosts a travelling circus at this time. Distinctive hooped *bolo-rei* (dried-fruit "king cake") appears in shops and

pastelarias. Christmas Day itself remains a family affair, with traditional midnight Mass celebrated on December 24, followed by a meal of bacalhau.

New Year's Eve
December 31 The best place to head for on New Year's Eve is Praça do Comércio, when fireworks light up the riverfront and there's a party which usually continues well into the next morning. There are also similar events at Cascais. The Parque das Nações hosts a *Noite Magica* (Magic Night) with a series of free events.

Directory

AIRLINES Air France, Avda 5 de Outubro 206 (Map 9, E5; ☎217 900 202); Alitalia, Praça Marquês de Pombal 1–5° (Map 8, D1; ☎213 536 141); British Airways, Avda da Liberdade 36–2° (Map 8, G5; ☎213 217 900); Iberia, Rua Rosa Araújo 2 (Map 8, D4; ☎213 558 119); KLM, Campo Grande 220b (Map 2, E3; ☎217 955 018); Lufthansa, Avda da Liberdade 192 (Map 8, F4; ☎213 573 722); TAP, Praça Marquês de Pombal 3 (Map 8, D1; ☎213 179 100); Varig, Praça Marquês de Pombal 1 (Map 8, D1; ☎213 136 830.

AMERICAN EXPRESS The local agent is Top Tours, Avda Duque de Loulé 108 (Map 8, E1; ☎213 155 885; Mon–Fri 9.30am–1pm & 2.30–6.30pm;

metro Marquês de Pombal).

BUSES The main terminal is at Avda João Crisóstomo (Map 9, G5; metro Saldanha; ☎213 545 439), for international and most domestic departures, including express services to the Algarve. Other bus services leave from Praça de Espanha (Map 9, A3; metro Praça de Espanha) for Transportes Sul do Tejo (☎217 262 740) departures to Caparica, Sesimbra and places south of the Tejo; from Parque das Nações (Map. p.106; metro Oriente) for AVIC services (☎218 940 238) to the north-west coast and Renex services (☎218 874 871) to the Minho and Algarve; and from Campo Grande 5 (Map 1, E3; metro Campo Grande) for Mafrense Empresa Barraqueiro services

(☏ 217 582 212) to Mafra and Ericeira. Stagecoach, Avda Atlântico 1, Colares (Map 1, B4; ☏ 219 291 166), operates between Lisbon airport and Sintra, Cascais and Estoril. You can buy advance bus tickets at most major travel agents – see below for a list. Fares and timetables for Portugal's main national coach service, Rede Expressos, can be found at ⓦ www.rede-expressos.pt.

CAR RENTAL Alamo/Guerin, Avda Alvares Cabral 45b ☏ 213 882 724 or 800 201 078; Auto Jardim, Rua Luciano Cordeiro 6 ☏ 213 549 182, airport ☏ 218 463 187; Avis, Avda Praia da Vitória 12c ☏ 213 514 560, airport ☏ 218 435 550; Budget, Rua Castilho 167b ☏ 213 860 516, airport ☏ 218 478 803; Europcar, Santa Apolónia station ☏ 218 861 573, airport ☏ 218 401 176; Hertz, Rua Castilho 72 ☏ 213 812 430, airport ☏ 218 463 154; Nova Rent, Largo Monterroio Mascarenhas 9 ☏ 213 870 808.

DISABLED TRAVELLERS The Secretariado Nacional Para a Reabilitação e Integração das Pessas com Deficiêcia, Avda Conde Valbom 63, ☏ 217 929 500, ⓦ www.snripd.mts.gov.pt, produces an Accessible Tourism Guide in English featuring disabled-friendly travel agents, restaurants, clubs, clinics, and so on. Lisbon airport offers a service for wheelchair users if advance notice is given (☏ 213 632 044), while the Orange Badge symbol is recognized for disabled car parking. The main public transport company, Carris, offers an inexpensive dial-a-ride minibus service, O Serviço Especial de Transporte de Deficientes (€1 per trip; Mon–Fri 6.30am–10pm, Sat & Sun 8am–10pm; ☏ 213 613 161, ⓦ www.carris.pt), though two days' advance notice and a medical certificate is required. The following museums have disabled access: Museu de Arqueologia; Museu de Arte Popular; Museu do Chiado; Museu dos Coches; Museu Nacional de Arte Antiga. For a list of hotels with disabled access, see p.116.

DRESS Conservative values exist on town beaches where

topless sunbathing is frowned upon, while shorts and skimpy clothes are best avoided in churches.

EMBASSIES AND CONSULATES Australia, Avda da Liberdade 198–2° (Map 8, F4; metro Avenida; ☎213 101 500); Canada, Avda da Liberdade 196–200, (Map 8, F4; metro Avenida; ☎213 164 600); Ireland, Rua da Imprensa à Estrela 1–4° (Map 6, H3; tram #28 to Estrela; ☎213 929 440); New Zealand, Avda António Aguiar 122 (Map 9, C6; metro São Sebastião or Parque; ☎213 509 690); UK, Rua de São Marçal 174 (Map 8, D7; metro Rato; ☎213 929 440); USA, Avda das Forças Armadas (Map 2, C5; metro Jardim Zoológico; ☎217 273 300).

ELECTRICITY Portugal uses two-pin plugs (220v). UK appliances will work with a continental adaptor.

EMERGENCIES Call ☎112 for police, ambulance and fire.

HOSPITAL British Hospital, Rua Saraiva de Carvalho 49 (Map 6, G2; ☎213 955 067), has English-speaking staff and doctors on call from 8.30am–9pm.

LAUNDRY Lavandaria Saus Ana, in the Centro Comércial da Mouraria, Largo Martim Moniz 9 (metro Socorro), does service washes for €5 (Mon–Sat 9.30am–8pm), or try the self-service Lava Neve, Rua da Alegria 37, Bairro Alto (Mon 9am–1pm & 3–7pm, Tues–Fri 10am–1pm & 3–7pm, Sat 9am–1pm), which charges €4.50 for 5kg of laundry.

LEFT LUGGAGE There are 24-hour lockers at the airport (€1.60–€5.50 per day depending on the size of luggage), and at Rossio, Cais do Sodré and Santa Apolónia stations (around €2 a day); and a left-luggage office at the bus terminal on Avda João Crisóstomo (Mon–Fri 6.30am–8pm, Sat & Sun 9am–1pm & 2–6pm; around €2.50 a day).

LOST PROPERTY Report any loss to the tourist police station in the Foz Cultura building in Palácio Foz, Restauradores

(Map 3, A9; daily 24hr, ☎213 421 634).

NEWSPAPERS There are several newsstands around Rossio and Restauradores, such as the one attached to the ABEP ticket kiosk, which sell foreign-language newspapers, as do the lobbies of many of the larger hotels.

PHARMACIES Pharmacies are open Mon–Fri 9am–1pm & 3–7pm, Sat 9am–1pm. Local papers carry information about 24hr pharmacies and the details are posted on every pharmacy door.

TIME Lisbon time is the same as Greenwich Mean Time (GMT). Clocks go forward an hour in late March and back to GMT in late October.

TIPPING Service charges are included in hotel and restaurant bills. It's usual to round-up restaurant bills to the nearest €1 or so; other than this, tips are not expected. Hotel porters, toilet attendants and

cinema ushers expect tips of at least €0.50.

TOILETS There are very few public toilets in the streets, although they can be found in nearly all museums and main tourist sights (signed variously as *casa de banho*, *retrete*, *banheiro*, *lavabos* or "WC"), and it is not difficult to sneak into a café or restaurant if need be. Gents are usually marked H (*homens*) or C (*cabalheiros*), and ladies M (*mulheres*) or S (*senhoras*).

TRAVEL AGENTS Marcus & Harting, Rossio 45–50 (Map 3, C6; ☎213 224 550), is a good, central option for bus tickets and general travel information. The well-informed Top Tours, Avda Duque de Loulé 108 (Map 9, E8; ☎213 155 885), near metro Marquês de Pombal, also acts as an American Express agent. USIT Tagus, Rua Camilo Castelo Branco 20 (Map 9, D9; ☎213 525 986), specializes in discounted student tickets and sells ISIC cards.

OUT OF THE CITY

21	Sintra, Queluz and Mafra	247
22	Estoril and Cascais	272
23	South of the Tejo	285

Sintra, Queluz and Mafra

I f you make just one day-trip during your stay in Lisbon the ride out to the beautiful hilltop town of **Sintra** is the one to choose. It's the most popular excursion from the city – served by regular trains from Rossio station – and the town ideally deserves several days' exploration. Home to two of Portugal's most extraordinary palaces, it also boasts a semi-tropical garden, a Moorish castle with breathtaking views over Lisbon, and one of the best modern art museums in the Iberian peninsula. To the west of town, the lighthouse and cape of the **Cabo da Roca** and the low-key beach resorts of the **Sintra** coast provide more reasons to stick around for a while.

The eighteenth-century Rococo **Palácio de Queluz**, on the same train line as Sintra, is worth a brief break in your journey to or from Lisbon. Finally, north of Sintra, about ninety minutes by bus from Lisbon, lies **Mafra** – an uninspiring town made famous by its extravagant **Palácio-Convento de Mafra**, the building of which virtually bankrupted the nation.

SINTRA

Map 1, C4. Trains every 15min from Rossio station (a 45min journey). Sintra's train station is in Estefânia, from where it's a 15min walk (or take bus #433 or #434) into the centre of Sintra-Vila. There are also regular buses from Estoril, Cascais, Cabo da Roca and Mafra; these stop opposite the train station.

As the summer residence of the kings of Portugal and of the Moorish lords of Lisbon before them, **Sintra**'s verdant charms have long been celebrated. British travellers of the eighteenth and nineteenth centuries found a new Arcadia in the town's cool, wooded heights, recording with satisfaction the old Spanish proverb: "To see the world and leave out Sintra is to go blind about". Byron stayed here in 1809 and began *Childe Harold*, his great mock-epic poem, in which the "horrid crags" of "Cintra's glorious Eden" form a first location. Writing home, in a letter to his mother, he proclaimed the village:

> *perhaps in every aspect the most delightful in Europe; it contains beauties of every description natural and artificial. Palaces and gardens rising in the midst of rocks, cataracts and precipices; convents on stupendous heights, a distant view of the sea and the Tagus . . . it unites in itself all the wildness of the Western Highlands with the verdure of the South of France.*

That the young Byron had seen neither the Western Highlands nor the South of France is irrelevant: his description of Sintra's romantic appeal is still exact.

Sintra loops around a series of green, wooded ravines and is a confusing place in which to get your bearings. Basically, it consists of three separate villages: the drab **Estefânia** (around the train station), **Sintra-Vila** (the attractive main town) and, 2km to the east, the functional **São Pedro de Sintra**. It's fifteen minutes' walk between the station –

where there's a small information desk – and Sintra-Vila, passing en route the fantastical Câmara Municipal (town hall); and around twenty minutes from Sintra-Vila to São Pedro. Sintra-Vila's **Turismo** (June–Sept daily 9am–8pm; Oct–May daily 9am–7pm; ☎219 231 157, ⓦwww.cm -sintra.pt) is just off the central Praça da República, where you'll find a post office and bank too. The *Turismo* can help out in times when accommodation is scarce, like during the village's annual **festival** in honour of São Pedro (June 28–29) and in July, during Sintra's music festival. The end of July also sees the Feira Grande in São Pedro, with crafts, antiques and cheeses on sale.

The old town of Sintra-Vila, with its narrow streets, bars and restaurants, is dominated by the **Palácio Nacional**, the former summer residence of Portuguese royalty. The lush surrounding hills shelter some of the area's grandest treasures, in particular the ruined Moorish castle, the **Castelo dos Mouros** (from which there are stunning views), and the ludicrously extravagant nineteenth-century **Palácio da Pena**. Other country retreats, like the **Palácio de Seteais**, now a splendid hotel, and the **Quinta da Regaleira**, both just outside Sintra, are worth a visit for even more opulence. Further afield lie the luxuriant gardens of **Monserrate** and, by way of contrast, the **Convento dos Capuchos**, a spartan hermitage in a stunning woodland location.

Stagecoach **bus #434** takes a circular route from Sintra station to the outlying sights, passing Sintra-Vila, the Castelo dos Mouros and the Palácio da Pena (daily every 40min, 10.20am– 5.15pm). Tickets can be purchased on board and cost a flat fare of €3 (or there's a day-rover pass for €6.23). Other useful buses include Stagecoach bus #418, which links Sintra with Estoril (hourly departures), and the #417 to Cacais (hourly departures). Both of these services leave from Sintra's main **bus station** at Portela da

SINTRA

SINTRA

0   100 m

N

To Ribeira de Sintra (tram)

To Colares & Praia das Maçãs

Centro Cultural O. Cadaval

Market

Museu de Arte Moderna

To Portela & bus station

ESTEFÂNIA

Câmara Municipal

Train Station

Palácio Nacional

SINTRA-VILA

Teatro Virtual

Parque da Liberdade

Museu do Brinquedo

To Monserrate, Seteais, Cabo da Roca & Quinta da Regaleira

Santa Maria

SÃO PEDRO DE SINTRA

Castelo dos Mouros

To Capuchos

To Lisbon & Queluz

São Pedro

To Capuchos

SANTA EUFÉMIA

Solar de São Pedro

(i) Tourist office

Steps

Pedestrianized street

Palácio da Pena

Youth Hostel

To Cruz Alta

To Youth Hostel (2 km)

Street labels: RUA VEIGA DA CUNHA, GEN. A. DE FIGUEIRA, AV. ADRIANO J. COELHO, RUA CÂMARA PESTANA, RUA DE CAMBURINHAL, AV. DE CAMBURINHAL, MEDINA JUNIOR, ESTRADA DO CARVALHEIRO, ESTRADA DA MACIEIRA, ALAMEDAS DOS COM. DA GUERRA, L. DE ALBUQUERQUE, R. DR. ÁLVARO DE VASCONCELOS, MONUMENTO DAS FORÇAS ARMADAS, RUA DA PENHA, CALÇADA DE S. PEDRO, LARGO Dr. VIRGILIO HORTA, R. ALFREDO COSTA, R. ANDRÉ DE ALBUQUERQUE, LARGO FERNANDO MORAIS, RUA FRANCISCO DOS SANTOS, AV. DR. M. BOMBARDA, VOLTA DO DUQUE, R. CÔNSUL SEIXAL, CAMINHO DE ST. CASTRO, RUA DA FERRARIA, RUA DO CASTELO, RUA GIL VICENTE, R. PEDRO I, R. EDUARDO F. NAVARRO, RUA VISCONDE DE MONSERRATE, RUA MARECHAL SALDANHA, CALÇ. DO LESENGO, RUA BERNARDIM RIBEIRO, ESTRADA DA PENA, CALÇ. DA TRINDADE, RUA DA TRINDADE, CALÇADA DA PENA, R. SERPA PINTO, RUA DO RIO DA TALA, RUA DO CANTÃO, ESTRADA

SINTRA

250

Sintra, the train stop before Sintra itself. Alternatively, there are **taxis** outside the train station and in Sintra-Vila's Praça da República, near the palace; the one-way trip to Monserrate, for example, costs roughly €8. Agree the price first – meters aren't always used and overcharging is common.

Museu de Arte Moderna

Map p.250, G1. Ⓦ www.berardocollection.com. Tues–Sun 10am–6pm; €3.

Just five minutes' walk from the train station in Estefânia (turn right out of the station; the museum is in Avda Heliodoro Salgado) is the **Museu de Arte Moderna**, a collection amassed by Madeiran tobacco magnate Joe Berardo, which art critics have compared favourably to the Guggenheim in Bilbão. Located in Sintra's former casino, the collection spreads over three floors, chronologically displaying the main modern movements, including pop art, minimalism, kinetic art and conceptual art.

The collection is so huge that exhibits change every two months and, depending on when you visit, you might see giant Gilbert and George panels, and works by Jackson Pollock, David Hockney, Roy Lichtenstein and Andy Warhol, including his wonderful portrait of Judy Garland. Lovers of kitsch will enjoy Jeff Koons' sculpture of a poodle and Bobtail the sheepdog. The top floor contains a café and restaurant, with an outdoor terrace offering great views towards the Palácio da Pena.

Further temporary exhibitions, performing arts and films can be viewed next to the modern art museum at the Centro Cultural Olga Cadaval, on Praça Dr Francisco Sá Carneiro. Details of current shows are available from Sintra's Turismo.

SINTRA

Palácio Nacional

Map p.250, C4. Mon, Tues & Thurs–Sun 10am–5.30pm; €3.

The extraordinary **Palácio Nacional** or Paço Real was probably already in existence at the time of the Moors. It takes its present form, however, from the rebuilding of Dom João I (1385–1433) and his fortunate successor, Dom Manuel, the chief royal beneficiary of Vasco da Gama's explorations. Its exterior style is an amalgam of Gothic – featuring impressive battlements – and the Manueline, tempered inside by a good deal of Moorish influence, adapted over the centuries by a succession of royal occupants. The last royal to live here, in the 1880s, was Maria Pia, grandmother of the country's last reigning monarch – Manuel II, "The Unfortunate".

Today the palace is a museum and is best seen early or late in the day to avoid the crowds. You first pass the kitchens, their roofs tapering into the giant chimneys that are the palace's distinguishing features, and then go on to the upper floor. First stop here is a gallery above the palace chapel, perhaps built on the old mosque. In a room alongside, the deranged Afonso VI was confined for six years by his brother Pedro II; he eventually died here in 1683, listening to Mass through a grid, Pedro having seized "his throne, his liberty and his queen". Beyond the gallery, a succession of state rooms climaxes in the Sala das Armas, its domed and coffered ceiling emblazoned with the arms of 72 noble families.

Highlights on the lower floor include the Manueline Sala dos Cisnes, so called for the swans (*cisnes*) on its ceiling, and the Sala das Pegas, which takes its name from the flock of magpies (*pegas*) painted on the frieze and ceiling, holding in their beaks the legend *por bem* (in honour) – reputedly the response of João I, caught by his queen, Philippa (of Lancaster), in the act of kissing a lady-in-waiting. He had

SINTRA

the room decorated with as many magpies as there were women at court in order to satirize them and put a stop to their gossip.

Museu do Brinquedo

Map p.250, C5. Tues–Sun 10am–6pm; €3.

Just south of the palace, the **Museu do Brinquedo** – the fascinating private toy collection of João Arbués Moreira – is housed in a former fire station on Rua Visconde de Monserrate. The building has been imaginatively converted – internal glass lifts take you from floor to floor – and not only is there a café but also a small play area for young children. The huge array of toys exhibited over three floors is somewhat confusingly labelled, but look out for the 3000-year-old stone Egyptian toys on the first floor; the 1930s' Hornby trains, and some of the first ever toy cars, produced in Germany in the early 1900s. There are cases of soldiers numerous enough to scare a real army, wooden toys from Senegal, wire bicycles from Zimbabwe, and a top floor stuffed with dolls and doll's house furniture. Perhaps the most interesting section is that on early Portuguese toys, containing old cars made from papier-mâché, tin-plate animals, wooden trams and trains, as well as a selection of 1930s' beach toys, including beautifully painted buckets and the metal fish that appears on the museum brochure.

Teatro Virtual

Map p.250, E5. June–Sept Tues–Fri 9.30am–12.30pm & 2–6pm; Sat & Sun 2–6pm; Oct–May same days and hours until 5.30pm; €1.50, children under 13 free.

A couple of hundred metres or so southeast of the toy museum, off Volta do Duque on the leafy slopes of the Parque da Liberdade, the **Teatro Virtual** is a tiny cinema

SINTRA

projecting a computer-animated film of the early voyages to Japan of the Portuguese discoverers. It's good entertainment on a rainy day or with bored children – who will relish seeing the Portuguese depicted with giant noses, which is how the Japanese saw them.

Castelo dos Mouros

Map p.250, C6–D7. June–Sept daily 10am–7pm; Oct–May daily 10am–5pm; €3. Bus #434 from Sintra station or Sintra-Vila.

From Calçada dos Clérigos, near the church of Santa Maria, a stone pathway leads up to the ruined ramparts of the **Castelo dos Mouros**. Taken in 1147 by Afonso Henriques, with the aid of Scandinavian Crusaders, the castle walls were allowed to fall into disrepair over subsequent centuries, though they were restored in the mid-nineteenth century as tourists increasingly began to make the climb. The Moorish castle spans two rocky pinnacles, with the remains of a mosque spread midway between the fortifications, and the views from up here are extraordinary: south beyond Lisbon's Ponte 25 de Abril to the Serra da Arrábida, west to Cascais and Cabo da Roca, and north to Peniche and the Berlenga islands.

Palácio da Pena

Map p.250, C9. Mid-June–mid Sept Tues–Sun 10am–7pm; mid-Sept–mid June Tues–Sun 10am–5pm; palace and gardens €5, gardens only €3. Bus #434 from Sintra station or Sintra-Vila.

The upper gate of the castle gives on to the road up to Pena, opposite the lower entrance to **Parque da Pena** (mid-June–mid-Sept daily 9am–7pm; mid-Sept–mid-June daily 10am–5pm), a stretch of rambling woodland with a scattering of lakes and follies, ideal for a picnic. At the top of the park, about twenty minutes' walk from the entrance, looms the fabulous **Palácio da Pena**, a wild fantasy of domes, towers, ramparts and walkways, approached through mock-Manueline gateways and a drawbridge that does not draw. A compelling riot of kitsch built in the 1840s to the specifications of Ferdinand of Saxe-Coburg-Gotha, husband of Queen Maria II, it bears comparison with the mock-medieval castles of Ludwig of Bavaria. The architect, the German Baron Eschwege, immortalized himself in the guise of a warrior-knight in a huge statue that guards the palace from a neighbouring crag. The interior is no less bizarre, preserved exactly as it was left by the royal family when it fled Portugal in 1910. The result is fascinating: rooms of stone decorated to look like wood, turbaned Moors nonchalantly holding electric chandeliers – it's all here. Of an original convent, founded to celebrate the first sight of Vasco da Gama's returning fleet, only a chapel and genuine Manueline cloister have been retained.

Above Pena, past the statue of Eschwege, a marked foot-path climbs in thirty minutes or so to the **Cruz Alta**, highest point of the Serra de Sintra.

Quinta da Regaleira

Map p.256. Ninety-minute tours: June–Sept, daily every 30min, 10am–6pm; March–May & Oct–Nov, roughly hourly, 10am–3.30pm; Dec–Feb, roughly hourly, 11am–3.30pm. Advance booking essential on ⓣ 219 106 650; €10.

The **Quinta da Regaleira**, a UNESCO World Heritage site, is one of Sintra's most elaborate private estates, lying just five minutes' walk west out of town on the Seteais-Monserrate road. The estate was designed at the turn of the twentieth century by Italian architect and theatrical set designer Luigi Manini for wealthy Brazilian merchant António Augusto Carvalho Monteiro. The Italian had worked at La Scala in Milan and his sense of the dramatic is

SINTRA

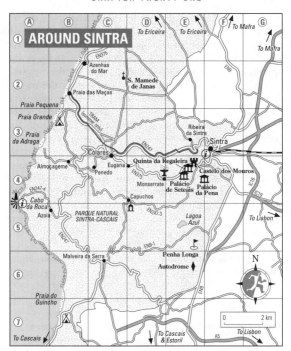

AROUND SINTRA

obvious: the principal building, the mock-Manueline
Palácio dos Milhões, sprouts turrets and towers, though
the interior is sparse apart from some elaborate Rococo
wooden ceilings and impressive Art Nouveau tiles. The surrounding **gardens** shelter fountains, terraces, lakes and
grottoes, with the highlight being the Initiation Well,
inspired by the initiation practices of the Knights Templar
and the Freemasons. Entering via an Indiana Jones-style
revolving stone door, you walk down a moss-covered spiral

SINTRA

staircase to the foot of the well and through a tunnel, which eventually resurfaces at the edge of a lake (though in winter you exit a shorter tunnel so as not to disturb a colony of hibernating bats).

For details of the Palácio de Seteais hotel, just beyond Quinta da Regaleira, see p.261.

Monserrate

Map p.256. June–Sept daily 9am–7pm; Oct–May daily 9am–5pm; €3.

Beyond the Palácio de Seteais, the road leads past a series of beautiful private *quintas* (manors or estates) to **Monserrate** – about an hour's walk from the centre of Sintra. It's one of the most romantic sights in Portugal, a Victorian folly-like mansion set in a vast botanical park of exotic trees and sub-tropical shrubs and plants, its charm immeasurably enhanced by the fact that it's only partially maintained. It would be easy to spend a day wandering around the paths laid out through the woods here.

The name most associated with Monserrate is that of **William Beckford**, author of the Gothic novel *Vathek* and the wealthiest untitled Englishman of his age. He rented Monserrate from 1793 to 1799, having been forced to flee Britain after he was caught in an uncompromising position with a sixteen-year-old boy, Kitty Courtenay. Setting about improving this "beautiful Claude-like place", he landscaped a waterfall and even imported a flock of sheep from his estate at Fonthill. In this dreamland he whiled away his days in summer pavilions, entertained by "bevys of delicate warblers and musicians" posted around the grounds.

Half a century later, a second immensely rich Englishman, **Sir Francis Cook**, bought the estate. His fantasies were

SINTRA

scarcely less ambitious, involving the construction of a great Victorian house inspired by Brighton Pavilion. Cook also spared no expense in developing the grounds, importing the head gardener from Kew to lay out succulents and water plants, tropical ferns and palms, and just about every known conifer. Ferdinand of Saxe-Coburg-Gotha, who was building the Pena palace at the time, was suitably impressed, making Cook a viscount for his efforts. For a time Monseratte boasted the only lawn in Iberia and it remains one of Europe's most richly stocked gardens, with over a thousand different species of sub-tropical trees and plants.

The house is closed but you can still admire the exterior, with its mix of Moorish and Italian decoration (the dome is modelled on the Duomo in Florence), and peer into a series of empty salons.

Convento dos Capuchos

Map p.256. Tours every 15–30min: Mon–Fri 9.30am–5pm, Sat & Sun 9.30am–5.15pm; advanced bookings essential on ☎ 219 237 300; €3.

One of the best long walks in the Sintra area is to the **Convento dos Capuchos**, an extraordinary hermitage with tiny, dwarf-like cells cut from the rock and lined in cork – hence its popular name of the "Cork Convent". Philip II, King of Spain and Portugal, pronounced it the poorest convent of his kingdom, and Byron, visiting a cave where one monk had spent thirty-six years in seclusion, mocked in *Childe Harold*:

> *Deep in yon cave Honorius long did dwell,*
> *In hope to merit Heaven by making earth a Hell.*

Coming upon the place after a walk through the woods, however, it's hard not to be moved by its simplicity and seclusion. It was occupied for three hundred years until being finally abandoned in 1834 by its seven remaining monks, who must have found the gloomy warren of rooms and corridors too much to maintain. Some rooms – the penitents' cells – can only be entered by crawling through 70cm-high doors; here, and on every other ceiling, door-frame and lintel, are attached panels of cork, taken from the surrounding woods. Elsewhere, you'll come across a wash-room, kitchen, refectory, tiny chapels, and even a bread oven set apart from the main complex.

There's no public transport to the hermitage. On foot, the most straightforward approach is by the ridge road from Pena (9km; allow a good two hours). There are other indistinct paths through the woods from Monserrate and elsewhere in the region, but without local advice and a good map you'll be hard pushed to find your way. Whichever route you take, the surroundings are startling: the minor road between Sintra, the convent and Cabo da Roca sports some of the country's most alarming natural rock formations, with boulders as big as houses looming out of the trees.

Accommodation

Residêncial Adelaide (Map p.250, D4), Rua Guilherme Gomes Fernandes 11, Sintra-Vila ⓣ 219 230 873.
Very clean, if spartan, rooms available at this simple guesthouse; quieter rooms at the rear face a patio. You're just five minutes' walk from the town-centre cafés and restaurants. ❷

Casa Miradouro (Map p.250, B3), Rua Sotto Mayor 55, Sintra-Vila ⓣ 219 235 900, ⓕ 219 241 836, ⓦ www. casa-miradouro.com.
Lovingly restored mansion, originally built in 1894, 500m beyond the Palácio Nacional, with friendly service, a terraced garden, and terrific views of coast

SINTRA

and castle from most rooms. The five charming rooms are stylishly furnished, and a good breakfast is included in the price. ❻

Casa da Paderna (Map p.250, B3), Rua da Paderna 4, Sintra-Vila ⓣ219 235 053.
Highly attractive accommodation with traditionally furnished rooms in a small house, reached down a steep cobbled track, just north of Sintra-Vila. There are great views from the house up to Quinta da Regaleira. ❺

Hotel Central (Map p.250, C4), Praça da República 35, Sintra-Vila ⓣ219 230 963.
Comfortable nineteenth-century two-star hotel, opposite the Palácio Nacional, with polished wood and tiles throughout. Triple rooms are available, too, and there are good off-season discounts. Breakfast is included. ❺

Lawrence's Hotel (Map p.250, B5), Rua Consigliéri Pedroso 38–40, Sintra-Vila ⓣ219 105 500, ⓕ219 105 505, ⓔlawrence_hotel@iol.pt.
This lays claim to being the oldest hotel in Portugal, dating from 1764 (and claiming a visit from Byron) but re-opened as a five-star under Dutch ownership in 1999. There are just eleven spacious rooms and five suites, all simply though elegantly furnished, and plenty of comfortable communal areas, including a highly rated restaurant which serves traditional but pricey Portuguese cuisine. The price includes a substantial buffet breakfast. The hotel can also organize golfing packages. ❾

Pensão Nova Sintra (Map p.250, F2), Largo Afonso d'Albuquerque 25, Estefânia ⓣ219 230 220, ⓕ219 107 033.
Very smart *pensão* in a big mansion, whose elevated terrace-café overlooks a busy street. The modern rooms all have TV and shiny marble floors, and a good breakfast is included. ❹

For an explanation of the accommodation price codes, see p.118.

SINTRA, QUELUZ AND MAFRA

Palácio de Seteais (Map p.256), Rua Barbosa du Bocage 8 ⊤ 219 233 200, ⓕ 219 234 277, ⓦ www.tivolihotels.com.

The "Seven Sighs", one of the most elegant palaces in Portugal, is on the Monserrate road, a few minutes' drive from the centre of Sintra-Vila. Completed in the last years of the eighteenth century and maintained today as an immensely luxurious hotel, it is entered through a majestic Neoclassical arch. The large rooms have period furniture and superior furnishings – they're very popular with honeymooners – while the landscaped garden has its own superb pool. With more modest money to blow, make for the bar and terrace – downstairs to the left, past a distinctly frosty reception. ❾

Piela's (Map p.250, G2), Avda Desiderio Cambournac 1–3, Estefânia ⊤ 219 241 691. Renovated town house above a cyber-café, with air-conditioned rooms with TV,

presided over by a welcoming and informative proprietor. *Piela's* is due to open in 2003, relocating from its old position above a café-*pastelaria* at Rua João de Deus 70–72. ❸

Pousada de Juventude de Sintra (Map p.250, E9), Santa Eufémia, São Pedro de Sintra ⊤ 219 241 210, ⓕ 219 233 176, ⓔ sintra@movijovem.pt.

Sintra's comfortable youth hostel is 6km from the train station, so it's best if you catch local bus #435 to São Pedro from the station via Sintra-Vila (roughly every 40min) and walk the remaining 2km from there. Meals are served if you can't face the hike down into town and back. Beds in the dorm cost from €9.50, double rooms from €21.

Residencial Sintra (Map p.250, G6), Trav. dos Alvares, São Pedro ⊤ & ⓕ 219 230 738, ⓔ pensao.residencial .sintra@clix.pt.
Rambling old pension with soaring ceilings, wooden floors and oodles of

SINTRA

character. There's a substantial garden with a swimming pool and the giant rooms can easily accommodate extra beds – so it's great for families. You'll need to book ahead in summer. ⑤

Hotel Tivoli (Map p.250, C4), Praça da República, Sintra-Vila ⓣ 219 237 200, ⓕ 219 237 245, ⓦ www.tivolihotels.com. Modern building sticking out like a sore thumb in the middle of the historic centre, though it has fine views from the room balconies. The rooms themselves have supremely comfortable beds and plush furniture, and there's internet access in the lobby. There's also an in-house restaurant, though the international food served here is unmemorable. Rates drop a category in winter. ⑥

Eating and drinking

Adega das Caves (Map p.250, C5), Rua de Pendora 2 (café) & 8 (restaurant), Sintra-Vila. Café daily 8am–2am, restaurant noon–3pm & 7–11pm. No credit cards. Inexpensive. Bustling café-bar in the basement of Café Paris, just off the main square, attracting a predominantly local and youthful clientele; the neighbouring associated restaurant serves good-value Portuguese grills.

Alcobaça (Map p.250, C5), Rua das Padarias 7–11, Sintra-Vila. Daily noon–4.30pm & 7pm–midnight. Inexpensive. The best central choice for a decent, straightforward Portuguese meal, on a small side street east of the main square. There's friendly service in the plain tiled dining room, and large servings of grilled chicken, *arroz de marisco* (seafood rice), pork or steak for around €13 a head.

Café Paris (Map p.250, C4), Largo Rainha D. Amélia, Sintra-Vila ⓣ 219 232 375. Café daily 8am–midnight, restaurant noon–10pm. Expensive.

The highest-profile café in town, opposite the Palácio Nacional, which means steep prices for not especially exciting food, although it is a great place to sit and nurse a drink in the sun. If you do want to eat, reservations are advised in high season.

Casa da Avo (Map p.250, C5), Rua Visdonde de Monserrate 46, Sintra-Vila. Mon–Wed & Fri–Sun noon–3pm & 7–11pm. Inexpensive.
Basic eating-house with few pretensions, but the house wine is cheap enough and it's hard to fault dishes like *caldeirada* (fish stew). There's a decent café attached, too.

Casa da Piriquita (Map p.250, C5), Rua das Padarias 1, Sintra-Vila. Mon, Tues & Thurs–Sun 9am–midnight. Inexpensive.
Cosy tea-room and bakery, which can get pretty smoky when it's busy with locals queueing to buy *queijadas da Sintra* (sweet cheesecakes) and other pastries. Another more modern branch, Piriquita Dois, is further up

the hill at no. 18 (closed Tues) and this has a big outdoor terrace.

O Chico (Map p.250, C5), Rua Arco do Teixeira 8, Sintra-Vila. Daily noon–midnight (bar open until 2am). Expensive.
Standard Sintra prices – ie, fairly high – for standard food, but come on Thursdays in summer for the fado and it's good-value entertainment. It's off the bottom of Rua das Padarias and has attractive outdoor tables on the cobbles. Fish *cataplana* for two people is a good bet at around €25.

Bar Fonte da Pipa (Map p.250, C5), Rua Fonte da Pipa 11–13, Sintra-Vila. Daily 9am–2am. Inexpensive.
Laid-back bar attracting a sophisticated clientele. It's up the hill from *Casa da Piriquita*, next to the lovely ornate fountain (*fonte*) that the street is named after.

Marquês de Sintra (Map p.250, D5), Parque das Castanheiro, Sintra-Vila. Daily 10am–8pm. No credit cards. Inexpensive.

SINTRA

Snack bar with plastic chairs on an outdoor terrace in this small park wedged between Rua Visconde de Monserrate and Volta do Duque, with great views over the Palácio Nacional.

Orixás (Map p.250, F1), Avda Adriano Coelho 7, Estefânia. Tues–Fri 4pm–midnight, Sat & Sun noon–4pm & 8pm–midnight. Expensive.
Brazilian bar, restaurant, music venue and art gallery housed in a lovely building complete with waterfalls and outdoor terrace, on the road behind the Museu de Arte Moderna. Go for the buffet to sample its range of Brazilian specialities; it costs around €30, but can last all night. With live Brazilian music thrown in, that's not bad value.

Toca do Javali (Map p.250, G7), Rua 1º Dezembro 18, São

Pedro de Sintra ⊤219 233 503. Mon, Tues & Thurs–Sun noon–midnight. Expensive.
Around 500 metres east of the main square in São Pedro, this is much the best place to eat in this part of town, with outdoor tables in summer in a terraced garden, combined with superb cooking at any time of year. Wild boar (*javali*) is the house speciality. Prices are fairly steep, around €25 a head. Reservations advised.

Tulhas (Map p.250, B5), Rua Gil Vicente 4, Sintra-Vila ⊤219 232 378. Mon, Tues & Thurs–Sun noon–3.30pm & 7–10pm. Moderate.
Imaginative cooking in a fine building, converted from old grain silos. The speciality is veal with Madeira at a reasonable €12 or so, but anything here is recommended. It's wise to book in advance.

For an explanation of the restaurant price codes, see p.138.

SINTRA

COLARES, CABO DA ROCA AND THE COAST

Map p.256.

West of Sintra, beyond the wine-producing village of Colares, a series of small-scale coastal resorts stretches north of Cabo da Roca ("cape of rock"), Europe's most westerly point. The sands make an attractive destination for an afternoon out (or even an overnight stop), but note that all the beaches have dangerous currents. There is public transport to the coast, though if you're planning on seeing more than one or two places in a short time you'll find having your own car useful. Sintra Turismo can provide details about local car rental.

Colares, around 11km northwest of Sintra, is a wealthy village famed for its rich red wine made from vines grown in the local sandy soil – an ancient vine that survived the nineteenth-century infestation that wiped out many other local varieties. The local producer, Adega Regional de Colares (℡ 219 288 082) hosts occasional tastings, concerts and exhibitions. Head uphill (signed "Penedo") for superb views back towards Sintra. Colares is on the Sintra–Cascais bus route #403, with buses leaving from outside the train stations in both towns; it is also on the tram route from Sintra to Praia das Maças (see below).

Cabo da Roca, 14km west of Sintra, is no more than a windswept rocky cape with a lighthouse, though the fact that it's also the most westerly point in Europe brings a steady stream of visitors – there's a tourist office (daily 9am–7pm; ℡ 219 280 892) and a café-restaurant (daily 9.30am–7.30pm) offering superb views; get there early to avoid the coach parties. Bus #403 from Sintra or Cascais train stations (departures roughly every 90min) makes the journey, and the ride out to the cape from Sintra along the EN247 takes about twenty minutes.

The string of small **beach resorts** lying north of the cape is reached on alternative roads from Sintra, or bus #441 from the town (departures every one to two hours). The southernmost beach, **Praia da Adraga** (no public transport; by car, follow the signs from the village of Almoçageme), is an unspoilt, cliff-backed, sandy bay with just one beach restaurant. Beyond here, **Praia Grande** is perhaps the best and safest beach on this strip of coast, with a row of inexpensive cafés and restaurants spreading up towards the cliffs; see p.134 for details of its campsite. Continuing north, the liveliest resort is **Praia das Maçãs**, with another big swath of sand backed by an array of bars and restaurants. The most fun way to get here is by **tram** from Ribeira de Sintra, just west of Estefânia, which calls at Colares on the way (May–Sept Sat & Sun only, departures at 9.30am, 10.30am, 2.30pm, 3.30pm & 6pm; returns at 10.30am, 12.15pm, 3.35pm 5.15pm & 7pm; €1). Finally, **Azenhas do Mar**, a kilometre further up the coast, is a pretty fishing village tumbling down the cliff face. There's only a small beach, but there are sea-pools for swimming in when the sea is too rough.

Accommodation

Hotel Arribus (Map p.256), Praia Grande ⊤ 219 289 050, ⊕ hotel.arribus@mail.telepac.pt. This modern three-star hotel is plonked ungraciously at the north end of the beach, the only building right on the sands. Rooms are enormous and those with a sea view are hard to fault. There are also sea-water swimming pools, a restaurant and café-terrace with more

great views. **6**

Pensão Oceano (Map p.256), Avda Eugénio Levy 52, Praia das Maçãs ⊤ 219 292 490. By far the best guesthouse in Praia das Maçãs, on the main road through the town. Rooms are spacious, the management is welcoming and there is an airy downstairs breakfast room. **4**

Eating and drinking

Colares Velho (Map p.256), Largo Dr. Carlos Franca 1–4, Colares. Tues–Sun 11am–11pm. Expensive.
Delightful restaurant and tea-house on Colares' tiny main square. The traditional Portuguese cuisine is pricey but superbly prepared (in autumn, game is a speciality), or just pop in for tea and cake.

Esplanada do Casino (Map p.256), Esplanada Vasco da Gama, Praia das Maças. Daily 10am–6pm. No credit cards. Inexpensive.
With an outdoor terrace facing the sands, this is the ideal spot for a cool drink, sandwich or ice cream. Daredevil specialities include a *salada de orelha de porco* (pig's ear salad).

O Loureiro (Map p.256), Esplanada Vasco da Gama, Praia das Maças. Mon–Wed & Fri–Sun 11am–3pm & 7–11pm. Moderate.
In a prime location overlooking the beach, this is the best place to try the local fresh fish and seafood; grilled squid is always a good and inexpensive choice.

PALÁCIO DE QUELUZ

Map 1, E5. Mon & Wed–Sun 10am–5pm; €3. Train (every 15min) from Rossio or Sintra to Queluz-Belas.

En route to Sintra (around 25 minutes from Rossio), it's worth a stopover to have a look at the royal **Palácio de Queluz**, an elegant, restrained structure regarded as the country's finest example of Rococo architecture. Its low, pink-washed wings enclose a series of public and private rooms and suites, as well as extensive eighteenth-century formal gardens. Although preserved as a museum, it doesn't quite feel like one, retaining instead a strong sense of its past royal owners. In fact, the palace is still pressed into service

PALÁCIO DE QUELUZ

to accommodate state guests and dignitaries.

To reach the palace, follow the signs from Queluz-Belas train station through the unremarkable town of Queluz until you reach a vast cobbled square, the Largo do Palácio, with the palace walls reaching out around one side – a fifteen-minute walk. The square also holds the local **Turismo** (Mon–Wed & Fri–Sun 10am–12.30pm & 2pm–7pm; ☎ 214 350 039).

You can still eat a meal in the original kitchen, the *Cozinha Velha* (daily 12.30–3pm & 7.30–10pm; ☎ 214 350 232), although the food doesn't always live up to its setting and you're looking at around €25 a head for a full meal. There is, however, a cheaper café in the main body of the palace.

The palace was built by Dom Pedro III, husband and regent to his niece, **Queen Maria I.** Maria lived here throughout her 39-year reign (1777–1816), for the last 27 years of which she was quite mad, following the death of her eldest son, José. William Beckford visited when the Queen's wits were dwindling and ran races in the gardens with the Princess of Brazil's ladies-in-waiting; at other times firework displays were held above the ornamental canal and bullfights in the courtyards.

Visitors first enter the **Throne Room**, which is lined with mirrors surmounted by paintings and golden flourishes. Beyond is the more restrained **Music Chamber** with its portrait of Queen Maria above a French grand piano. Smaller quarters include bed- and sitting rooms, a tiny oratory overwhelmed with red velvet, and the **Sculpture Room**, whose only exhibit is an earthenware bust of Maria. Another wing comprises an elegant suite of **public rooms** – smoking, coffee and dining rooms – all intimate in scale and surprisingly tastefully decorated. The **Ambassador's Chamber** – where diplomats and foreign ministers were received during the nineteenth century – echoes the Throne Room in style, with one side lined with porcelain chinoiserie. In the end, though, perhaps one of the most pleasing rooms is the simple **Dressing Room**, with its geometric inlaid wooden floor and spider's-web ceiling.

Entry to the formal **gardens** is included in the ticket price. Low box hedges and elaborate (if weatherworn) statues spread out from the protection of the palace wings, while small pools and fountains, steps and terracing form a harmonious background to the building. From May to October there's a display of Portuguese horsemanship here every Wednesday at 11am (€1).

Accommodation

Pousada Dona Maria I (Map 1, E5), Largo do Palácio, Palácio de Queluz, Queluz ⓉＴ 214 356 158, ⒻＦ 214 356 189, ⓌＷ www.pousadas.pt. The pink-faced *pousada* (government-run inn), with its distinctive clock tower, gives you the chance to stay in an annexe of one of Lisbon's grandest palaces. It was once used as the palace staff quarters, and they must have lived very comfortably: the rooms are huge and the furnishings are lavish, with ornate drapes and big comfy chairs. Evening meals are served at the Cozinha Velha (see above). ❽

PALÁCIO-CONVENTO DE MAFRA

Map 1, D2. Mon & Wed–Sun 10am–5pm, last entry 4.30pm; €3. Mafrense buses hourly from metro Campo Grande in Lisbon or from Sintra station.

The town of **Mafra** is distinguished – and utterly dominated – by just one building: the vast **Palácio-Convento** built in emulation of Madrid's Escorial by João V, the wealthiest and most extravagant of all Portuguese monarchs. It takes about ninety minutes to reach Mafra by bus from Lisbon, or around 45 minutes from Sintra. **Guided tours** of the complex take around an hour; there are English-language tours daily (except Tuesdays) at 11am and 2.30pm; at other times, the language of the tour depends on the number of people present. If you don't mind a foreign-language commentary, you don't usually have to wait long to be shown around.

Begun in 1717 to honour a vow made on the birth of a royal heir, **Mafra Convent** was initially intended for just thirteen Franciscan friars. But as gold and diamonds poured in from Brazil, João and his German court architect, Frederico Ludovice, amplified their plans to build a massive basilica, two royal wings and monastic quarters for 300 monks and 150 novices. The result, completed in thirteen years, is quite extraordinary and – on its own bizarre terms – extremely impressive.

In style the building is a fusion of Baroque and Italianate Neoclassicism, but it is the sheer magnitude of the edifice that distinguishes it. There are 5200 doorways, 2500 windows and two immense bell towers each containing over fifty bells; in the last stages of construction more than 45,000 labourers were employed, while throughout the years of building there was a daily average of nearly 15,000. An apocryphal story records the astonishment of the Flemish bellmakers at the size of this order: on their querying it, and asking for payment in advance, Dom João retorted by doubling their price and his original requirement.

Parts of the convent are used by the military, but you'll be shown around a sizeable enough portion. The **royal apartments** are a mix of the tedious and the shocking: the latter most obviously in the **Sala dos Troféus**, with its furniture (even chandeliers) constructed of antlers and upholstered in deerskin. Beyond are the **monastic quarters**, including cells, a pharmacy and a curious infirmary with beds positioned so the ailing monks could see Mass performed. The highlight, however, is the magnificent Rococo **library**, containing some 35,000 volumes. The **basilica** itself, which can be seen separately to the main palace, is no less imposing, with the multicoloured marble designs of its floor mirrored in the ceiling decoration.

With your own transport, you can also visit the **Tapada de Mafra**, the palace's extensive walled hunting grounds, with its entrance lying 10km out of Mafra on the Torres Vedras road. The grounds are open daily for guided walking tours (at 10am & 2pm; €4). At weekends, you can also tour the grounds in a toy train (at 10.15am & 3pm; €8.50). Both tours take in a coach museum, the deer park and wilderness areas where wild boars, civet cats and mongooses still roam.

PALÁCIO-CONVENTO DE MAFRA

271

Estoril and Cascais

The most straightforward escape from Lisbon is to the string of beach resorts along the coast west of Belém. From the city centre, the appealing **Linha de Cascais** (Cascais Line) train from Cais do Sodré station wends up the Tejo estuary – at times so close to the water that waves almost break over the tracks – and along the coast past a string of sprawling seaside suburbs, of which **Carcavelos** has most to offer, before ending at the popular resorts of **Estoril** and **Cascais**. Sadly, the water along this stretch has suffered badly from pollution, and though steps are being taken to clean it up, it remains something of a health hazard. Nonetheless, the coast retains its attractions and Cascais, in particular, has a very relaxed atmosphere.

Trains leave every twenty minutes (Mon–Thurs & Sun 5.30am–1.30am, Fri & Sat 5.30am–2.30am) from Cais do Sodré station, taking 35 minutes to reach Estoril and 40 minutes to Cascais.

CARCAVELOS

Map 1, D6.

The first stop of any note along the line is **Carcavelos**, just over half way from Lisbon to Cascais, which has the most extensive sandy beach on this part of the coast. Swimmers chance the waters in high summer, and at other times it's a lively spot for beach soccer, surfing and breezy winter walks. To reach the beach, it's a ten-minute walk from the station along the broad Avenida Jorge V. Try to visit Carcavelos on Thursday morning, when the town hosts a huge **market**; turn right out of the station and follow the signs. Street upon street is taken over by stalls selling cheap clothes (many with brand-name labels), ceramics and general bric-a-brac.

ESTORIL

Map 1, C6.

Estoril gained a postwar reputation as a haunt of exiled royalty and the idle rich, and it continues to maintain its pretensions towards being a "Portuguese Riviera", with grandiose villas, luxury hotels and top-rated golf courses. Its beach is highly appealing but the town itself is something of a disappointment, lacking the character and buzz of neighbouring Cascais. It is at its nicest around the central **Parque do Estoril**, a lovely stretch of fountains and exotic trees, surrounded by bars and restaurants. For a leisurely tour of Estoril, a **toy train** departs from the eastern end of the park (daily every 50min, 11am–12.40pm & 2.20–4pm; free). The town's tourism revolves around Europe's biggest **casino** (3pm–3am; free), sited at the top end of the park, where Ian Fleming gained much of his inspiration for Bond's exploits. This requires some semblance of formal attire to enter; once inside, you have the choice of roulette, cards, slot machines, restaurants, shops, an art gallery, and live shows every night at 11pm.

Estoril's fine sandy **beach** is backed by a seafront promenade that stretches all the way to Cascais. A stroll between the two towns is recommended, drifting from beach to bar; the walk takes around twenty minutes. From July to mid-September, a free **firework display** takes place above Estoril's main beach, the Praia de Tamariz, every Saturday night at midnight.

Estoril's **train station** is next to Avenida Marginal, the coast road which, along with the railway, separates the beach from the town; the two sides are connected by an underpass. Directly opposite the underpass you'll find the very helpful **Turismo** (Mon–Sat 9am–7pm, Sun 10am–6pm; ☎214 663 813; ⓦwww.estorilcoast-tourism. com), which offers free maps, sound advice on the area and help with accommodation.

Accommodation

Estoril Sol Parque Palmela, ☎214 839 000, Ⓕ214 832 280, ⓦwww.hotelestorilsol.pt.

It may not win any beauty prizes from the outside, but this top-of-the-range, old-fashioned high-rise between Cascais and Estoril offers dazzling views over Cascais bay from many of its spacious rooms. Facilities include a restaurant, indoor and outdoor pool and a health club, and there's a tunnel linking the hotel with the beach. It's around ten minutes' walk northwest of the centre of Estoril. ⑧

Pensão-Residencial Smart Rua José Viana 3 ☎214 682 164, Ⓕ214 649 030, Ⓔresidencial.smart@netcabo .pt.
One of the best budget options in Estoril, with pleasant rooms and breakfast included. It's east of the park – turn right out of the station, then left when you reach Avda Bombeiros Voluntários. ④

Eating and drinking

English Bar (Cimas) Avda. Sabóia 9, Monte Estoril ☎214 680 413. Mon–Sat 12.30–4pm & 7.30–11pm. Expensive.

Despite the name, this is actually one of the region's best restaurants. Named for the Englishman who built the mansion in the 1940s, it has been run by the same Hispano-Portuguese family since 1952. The sumptuous wood-panelled decor, sea views and top-quality fish, meat and game have attracted leading politicians, journalists and even Spanish royalty. It is signed just northwest of the train station, around ten minutes from the centre of town.

Frolic Avda Clotilde 2765. Tues–Thurs 8am–midnight, Fri & Sat 9am–2am. Moderate. Restaurant (specializing in grilled meats and seafood), *pastelaria* and pricey club (entrance around the side). The outdoor seats facing the park are good spots for a late-night drink.

Jonas Bar Paredão do Estoril, Monte Estoril. Daily 10am–2am (Sept–May until 6pm). No credit cards. Inexpensive. Right on the seafront between Cascais and Estoril, this is a fun spot day or night, selling cocktails, juices and snacks.

Pintos Arcadas do Parque 18b. Daily 8am–2am. Moderate. Multi-faceted place which quadruples as a restaurant, *marisqueira*, *pastelaria* and pizzeria; the main draw is the outdoor seating facing the park.

CASCAIS

Map 1, B6.

With three fair beaches along its esplanade and a modern marina, **Cascais** is a major resort, positively bursting at the seams in high season, which nowadays lasts from around May to early October. At these times, the commercialism can be trying, though it's not too large or difficult to get around and has a much younger and less exclusive feel than Estoril. Go out of season and the whole place becomes delightful, even retaining a few elements of its previous existence as a fishing village.

Cascais is at the end of the train line from Lisbon. The **train station** (Map p.276, F1) is a short walk north from the town's main street, Rua Frederico Arouca; **buses** to Guincho, Cabo da Roca and Sintra leave from the stands outside the station. It's a five-minute walk down to the **Turismo** (Map p.276, D3; Mon–Sat 9am–7pm, Sun

10am–6pm; ☏ 214 868 204), set in an old mansion on Rua Visconde da Luz, which has maps and information about local events.

Stagecoach day-rover bus passes (€6.23) represent good value if you want to explore the surrounding area. Bus services link Cascais with Sintra (p.248), and with Cabo da Roca and the beaches of the Sintra coast (p.265). Passes are also valid on Stagecoach buses from Cascais to Lisbon airport.

You'll find the main concentration of bars and nightlife on **Rua Frederico Arouca**, the main pedestrian thoroughfare. East of here is Cascais's largest beach, **Praia da Conceição** (Map p.276, G2); the smaller beaches of Praia da Rainha and Praia da Ribeira are in the middle of town. For a wander away from the crowds, stroll up beyond Largo 5 de Outubro (behind the Town Hall) into the old and surprisingly pretty west side of town, which is at its most delightful in the streets around the graceful **Igreja da Assunção** (Map p.276, D5). This is worth a look inside for its azulejos, which predate the earthquake of 1755. Beyond the church, the walls of the largely seventeenth-century fortress now guard the entrance to the **Marina de Cascais** (Map p.276, G7), an enclave of expensive yachts serviced by restaurants, bars and boutiques.

West of the church and fort lies the pleasant **Parque Municipal da Gandarinha** in whose southern reaches stands the mansion of the nineteenth-century Count of Guimarães, preserved complete with its fittings as the **Museu Biblioteca Conde Castro Guimarães** (Map p.276, C7; Tues–Sun 10am–5pm; €1.30); most days, there's someone around to give you a guided tour of the furniture, paintings and antiques that the count bequeathed to the

CASCAIS

nation. On the north side of the park, opposite the Pavilhão de Cascais, signs direct you to the modern **Museu do Mar** (Map p.276, A5; Tues–Sun 10am–5pm; €1.30), an engaging little collection of model boats, sea-related arte-facts, old costumes and pictures.

As well as the **Fish Market** (Map p.276, E3; Mon–Sat 6am–noon) just south of Rua Frederico Arouca, there's a lively **Wednesday market** on Rua do Mercado – head up Alameda C. da Grande Guerra, bear left at the roundabout and it's on the right. You may also want to catch the Sunday evening **bullfights** (held from April to September) in the Praça de Touros, along Avenida Pedro Alvares Cabral, west of the centre.

West from Cascais

Keeping to the coastal road out of town, it's about twenty minutes' walk west to the **Boca do Inferno** – the "Mouth of Hell" – where waves crash against caves in the cliff face. The viewpoints above are always packed with tourists (as is the very tacky market on the roadside), though the whole affair is rather unimpressive except in stormy weather. Boca do Inferno is also served by a **toy train** (every 45min, daily 11.15am–1.30pm & 3–4.30pm; free), which trundles through town from Cascais train station. En route, look out for the little beach of **Praia de Santa Marta** (Map p.276, C8), with a nice café on a terrace above the sands.

There are buses every one or two hours (daily 7.15am–7.15pm) from outside Cascais train station which run the 6km west to **Praia do Guincho**, a great sweeping beach with body-crashing Atlantic rollers. It's a superb place to surf or windsurf – Windsurfing Championships are usu-ally held here in August – but also a dangerous one. The water is clean but the undertow is notoriously strong and people are drowned almost every year. The beach has become increasingly popular in recent times and the coastal approach road is flanked by half a dozen large terrace-restaurants, and a couple of hotels, all with varying views of the breaking rollers and fish-dominated menus. There is also a well-equipped campsite just back from the beach (see p.134).

Accommodation

Adega do Gonçalves (Map p.276, C3), Rua Afonso Sanches 54 ⓣ 214 831 519.

Basic rooms above a reasonable restaurant. The situation is nice and central, though it is guaranteed to be fairly noisy, scuppering hopes of an early night. ❷

Hotel Albatroz (Map p.276, F2), Rua Frederico Arouca 100 ⓣ 214 832 821, ⓕ 214 844 827, ⓦ www.albatrozhotel.pt. Built in the nineteenth century as a royal retreat, seaside hotels don't come much grander than this – one of the best in the region, with glorious views from some rooms (for which you pay extra) and top-of-the-range facilities. There's a lovely swimming pool on the ocean terrace, and a restaurant. Big winter reductions apply, when the price drops a category. ❾

Hotel Baía (Map p.276, E4), Avda C. Grande Guerra ⓣ 214 831 033, ⓕ 214 831 095, ⓦ www.hotelbaia.com. Modern seafront hotel whose front rooms have balconies overlooking the beach and harbour. Rooms are very good value out of season, and not bad in summer; it's worth booking ahead for one with a sea view. ❻

Estalagem O Muchaxo Praia do Guincho ⓣ 214 870 221, ⓕ 214 870 044, ⓔ muchaco@ip.pt. With a stone-flagged bar and picture windows looking across the beach, this old inn has a slightly fading, windswept charm. There's a sea-water pool for when the

CASCAIS

sea's too rough, and an attached restaurant. Rooms without sea views fall into the price category below. ❺

Fortaleza do Guincho Praia do Guincho ⓣ 214 870 491, ⓕ 214 870 431, ⓔ reservations@guinchohotel.pt.

Five-star hotel set in a converted fort overlooking Guincho beach. Guests are welcomed in the central courtyard by knights-in-armour; beyond lie a bar, a renowned French restaurant with a Michelin star and even a ballroom. There are 27 tastefully decorated rooms with sea views and others gathered round the internal courtyard; a limousine service takes guests to and from the airport on request. ❾

Solar Dom Carlos (Map p.276, C4), Rua Latino Coelho 8 ⓣ 214 828 115, ⓕ 214 865 155.

Sixteenth-century mansion on a quiet backstreet in the pretty western side of town. Dom Carlos once stayed here, hence the royal chapel, which still survives. There

are cool tiles throughout, attractive rooms, a garden, and the price includes breakfast. ❹

Villa Cascais (Map p.276, E4), Rua Fernandes Tomás 1. ⓣ 214 863 410, ⓕ 214 844 680, ⓦ www.albatrozhotels.com.

Deluxe five-star hotel set in a superb renovated mansion overlooking the fishing harbour. The villa superbly blends modern touches (such as chrome-and-glass sinks) with traditional decor and, with just ten individually styled rooms, personalised service is guaranteed. Even if you're not staying here, take a drink on the first-floor terrace to sample the atmosphere and view. The price includes breakfast. ❼

Village Cascais (Map p.276, A8), Rua Frie Nicolau de Oliveira. ⓣ 214 826 000, ⓕ 214 837 319, ⓦ www.vilagale.pt.

Occupying a superb position near an unspoilt part of the coast, the Village Cascais is one of the area's more tasteful hotel complexes, set

CASCAIS

●

in palm-studded grounds a short walk from Cascais town centre (head down Avda Rei Humberto II de Itália and it is on the right).

The spacious rooms have satellite TV and kitchenettes – so they're good for families – and there's also a bar and restaurant. ➏

For an explanation of the accommodation and restaurant price codes, see p.118 and p.138 respectively.

Eating

Adega do Gonçalves (Map p.276, C3), Rua Afonso Sanches 54. Daily noon–11pm. Inexpensive.
Traditional *adega* (wine cellar) not yet overwhelmed by tourists, serving huge portions of good food. The locally caught grilled fish is always a good bet.

Bangkok (Map p.276, C1), Rua Bela Vista 6. ☎ 214 847 600. Daily 1–2.30pm & 7.30–10.30pm. Expensive. Sublime Thai cooking in a traditional Cascais town house, beautifully decorated with inlaid wood and Oriental furnishings. This place attracts media stars and politicians so it's best to reserve in advance. The ground floor is divided into individual rooms, and there's a small back patio; the upstairs area is better for larger groups. Highlights include lobster in curry paste and the assorted Thai snacks; expect to pay upwards of €30 a head.

Casa de Pasto 011 (Map p.276, C3), Trav dos Navegantes 11. Mon–Sat 7am–midnight. No credit cards. Inexpensive.
With just half a dozen tables, this local grill-house gets packed thanks to its bargain-value house wine and very tasty fish and meat dishes. Service is slow, so sit back

CASCAIS

and enjoy.

Dom Manolo's (Map p.276, D3), Avda Com. Grande Guerra 11. Daily 10am–midnight. Inexpensive.
Busy grill-house just down from the *Turismo*, where the alley runs through to Largo Luís de Camões. Superb chicken and chips; add a salad, local wine and home-made dessert and you'll pay around €10.

Esplanada Santa Marta (Map p.276, C8), Praia de Santa Marta. Mon–Sat 7am–2am, Sun 7am–10pm. No credit cards. Moderate.
One of the best places to enjoy charcoal-grilled fish, which is served on a tiny terrace overlooking the sea and the little beach. The café is on the road out to the Boca do Inferno.

Jardim dos Frangos (Map p.276, D3), Avda Com. Grande Guerra 66. Daily 10am–midnight. Inexpensive.
Permanently buzzing with people and sizzling with the speciality, grilled chicken, which is devoured by the

plateful at indoor and outdoor tables.

Mar e Mar (Map p.276, G2), Praia da Conceição. Daily 8am–2am (weather permitting; closed in bad weather). Moderate.
Little more than a kiosk on the seafront promenade, but nevertheless it turns out surprisingly good and reasonably priced seafood, including squid kebabs. Outdoor tables overlook the attractive beach.

O Marégrafo (Map p.276, F5), Passeio Dona Maria Pia ⓣ214 842 104. Mon & Wed–Sun 12.30–3pm & 7.30–11pm. Expensive.
Enjoys a fantastic position below the fort, with a terrace overlooking the town, harbour and marina. Superb grilled tiger prawns and mixed seafood kebabs cost an arm and leg, though meat dishes are more affordable. Reservations are advised.

O Muchaxo Praia do Guincho ⓣ214 870 221. Daily noon–3.30pm & 7.30–10.30pm. Expensive.

CASCAIS

This restaurant, overlooking the crashing waves, is rated one of the best in the Lisbon area. A meal will set you back around €25 a head, but that's not bad value for some delicious Portuguese fish and meat delicacies. Tables at lunch are usually easy to come by, though you might want to book for dinner.

O Pescador (Map p.276, F3), Rua das Flores 10 ⊤214 832 054. Mon–Sat 12.30–3pm & 7.30–11pm. Expensive.

One of several places close to the fish market, this one offers superior fish meals. Good food, smart decor and efficient service; bookings advised for dinner.

Bars and clubs

Chequers (Map p.276, D3), Largo Luís de Camões 7. Daily 10.30am–2am.

Not quite as "legendary" as it would have you believe, but it's a lively enough English-style pub, especially once the pumping rock music strengthens its grip.

Coconuts (Map p.276, A8), Avda Rei Humberto II de Itália 7. Daily 11pm–4am; closed Sun in winter.

A club about 1km along the road to Boca do Inferno, which attracts an odd mix of trendy locals and raving tourists. There's a sea-facing terrace, karaoke bar and theme nights (from foam parties to "ladies" night). Guest DJs appear on Thursdays.

John Bull (Map p.276, D3), Praça Costa Pinto 31. Daily 10am–2am.

Backing onto Cascais's most attractive square – an extension of Largo Luís de Camões – this is an English-style pub that fills up early with a good-time crowd; it serves meals, too, at tables outside in the square during the day.

Music Bar (Map p.276, F3), Largo da Praia da Rainha. Tues–Sun 10am–10pm.

One of the few café-bars in Cascais with decent sea

CASCAIS

views. It's a fine spot to have a sunset beer, while the outside tables on the patio above the beach are packed throughout the day with tourists drinking coffees and rehydrating with an *água com gás* (fizzy water).

News Estrada da Malveira da Serra. Daily 11pm–4am.

Happening club with a terrace and a lively night guaranteed, Fridays especially, when there are live shows. It's around 4km north of Cascais, on the road to Malveira; take Avda 25 de Abril past the Wednesday market and head right along Avda Eng. Adelino Amaro da Costa.

South of the Tejo

s late as the nineteenth century, the **southern bank of the Tejo estuary** was an underpopulated area used as a quarantine station for foreign visitors; the village of Trafaria was so lawless that police only patrolled the area when accompanied by members of the army. The development of Lisbon's port and its related industries in the twentieth century gave this side of the river a more industrial hue, but it was not until the huge **Ponte 25 de Abril** suspension bridge – inaugurated as the "Salazar Bridge" in 1966 and renamed after the 1974 revolution – that the separation between town and country was finally ended.

Since then, over a million people have settled over the river in a string of grim and largely industrial suburbs that spread east of the bridge, in and around the district of Almada. Almada's port area, **Cacilhas**, a ferry ride south of Lisbon, makes a pleasant excursion, with its excellent seafood restaurants and views back over the estuary. East of here, **Caparica** was once a remote fishing village, but its fine expanse of Atlantic beach has led to its transformation into a high-rise resort, and made it Lisbon's favourite seaside escape. Further south, along the **Costa da Caparica**, there are more fine beaches – like those at **Lagoa de Albufeira** and **Aldeia do Meco** – before the coast ends at the wild headland of **Cabo Espichel**. East of here lie the

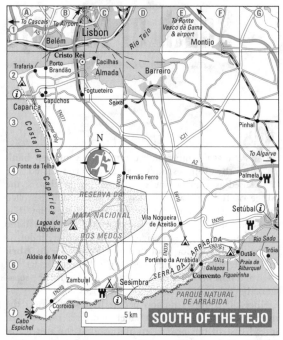

SOUTH OF THE TEJO

0   5 km

calmer waters of the Baia de Setúbal, whose one main resort is the lively fishing town of **Sesimbra**. Continuing east, between here and the city of Setúbal, lies the **Parque Natural da Arrábida**, a craggy mountain range fronted by some superb, calm-watered beaches.

CACILHAS

Map p.286. Cacilhas is a short ferry ride from Estação Fluvial by

CACILHAS

Praça do Comércio (every 10min, Mon–Fri 6.10am–9.45pm, Sat &
Sun 6.15am–9.50pm; last return 9.30pm; or take the car and passenger ferry from Cais do Sodré (every 10min, 5.30am–2.30am).

Despite the bridge, **Cacilhas** remains dependent mainly on
the little orange ferries that connect it to the capital. The
blustery ride is great fun – especially on the car-ferries,
which are more open to the elements – and grants wonderful views of the city, as well as of the enormous Ponte 25 de
Abril. From the ferry terminal in Cacilhas, head west
towards the bridge along the waterfront, past *O Ponto Final*
restaurant, and it's around fifteen minutes' walk to the
Elevador Panorâmico da Boca do Vento (daily
8am–11.45pm; €1 return), a sleek lift which whisks you up
the cliff face to the old part of Almada. If the lift is in the
wrong place when you arrive, the guard will blow his whis-
tle to alert the operator at the other end. From the top there
are fantastic views over the river and right over the city.

On the heights above Almada stands the **Cristo Rei**
(June–Sept daily 9am–7.30pm; Oct–May daily 9am–6pm;
€1.50), a relatively modest version of Rio de Janeiro's
Christ statue, built in 1959. It's best reached by bus #101
from outside the Cacilhas ferry terminal. A lift at the statue
shuttles you 80m up to a dramatic viewing platform, from
where, on a clear day at least, you can catch a glimpse of
the glistening roof of the Pena palace at Sintra. Back on
ground level, there's a **visitor centre,** which hosts occasional exhibitions and has a handy bar.

Eating

Atira-te ao Rio Cais do Ginjal
69–70. Tues–Fri 8pm–midnight,
Sat & Sun 1–4pm & 8pm–midnight. Expensive.

Considering how many of
Lisbon's warehouses have
been turned into bars and
restaurants, it's surprising

CACILHAS

that this is one of only two restaurants in similar conversions south of the Tejo. Superior Brazilian dishes are offered and on Saturday there is a *feijoada* (bean stew) buffet lunch. To reach the restaurant, turn right from the ferry and keep walking along the quay for ten minutes. There are a few outdoor tables, too.

Cervejaria Farol Alfredo Dinis Alex 1–3. Mon, Tues & Thurs–Sun 9am–midnight. Moderate.

The most high-profile beer hall and seafood restaurant in Cacilhas, with some of the best views across the Tejo to match. If you feel extravagant, it's hard to beat the lobsters. Azulejos on the wall show the old *farol* (lighthouse) that once stood here – the restaurant is located along the quayside, on the right as you leave the ferry.

Escondidinho de Cacilhas Alfredo Dinis Alex. Mon–Wed & Fri–Sun 9am–midnight. No credit cards. Inexpensive.

The specialities are, of course, fish and seafood though does meat is also on the menu. You don't get a river view, but this is a genuine, cosy port restaurant visited mainly by locals. It's on the right of the square as you leave the ferry.

O Ponto Final Rua do Ginjal 72. Mon & Wed–Sun 12.30-11pm. Moderate.

Near the foot of the lift to Almada, this moderately priced restaurant has a menu packed with well-cooked Portuguese dishes; try the *carapauzinhas* (little mackerel) with tomato rice. If you want to sit outside while eating and enjoying the views, this is the place to come.

CACILHAS

For an explanation of the restaurant price categories, see "Eating" p.138.

CAPARICA

Map p.286. Regular express or slower local buses from Cacilhas (every 15–30min, daily 7am–9pm), or from Lisbon's Praça de Espanha (every 30min, daily 7am–12.45am). It's 30min from Cacilhas, around 40min from Praça de Espanha. Regular buses also link Caparica with Trafaria, which has ferry connections to Belém.

Lisbon's main seaside resort, **Caparica** is high-rise, tacky and packed at weekends in summer, but don't let that put you off. Its family atmosphere, restaurants and beachside cafés full of tanned surfers make it a thoroughly enjoyable day out, while on the southern edges of town there's still a minor fishing industry, with tractors hauling in drift-nets once a day.

During the summer (roughly May to early October), **buses** stop at the bus park near the beginning of the sands. In winter – when the beaches are dotted with fishermen casting into the exhilarating surf – buses use the station in Praça Padre Manuel Bernardes, in which case it's best to get off at the first stop in Caparica, on the edge of the leafy Praça da Liberdade, five minutes from the beach. If you arrive here, walk diagonally across the square, turn right and at Avenida da Liberdade 18 you'll find the **Turismo** (Mon–Fri 9am–1pm & 2–5.30pm, Sat 9am–1pm; ☎212 900 071), which can supply information about local accommodation. The campsite is reviewed on p.135. Be warned that there's little space available in July and August; it's best to book ahead. Day-trippers should note that the last bus back to Lisbon departs at around 9pm.

From Praça da Liberdade the pedestrianized Rua dos Pescadores – lined with cafés, restaurants and inexpensive guesthouses – heads down to the seafront. Caparica's **beach** is a huge sandy expanse freshened by Atlantic breakers. From the beach in front of Rua dos Pescadores, a narrow-gauge **mini-railway** (June–Sept daily departures, every

CAPARICA

20min, 9am–7.30pm) runs south along 8km or so of dunes to **Fonte da Telha**, a scattered resort of beach huts, cafés and restaurants. Buy your ticket at the kiosk by the terminal (€3.40 return to Fonte da Telha; tickets bought on board cost a few cents more) and ring the bell to jump off at any one of the twenty stops en route. Earlier stops tend to be family-oriented, while later ones are, on the whole, younger, with nudity (though officially illegal) more or less obligatory. This is especially true around stops 18 and 19, a predominately gay area. If you're after solitude you'll need to ride to Fonte da Telha and walk south, though always take care while swimming, especially in unsupervised areas. Fonte da Telha also has bus links with Cacilhas; the circuitous and infrequent service leaves from the top of the hill roughly every one or two hours.

Accommodation

Residencial Capa-Rica Rua dos Pescadores 9 ⓣ 212 900 242, ⓕ 213 541 427, ⓔ benvindo.tours@mail.telepac.pt.

Clean, bright rooms just off the main drag – some face the beach. There's also a garage for drivers and a sunny breakfast room. Breakfast is included in the price. ❸

Hotel Costa da Caparica Avda Gen. Delgado 47 ⓣ 212 918 900, ⓕ 212 910 687, ⓦ www.hotelcostacaparica.pt.

Large, modern seafront hotel with its own restaurant and pool. It's not cheap, but with over 350 rooms it usually has space. Some rooms have sea-facing balconies, though the price rises a category for these (and you'll want to book in advance to make sure you get one in high season). There's also a restaurant, bar, disco and disabled access. ❻

Pensão Real Rua Mestre Manuel 18 ⓣ 212 918 870, ⓕ 212 918 879.

Friendly and reasonable central *pensão*, a few minutes' walk from the beach, just off Rua dos Pescadores. Small but pleasant rooms come with TV and bath and some have balconies and distant sea views. The price includes breakfast. ❹

For an explanation of the price codes used in this chapter, see "Accommodation" p.118 and "Eating" p.138.

Eating and drinking

O Barbas Praia da Costa. Mon & Thurs–Sun noon–2am, Tues noon–3am. Moderate.
With window seats looking out over the sands, *O Barbas* (The Beard) is an atmospheric beach restaurant with fish to die for. You'll probably see the owner – he's the one with the huge amounts of facial hair. From Rua das Pescadores, head north up the esplanade; the restaurant is on your right.

Novo Sabor Rua dos Pescadores 15. Daily 8.30am–midnight. Inexpensive.
Lively café with a good range of fruity *batidas* (milk shakes), toasted sandwiches and ice creams, with outdoor tables to watch the world go by.

Primoroso Praia da Costa. Mon–Wed & Fri–Sun 10am–11pm. Moderate.
Continuing north past *O Barbas* along the seafront esplanade, *Primoroso* sits on the right. Plenty of freshly caught fish to choose from, but if in doubt, try the *cataplana* (fish or shellfish stew). The outdoor tables facing the beach are the perfect spot from which to watch the sun go down.

Tarquinho Bar Praia da Costa. Mon–Thurs & Sun 10am–7pm, Fri & Sat 10am–midnight. Inexpensive.
Popular surfers' hangout

CAPARICA

right on the seafront promenade, with cocktails, sangria and snacks served at wooden outdoor tables shaded by straw-mat roofs.

Bar Terminal Fonte da Telha. Tues–Sun 10am–10pm (weekends only in winter).

Inexpensive.

Doubling as the terminal for the mini-railway, this is an idyllic little bar-restaurant on a wooden platform raised above the beach. Just right for a beer, but also serves snacks and the ubiquitous grilled sardine.

COSTA DA CAPARICA AND CABO ESPICHEL

Map p.286.

South of Fonte da Telha the **Costa da Caparica** stretches for another 18km, as far as Cabo Espichel, the distant southwestern cape. The southern reaches of the coastline are protected by the **Reserva da Mata Nacional dos Medos**, a delightful area of fragrant pinewoods and agricultural smallholdings. Accommodation along the coast is limited to three good campsites (reviewed on pp.134–135), while public transport here is virtually non-existent, but with a car you can reach the reserve by following the busy EN378 (signposted to Sesimbra) off the main A2 highway. Around 10km down the EN378, a small side road takes you on a delightful drive to the **Lagoa de Albufeira**, a lagoon filled in summer with swimmers and windsurfers and at other times frequented by fishermen. It's a lovely spot, home to mallards, shovellers and woodcocks, and there's a superb neighbouring beach pummelled by surf. Just back from the beach, overlooking the lagoon, *O Lagoeiro* (Tues–Sun noon–3pm & 7–10pm) is the best place for grills, drinks or snacks.

Around 4km further south is the village of **Aldeia do Meco,** an attractive place that is being swamped by a fair bit of development. Its low cliff-backed beach, **Praia do Meco**, is popular with nudists. Like the other beaches on this coast, it is prone to overcrowding in July and August, but can be almost deserted out of season; in winter the crashing surf is a tremendous sight, though take care when swimming as the currents can be lethal. The village has several averagely priced café-restaurants, and there's a seasonal café on the beach.

From Aldeia do Meco, it is around 6km southwest to **Cabo Espichel**, an end-of-the-world plateau where the road stops at a wide church square resembling a scene from a Spaghetti Western. This is enclosed on three sides by ramshackle, arcaded eighteenth-century pilgrimage lodgings, whose desolate air have made them a popular location for film directors. Beyond, wild and windswept cliffs drop almost vertically several hundred feet into the Atlantic; dinosaur footprints have been found on the nearby **Praia dos Lagosteiros**. Twice a day (both departures in the afternoon, making a brief day-trip feasible), buses make the eleven-kilometre journey west to the cape from Sesimbra (see below).

SESIMBRA

Map p.286. Frequent buses from Lisbon's Praça de Espanha (8am–7.30pm). Coming from Lisbon in summer, it's usually much quicker to take the ferry across to Cacilhas and pick up a bus there (every 30min, 7am–midnight), as the main bridge road is often jammed solid with traffic.

If you get up early enough in **Sesimbra**, you'll still see fishermen mending their nets on the beach, but that's about the extent of the surviving fishing tradition. Instead, the town is largely a holiday destination for Lisboetas, and apartment buildings and hotels have mushroomed in the bare hills beyond the steep, narrow streets of the old centre. Nonetheless, it's still an admirable spot, with excellent swimming from the long beach and an endless row of café-restaurants, each with an outdoor charcoal-grill wafting fine smells across the town.

The **bus station**, halfway up Avenida da Liberdade, is a five-minute walk from the seafront. Walk down to the water, turn right, and the **Turismo** (June–Sept daily 9am–8pm; Oct–May daily 9am–12.30pm & 2–5.30pm; ☎212 288 540) is underneath the terrace, a step back from the seafront Avenida dos Náufragos. Accommodation can be hard to come by in high season, with just a dozen or so *pensões* and pricey hotels in town. If you haven't booked in advance, your best bet is to try for private rooms through the *Turismo*. At night, families crowd the line of restaurants east of the fort, along Avenida 25 de Abril, and round the little Largo dos Bombaldes. Cheaper places abound in the back streets on either side of the central spine, Avenida da Nova Fortaleza.

At the time of the Discoveries Sesimbra was an important port and the waterfront **Fortaleza de Santiago**, built in the seventeenth century, later formed a vital link in Portugal's coastal defence. The **Museu Municipal** (Mon–Fri 10am–12.30pm & 2–5.30pm; free), just off Avenida da Liberdade (take the steps by *Restaurante Xurrex*), features archeological and historical finds from the area, while the best of the churches, the Manueline **Igreja da Mai**, is on nearby Rua João de Deus. The original fishing port, **Porto de Abrigo**, is a pleasant walk along Avenida dos Náufragos. There are daily fish auctions here, shellfish stalls, and a variety of **boat trips** departing most days during the summer. The Clube Naval (☎212 233 451, Ⓦwww.naval-sesimbra.pt) offers cruises on a traditional sailing boat, the *Santiago*; in high season there are usually two departures a day (at 10am & 1pm; from €40 per person). From May to September, *Aquarama* (☎965 263 157) operates daily "floating submarine" trips in a boat with a glass bottom, either up to Cabo Espichel or on evening cruises. Tickets cost €15 and can be bought on the boat or from the kiosk on Avenida dos Náufragos.

For panoramas over the surrounding countryside and coastline make the short drive (or a stiff half-hour climb from the centre) to the battlemented **Moorish castle** (Sun–Thurs 7am–7pm, Fri & Sat 7am–8pm; free), which sits on the heights above town. Within the walls are a pretty eighteenth-century church, café and cemetery.

Sesimbra's main festival, Festa de Senhor Jesus das Chagas in late April /early May, consists of one of Portugal's largest religious processions, followed by a lively street party.

Accommodation

Residencial Chic Trav. Xavier da Silva 2–6 ☎212 233 110. Central choice just back from the sea, on the corner with Rua Candido dos Reis. It has bright rooms, some with restricted sea views. The price includes breakfast. ❸

Residencial Náutico Bairro Infante D. Henrique 3 ☎212 233 233.
A good budget choice, though it's a steeply ten-minute walk uphill from the centre. Rooms are comfortable and it's a little

quieter than the more central options. The price includes breakfast. ❸

Sana Park Avda 25 de Abril, ☎212 289 000, ☏212 289 001, ⓦwww.sanahotels.com. The best upmarket choice, right on the seafront. The plush rooms have TVs and baths, and there's a sauna and pool (open to non-guests), a restaurant and groovy rooftop bar. Prices are a category higher with sea views. ❻

SESIMBRA

For an explanation of the price codes used in this chapter, see "Accommodation" p.118 and "Eating" p.138.

Eating

Marisqueira Filipe Avda 25 de Abril. Mon, Tues & Thurs–Sun 11am–3pm & 7.30–11pm. Expensive.

Extremely popular seafood restaurant, and one of the more expensive places in town – €20 and upwards – but it serves great grilled fish, a bumper *arroz de marisco* (seafood rice) and some decent wines.

Nova Fortaleza Largo dos Bombaldes. Mon & Wed–Sun noon–3.30pm & 7.30–11pm. Moderate.
On the edge of the square, facing the beach, with a great terrace, serving well-priced fish and good salads.

A Sesimbrense Rua Jorge Nunes 17–19. Mon & Wed–Sun 12.30–3pm & 7.30–11pm. Inexpensive.
Bustling local joint just back from Largo dos Bombaldes (keep going past the *Toni Bar*), serving no-nonsense soups, fish and grills with a TV for company.

A Tasca de Ratinho Rua Plinio Mesquita 17. Mon–Wed & Fri–Sun noon–3.30pm & 7.30–11pm. Moderate.
Tucked up a side street behind Largo dos Bombaldes, this cosy place specializes in swordfish cooked in cream and port, and has a terrace overlooking the sea.

Toni Bar Largo dos Bombaldes ☎ 212 233 199.
Daily noon–2am. Expensive.
For a quality fish or shellfish meal, the *Toni Bar* at the back of the square is hard to beat. Reservations are advised in high season.

Bars and clubs

Bolina Rua Prof. Fernandes Marques 13. June–Sept Tues–Sun midnight–4am, Oct–May Fri & Sat midnight–4am.
The best club in Sesimbra, attracting a happy dancing crowd, though outside the

summer months it can be pretty quiet. If you don't like it, *Central*, next door at no. 11, is the other club with a summer reputation.

Bote Douro Avda dos Náufragos 10. Mon & Wed–Sun noon–midnight.
Laid-back bar facing the waves where you can chill out over a beer.

A Galé Rua Capitão Leitão 5. Daily 7am–midnight.

On a raised terrace overlooking the sea, next to the Safari surf shop, this popular no-frills café-bar attracts students and youthful Lisboetas. The house wine is extremely rough.

Mareante Avda dos Náufragos 13. Daily 10am–2am.
Sleek place that's a café-bar by day, and a booming music bar after dark, with occasional live music.

PARQUE NATURAL DA ARRÁBIDA

Map p.286.

With your own transport, it is an easy drive to the **Parque Natural da Arrábida**, around 12km east of Sesimbra along the EN379-1. Considering it is only an hour or so south of the capital (take the EN10 off the A2 from Lisbon, signed Vila Nogueira de Azeitão), the park is surprisingly wild and unspoilt, with a coastline sheltering some of Portugal's calmest sandy bays. The beautiful park spreads across a 500-metre-high granite ridge known as the Serra da Arrábida, visible for miles around and home to wildcats, badgers, polecats, buzzards and Bonelli eagles. The most dramatic sections of the park are crossed by two roads, the twisting N379–1, which winds across its upper stretches, and the EN10-4 coastal road. Apart from the views, the main highlight of the upper road is the **Convento da Arrábida** (Map p.286; Wed–Sun 3–4pm; €3; to visit at other times, call ☎212 180 520), a convent made up of dazzling white buildings that tumble down a steep hillside, offering stunning ocean views. The convent was built by Franciscan monks in the sixteenth century and is only open for limited hours, but it's an impressive sight even from the outside.

The EN10 winds down to the coast, around 3km west of the convent, to the tiny harbour village of **Portinho da Arrábida** (Map p.286), which has one the region's best beaches – wonderful out of season, when it is often deserted. The harbour is guarded by a tiny seventeenth-century fort, now housing the **Museu Oceanográfico** (Tues–Fri 10am–4pm, Sat & Sun 3–6pm; €1.75), displaying marine animals from the region either live – in a small aquarium – or stuffed. If you hold a diving certificate, you can see some of the fish for real by renting equipment from the **diving school** on the beach, the Centro de Mergulho (☎212 183 197, ℻212 183 656); this also lets out a couple of spacious double rooms or a self-catering apartment sleeping up to five. At weekends, day-trippers head for the *Restaurant Beira Mar* (closed Wed & Sept–March) on the seafront, which serves a good range of moderately priced fish and seafood. *Galeão*, next door (open daily) has a similar menu and a fine outdoor terrace.

DOLPHIN WATCHING

The Sado estuary and the coast off Arrábida is one of the best places in Portugal to see bottle-nosed dolphins. Vertigem Azul (☎265 238 000; ℮vertigemazul@mail.telepac.pt) organizes year-round dolphin-watching trips (Oct–April daily 9.30am & 3pm, dependent on the weather; minimum six people required; €28) with the chance to go snorkelling too. It also organizes all-day jeep safaris, including the dolphin trip, a tour of Arrábida and a visit to the Convento da Arrábida (minimum five people required; €58). Departures are from the harbour at Setúbal, a port town just east of the Parque Natural and 28km east of Sesimbra.

José Maria da Fonseca wine vaults and museum

Map p.286. Hourly buses from Lisbon's Praça de Espanha (8am–7.30pm; 45min). Mon–Fri 9am–noon & 2.15–4.15pm; Sat 10am–12.15pm & 2.15–4.30pm; €2, though €3 on Sat; advance bookings essential ⓣ 212 198 940.

On the northern borders of the Parque Natural da Arrábida, 12km northeast of Sesimbra, the big highlight in the otherwise dull town of Vila Nogueira de Azeitão is the **José Maria da Fonseca wine vaults and museum** on the main Rua José Augusto Coelho. Tours, which last 45 minutes, take in the vaults, lined with a superb series of azulejos – some dating back to the fifteenth century – and include a free tasting, providing an interesting introduction to the local wine, a Setúbal Moscatel.

PARQUE NATURAL DA ARRÁBIDA

CONTEXTS

History	303
Books	316
Language	324

History

Beginnings

The tourist board likes to promote the romantic idea that Lisbon was founded by Ulysses, though there's little evidence to support either this claim or the theory that the word "Lisboa" is a corruption of his name. It is far more likely that the true founders of the city were the **Phoenicians**, who called the place Allis Ubbo – "calm harbour" – which later became Olisipo. They established an outpost here around 900 BC and were subsequently succeeded by the Greeks and then the Carthaginians, though neither had much effect on the development of the city.

The city's prosperity grew with the **Romans**, who entered the Iberian peninsula in around 210 BC; Olisipo (Lisbon) became administrative capital of Lusitania, the western part of Iberia, under Julius Caesar in 60 BC. The city's wealth was increased by its fish-preserving industries – fittingly enough, in a city whose favourite dish remains dried cod – and the remains of a Roman fish-preserving factory can still be seen in the Baixa (see p.33). Other remains include the scant ruins of a Roman theatre near Rua Augusto Rosa (see p.48), just above Alfama; there was probably also a Roman fort on the site of today's castle.

Christianity reached Portugal at the end of the first century AD, and within two hundred years there was a bishopric in Lisbon. As the Roman Empire declined, a wave of barbarian invaders moved in. First came the Suevi, followed by the Visigoths, though neither made any sort of lasting impact on Lisbon. At the end of the seventh century, one quarrelling faction of Visigoths appealed for aid from Muslim North Africa, and in 711 a force of Moors crossed over to Spain and swept up into Portugal, establishing a new, Moorish kingdom.

Moorish rule

The Moors proved to be tolerant and productive rulers. **Moorish** Lishbuna thrived on its wide links with the Arab world, Roman irrigation techniques were improved and crop-rotation was introduced, exploiting the rich territories of the south. Urban life prospered too, and Lisbon became a major town. The Alcáçova – a Muslim palace – was constructed on the site of today's castle. The Moors named the grandest part of their settlement *alhama* (hot springs) because of the waters that rose to the surface there; over the years, the name changed to Alfama.

Moorish advances were halted in the north and, in the eleventh century, a tiny Roman Catholic kingdom called Portucale was established between the Douro and Minho rivers under Afonso VI. In 1086, pressure exerted by a new wave of Muslim invaders from North Africa forced Afonso to turn to European Crusaders for assistance. His successor, Afonso Henriques, extended his kingdom southwards, and by 1147 had pushed the Moors back almost as far as Lisbon. In the same year, the king persuaded other European Crusaders to help him in the **siege of Lisbon** (see p.51). With the promise of land rights and material goods as a reward, the Crusaders murderously sacked the city. Those

Moors that survived were forced out of Alfama to live in the quarter still known as Mouraria, and Alfama was given over to Christian fishermen and artisans.

The one positive outcome of the siege was the establishment of **Afonso Henriques** as the first monarch of modern Portugal. In 1150, Lisbon's cathedral, the Sé, was founded to commemorate the reconquest of the city. It was not until 1260, however – with the Moors finally expelled from the south and the frontiers of today's Portugal almost in place – that the more centrally located city of Lisbon took over from Coimbra as capital.

The discoveries

In 1290, Lisbon University was founded by the far-sighted king, Dom Dinis (1279–1325), who also set about strengthening the new country's frontiers – in 1297 these were acknowledged by Spain in the Treaty of Alcañices. Castile, however, still had its eyes on the Portuguese throne, which it looked to acquire by a series of royal marriages between the two countries. War followed when the future Portuguese king, João I, backed by Portuguese commoners and English archers, led a famous victory over the Spaniards at Aljubarrota in 1385. To give thanks for a victory that sealed Portugal's independence, the victors set about building Batalha Abbey and the Carmelite Convento do Carmo in Lisbon, which was completed in 1389.

It was only after peace was fully restored in 1411 that the king, Dom João I could turn his resources towards Morocco in expeditions that were part crusade and part strategic strike against the Moors. The third son of João I, **Prince Henry the Navigator**, founded a School of Navigation in the Algarve, which initiated Portugal's great seafaring traditions and led to the exploration of Madeira, the Azores and the west coast of Africa between 1419 and 1460.

CONTEXTS

Over the following centuries, Lisbon was twice at the forefront of European development. The first phase came with the great Portuguese **discoveries** of the late fifteenth and sixteenth centuries. In 1498, Vasco da Gama opened the sea route to India and the Portuguese monarchy, already doing well out of African gold, now became the richest in Europe as a result of taxes levied on the Indian trade. In 1494, the Treaty of Tordesillas saw Portugal and Spain divide up the world between them. As they were discovered, more areas fell under Portuguese control, including Brazil (1500), Goa (1510) and Macau (1557).

The reign of Manuel I (1495–1521) marked the apogee of Portuguese wealth and strength. In 1511, he moved into the Terreiro do Paço, a grand palace on Praça do Comércio, later destroyed in the Great Earthquake. His reign found its expression in the extraordinary **Manueline** style of architecture, an elaborately decorative genre inspired by marine motifs (see p.79), as can be seen on the Tower of Belém and the royal palace at Sintra.

Spanish domination

Despite this enormous wealth there was no entrepreneurial class in Lisbon, the development of a middle class having been stifled by the aristocracy's dominance of commerce. Banking and commerce was also left in the hands of the **Jews**, who were banned from taking up most other professions. Though the citizens of Lisbon marvelled at the exotic wares brought back from abroad (such as the elephant which was paraded around the waterfront), few of them could afford to buy any of these goods, most of which were exported to northern Europe.

Popular resentment of Jewish prosperity and pressure from Spain persuaded Manuel I to expel the entire Jewish population from the city in 1496. His successor, João III (1521–57) established the Inquisition in 1536, setting up an Inquisitional Palace in Rossio and victimizing those converted Jews known as New Christians, many of whom were killed in *autos-da-fé* (public executions by burning). Inquisitions were to continue until the social reforms instigated by the Marquês de Pombal in the eighteenth century. Without Jewish professionals, Portugal found itself with an empire based on commerce but deprived of its commercial expertise. By the 1570s, with the economy close to collapse, the country became vulnerable to Spain once more. After the death of Dom Sebastião in 1578 the next king, Cardinal Henrique, ruled without an heir. When he died in 1580, Sebastião's uncle, the Habsburg Philip II of Spain – Felipe I of Portugal – defeated rival claims to the throne and, in 1581, began a period of **Spanish rule** which was to last for sixty years.

In fact, Felipe I allowed Portugal to continue with a large degree of autonomy, whilst attempting to help develop the city, even bringing over his favourite architect, Juan de Herrera, to begin the construction of São Vicente de Fora. Resentment of Spain came about because of its foreign policy. Part of the Armada was prepared in Lisbon, provoking the enmity of the Dutch and British, old allies of Portugal who were never to be as supportive again. By the time Felipe III tried to conscript Portuguese troops to quell a rising in Catalonia, Portuguese resentment had reached boiling point. In 1640, a group of conspirators stormed the palace in Lisbon and the **Duke of Bragança** took the throne as João IV. Spain, preoccupied with events elsewhere, accepted the situation formally under the Treaty of Lisbon in 1668.

The second golden age and the Great Earthquake

The opening decades of the eighteenth century witnessed Portugal's second period of splendour, when a colonized

Brazil began to yield both gold and diamonds. This new golden age, though more extravagant than the first, had a less brilliant effect. Dom João V (1706–50) virtually bankrupted the state with the construction of the extravagant **Palácio-Convento de Mafra**, created to rival El Escorial in Spain. He also commissioned the phenomenally expensive Capela de São João Baptista in the Igreja de São Roque (see p.60) and the hugely ambitious – albeit more useful – Aqueduto das Águas Livres, which brought supplies of fresh water to the whole of Lisbon for the first time. The **Methuen Treaty** of 1703 established a military and trading alliance between Britain and Portugal. For the Portuguese, it meant the reassuring protection of the British against the threatening powers of Spain and France, as well as a guaranteed export market for its wines. The downside was that it helped destroy the native textile industry by letting in British cloth at preferential rates. João V's apathetic successor José I (1750–77) left almost complete power in the hands of his minister, the **Marquês de Pombal**. The **Great Earthquake** (see p.30) struck Lisbon on November 1, 1755, killing around 40,000 of the city's 270,000 inhabitants. For Portugal, and for the capital, it was a disaster that in retrospect seems to seal an age, marking the end of Lisbon's role as the most active port in Europe.

Pombal immediately started rebuilding the city to his own designs; the grid-pattern of the Baixa was quickly laid out and a new palace was built around Praça do Comércio. Pombal also set about modernizing post-earthquake Lisbon's institutions, establishing an efficient and secular bureaucracy, renewing the system of taxation, setting up export companies, outlawing slavery and abolishing the Jesuit order, which had long dominated education and religious life in Portugal.

The nineteenth century

Already diminished following the devastating earthquake, Lisbon's trade routes were further threatened by **Napoleon**, and it was only with the protection of the British fleet that Portugal could trade at all. When the country refused Napoleon's demand to call off this protection in 1807, Napoleon's General Junot marched into Lisbon, setting himself up at the palace in Queluz. On British advice, the royal family fled to Brazil, leaving the war in the hands of British generals, Beresford and Wellington. The French were finally driven back in 1811, leaving Portugal little choice but to allow Britain to trade freely with its colony Brazil, which soon declared its independence. The result was that Portugal became almost a colony of Brazil – where its royal family now resided – and a protectorate of Britain under Beresford. The Portuguese army, however, remained intact, and it was it which forced a new assembly and the return of the king, João VI, from Brazil in 1821.

João VI's son, the reactionary Miguel, acceded to the throne in 1826 and at once returned Portugal to its old absolutist ways. The rest of the nineteenth century saw a constant struggle between supporters of an absolutist monarch and those who favoured a new liberal charter, but despite the political turmoil, Lisbon flourished economically and culturally. The Botanical Gardens were considered the best in Europe, the Teatro Nacional de Dona Maria II (built in 1840) became the place to be seen, and the cafés of Rossio – newly laid with its distinctive black and white cobbles – and Chiado were frequented by the likes of novelist Eça de Queiroz. A public works programme was started in 1851 to help curtail unemployment, a national post office established, and the triumphant arch on Praça do Comércio erected in 1873. The development of Avenida da

Liberdade during the 1880s began to change the shape of Lisbon, creating a central axis that allowed the city to spread north up the slopes around the new Parque Eduardo VII. At around the same time the Elevador da Glória (1885) and Elevador de Santa Justa (1902) were constructed as part of a new network of trams and funiculars.

Meanwhile, **republicanism** took root in the army and among the urban poor, especially after Portuguese claims to Zambesi – the area between the colonies of Angola and Mozambique – failed in 1890, causing Portugal to fall out with Britain. The dictatorial Dom Carlos (1898–1908) was assassinated in Praça do Comércio in a failed coup in 1908 and finally, in 1910, the monarchy was overthrown by a joint revolt of the army and navy. Portugal's last king, Dom Manuel I, was sent into exile in Britain. The new republic was declared in Praça do Município, and the palace at Praça do Comércio turned into government offices.

The republic and Salazar

Lisbon and Portugal remained in turmoil because of divisions among republicans, briefly culminating in victory for the army, which – led by Sidónio Pais – bombed the government offices in Praça do Comércio from Parque Eduardo VII. Pais's rule ended with his assassination in 1918. Economic turmoil followed World War I, with no fewer than 45 changes of government, before General Carmona became president in 1926 and suspended the Republican constitution. In 1928, **Dr António de Oliveira Salazar** became the cabinet's finance minister and managed, with his strict monetarist line, to balance the budget for the first time in years. From then on, he effectively controlled the country, becoming prime minister in 1932 and staying in power until 1968.

Salazar's policies bore many similarities to those of a fascist state: only one political party was permitted, workers' organizations were controlled by their employers, education was managed by the state and censorship was strictly enforced. Opposition to the regime was monitored by the PIDE – a secret police force set up with Gestapo assistance, which used torture and long-term detention in camps in the colonies to defuse resistance. During World War II, a neutral Portugal became a hotbed of spies and an outlet for refugees, remaining on good terms with its old ally, Britain, even though Salazar's policies were closer to those of the Nazis.

Salazar's rule produced a modern economy and much of Lisbon prospered. Despite World War II, in 1940 Salazar staged an exhibition of the Portuguese world, which saw Belém remodelled, with the creation of the Praça do Império and the new Museu de Arte Popular. High-rise buildings appeared around Avenida Roma, the vast Cristo Rei statue was erected in Almada and, in 1959, the city's metro opened. A building boom saw the construction of the Monument to the Discoveries in Belém in 1960, the Ponte 25 de Abril suspension bridge in 1966 (originally called Salazar Bridge) and – shortly after Salazar's demise – the Museu Calouste Gulbenkian in 1969.

But although Lisbon prospered, the majority of Portugal's population suffered under the regime and agriculture was allowed to stagnate. There was internal dissent, but the New State's downfall was largely due to Salazar's imperialism and his obsession with colonial wars. From 1968 Salazar's successor, Marcelo Caetano, attempted to continue with the colonial policies despite growing discontent within the army. Young conscripts had come to sympathize with the freedom movements in the colonies that they were intended to suppress, and from their ranks grew the revolutionary Movimento das Forças Armadas (MFA).

From revolution to Expo 98

On April 25, 1974, the MFA, led by Major Otelo Saraiva de Carvalho, gave the signal for a **revolution**, leading to a virtually bloodless coup, with no serious attempt made to defend the government. Almost immediately the colonies were granted independence and Portuguese military forces withdrawn, leading to the arrival in Lisbon of some half a million **colonial refugees**, further complicating an already unstable post-revolutionary period. Despite an acute housing shortage, rigid pre-revolution rent laws left landlords with insufficient funds to maintain or improve their properties. Lisbon became a grandly decaying city covered in political graffiti and surrounded by shantytowns, some of which still exist today.

In 1985, Dr Aníbal Cavaco Silva's PSD party came to power and, a year later, presided over Portugal's entry into the **European Community**. A massive injection of funds helped Portugal experience unprecedented economic growth and much of Lisbon was reconstructed with a combination of European funds and overseas business investment. The Amoreiras shopping centre, opened in 1986, seemed a suitable symbol for the new rush to consumerism. A massive fire in 1988 was only a temporary setback; though much of the historic Chiado district burnt down, within a decade the area had been impressively rebuilt to its original design.

In the 1990s, Lisbon echoed to the sound of a building programme on a scale not witnessed for two hundred years. Many of the grand mansions on Avenida da República and Avenida da Liberdade were replaced by gleaming office buildings; cobbled streets served by trams were ploughed under tarmac for fast dual carriageways and underpasses; and decaying houses were either renovated or swept away. In 1992, Portugal's **presidency of the European Union** was commemorated by the hurried and controversial construction of presidential headquarters in Belém – now the Centro Cultural de Belém. Then in 1994 came the recognition of Lisbon as **European City of Culture**, lifting the city's European profile still higher.

Despite the optimism engendered by Cavaco Silva's policies of free enterprise and privatization in the 1980s and early 1990s, there were still noticeable **inequalities** in the distribution of wealth, while large areas of the real estate and financial sectors were bought up by Spanish companies. There was also little awareness of the tourist potential of the city, and though much had been done to lure in foreign business, visitor attractions were either often neglected altogether or poorly advertised. The Portuguese reaction to all this was to vote in a fresh government. In 1995, António Guterres was elected prime minister; the following year, Jorge Sampaio, former mayor of Lisbon, became president, giving Portugal a socialist head of state and prime minister for the first time since the revolution.

The new team presided over a further period of growth as more funds poured into Lisbon for the ambitious World Exposition, or **Expo 98**, which saw the redevelopment of the Olivais docklands, the opening of the Vasco da Gama bridge, and a revamped transport network, including a spanking new metro system. A series of new hotels also appeared as the potential for tourist revenue was fully realized. The resulting construction boom led to an increasing number of **Eastern European immigrant workers** arriving in the capital, attracted by the fact that the authorities tended to turn a blind eye to their lack of work visas. Immigration rules have subsequently been tightened up, but you will still see plenty of Eastern European characters in Lisbon's markets and on public transport, selling everything from belts to night-vision glasses.

Meanwhile, the uncomplicated handover of former Portuguese colony Macau to the Chinese in 1999, and the solid support Portugal gave to East Timor during the Indonesian suppression of the former Portuguese colony in the same year, showed the country's growing stature as an international player.

Contemporary Lisbon

Although Expo 98 was a huge success, the social problems and unemployment that plagued Lisbon during the late twentieth century have continued into the new millennium. Lisbon today remains capital of one of the EU's poorest countries. Various schemes aimed at relieving the city's chronic **housing shortage** have been poorly planned, producing grim suburbs of Soviet-style estates which now house a sizeable chunk of the city's population. Over the river, the working-class city of Almada has a population nearing that of the capital itself, though most of its residents work in Lisbon, relying on the Ponte 25 de Abril, the worst bottleneck in Lisbon's increasingly congested traffic system. Inadequate housing has inevitably formed the breeding ground for an acute **drugs problem**, which the government sought to tackle by decriminalizing drug usage. Scaremongers worry that the city will become a "new Amsterdam" attracting drug tourists, though the move is actually a forward-thinking approach to help drug addicts rather than attract new ones.

These problems helped explain why Lisboetas, along with voters all over the country, finally lost patience with António Guterres' PSP, which was resoundingly trounced in local elections in December 2001. Guterres' previously unflappable and highly popular government had also been given the unenviable task of overseeing the change in the country's currency, from the escudo to the euro. Just one month before the change took place, Guterres resigned and the PSD's José Manuel Durão Barroso won the **general election** in March

2002. The fall-out also saw Pedro Santana elected as Lisbon's new mayor; one of his first pledges was to pedestrianize large stretches of the Baixa. The first Portuguese **euros** were withdrawn from a cash machine in Porto in January 2002 and, on the whole, the currency transfer seems to have been relatively painless. It's still too early to say what effects the euro will have on Portugal's economy, though many Lisboetas worry that conversion will almost certainly edge prices of some goods upwards.

However, for the most part Lisbon's future looks bright. The Expo 98 site, renamed Parque das Nações, is becoming a new eastern axis for the city's growth, while there are further ambitious plans to extend the metro, build a new rail crossing over the Tejo to create a direct link with the Algarve, and open a larger international airport northwest of Vila Franca – though the latter two projects were put on hold after José Manuel Durão Barroso's election victory, as part of his pledge to cut back on government spending. The new transport links helped persuade the soccer body, UEFA, to choose Lisbon as the main venue for Portugal's **2004 European Championships**, which will see a further wave of improvements to Lisbon's tourist facilities, as well as the rebuilding of Benfica's Stadium of Light and a brand new stadium for city rivals, Sporting (see p.210).

Lisbon no longer qualifies for the top European grants and many economists worry that the funds for such grandiose projects can never be paid back and will burden the country with permanent debt. However, tourist numbers continue to increase and the city has become one of the most popular stopping-off points for giant cruise ships – indeed a new cruise terminal is earmarked for the riverside between Santa Apolónia and Praça do Comércio. The city's cultural life is flourishing, and social problems largely remain on the periphery of the city's historic core, which looks better than it has done for decades.

Books

n the reviews below, publishers are listed in the format UK/US unless the title is available in one country only, or from a Portuguese publisher, in which case we've specified the country. A reliable specialist source for out-of-print books on all aspects of Portugal is Keith Harris Books, PO Box 207, Twickenham, TW2 5BQ ☎020/8898 7789, Ⓦwww.books -on-portugal.com. For contemporary publications, it's worth checking the latest books available from Carcanet Press, 4th Floor, Conavon Court, 12–16 Blackfriars Street, Manchester, M3 5BQ ☎0161/834 8730, Ⓦwww.carcanet.co.uk, which has a fiction series entitled "From the Portuguese" and a non-fiction series entitled "Aspects of Portugal".

Portuguese writers

António Lobo Antunes *An Explanation of the Birds*; *The Natural Order of Things*; *Act of the Damned* (all Secker & Warburg/Grove-Atlantic); *South of Nowhere* (Chatto & Windus/Random House). Many consider Antunes to be Portugal's leading contemporary writer, with most of his novels set in modern-day Lisbon. Antunes is a psychologist and writes helter-skelter prose, notably in the recent *Act of the Damned*, whose narrative voice changes ceaselessly.

Eugénio Lisboa and Helder Macedo (eds) *The Dedalus Book of Portuguese Fantasy* (Dedalus, UK). A rich feast of literary fantasy, comprising short stories by the likes of Eça de Queiroz and José de Almada Negreiros.

José Rodrigues Miguéis *Happy Easter* (Carcanet, UK). A powerful and disturbing account of the distorted reality experienced by a schizophrenic, whose deprived childhood leads him to a self-destructive and tragic life in Lisbon. An evocatively written and gripping read.

Fernando Pessoa *The Book of Disquiet* (Carcanet, UK); *A Centenary Pessoa* (Carcanet, UK). The country's best-known poet (see p.68) wrote *The Book of Disquiet* in prose: a kind of autobiography, set in Lisbon and posthumously compiled from a truckload of material. Regarded as a modernist classic, this is the first complete English version. *A Centenary Pessoa* includes a selection of his varied prose and poetry, including his works under the pseudonym of Ricardo Reis.

Eça de Queiroz *The Sin of Father Amaro* (Carcanet, UK); *The Maias* (Carcanet, UK); *Cousin Bazilio* (Carcanet, UK); *The Illustrious House of Ramires* (Carcanet, UK); *The Tragedy of the Street of Flowers* (Dedalus, UK); *To the Capital: the start of a career* (Carcanet, UK). Queiroz introduced realism into Portuguese fiction with *The Sin of Father Amaro*, first published in 1876, and over half a dozen of his novels have since been translated into English. *The Illustrious House of Ramires* and *The Maias* are both entertaining narratives which give a comprehensive account of nineteenth-century Portuguese society. *The Tragedy of the Street of Flowers*, which was published posthumously, is particularly scathing of Lisbon's bourgeois society. *Cousin Bazilio* is a gripping story of a woman's daring affair in the confines of Lisbon's middle-class, while *To the Capital* traces the disillusionment of a provincial man who seeks a literary career in the capital.

CONTEXTS

JOSÉ SARAMAGO

Portugal's most famous living writer, José Saramago achieved global recognition when he won the Nobel Prize for Literature in 1998. Despite comparisons with Gabriel García Márquez, Saramago's blend of magical realism and an almost Joycean stream of consciousness give his novels a uniquely dense but surprisingly readable style. Saramago went to school in Lisbon during the time of Salazar, a background that engendered an antipathy to politics and the Church. As a result, his novels often deal with themes of resistance and the emergence of personal identity. After periods as a metalworker and draughtsman, he moved into publishing and translation before becoming a political commentator for a Lisbon newspaper. In 1969, Saramago joined the then-prohibited Communist Party; in 1989, he was elected as a Communist councillor for Lisbon City Council before he decided to concentrate on being a full-time author. His novels have since come thick and fast but continue to be experimental, often dispensing with punctuation altogether; his novel The Blind even avoided naming a single character in the book. Now in his seventies, Saramago lives in Lanzarote with his Spanish wife.

Mário de Sá-Carneiro The Great Shadow; Lucio's Confessions (both Dedalus, UK). The Great Shadow is a collection of short stories set against the backdrop of Lisbon, as the author describes his obsession with great art and laments Lisbon's inferiority to Paris. Sá-Carneiro, who committed suicide at 26, writes with stunning intensity and

originality about art, science, death, sex (including homo-sexuality) and insanity. Similar themes appear in Lucio's Confessions, in which a ménage á trois between three artists ends in a death.

José Saramago Baltasar and Blimunda (Harvill, UK); The Year of the Death of Ricardo Reis (Harvill/Harcourt Brace);

The Stone Raft
(Harvill/Harcourt Brace); *The History of the Siege of Lisbon* (Harvill/Harcourt Brace). Though many of Saramago's novels feature Lisbon at some stage, the city is most wonderfully evoked in *The Year of the Death of Ricardo Reis*, a book about Pessoa's alter ego, which won *The Independent*'s foreign fiction award. In *Baltasar and Blimunda*, Saramago mixes fact with myth in an atmospheric novel set around the building of the Convent of Mafra and the construction of the world's first flying machine. In *The History of the Siege of Lisbon,* contemporary Lisbon is superimposed on an account of the Crusader siege of the city. A proofreader's own emotions come under siege when he falls in love with his boss – who had been appointed to keep an eye on him after he deliberately alters a historical fact.

Other books set in Lisbon

Cees Nooteboom *The Following Story* (Harcourt Brace, UK). Dutch author Nooteboom successfully evokes the famous Portuguese feeling of melancholy – or *saudade* – in a tale of a classics teacher who falls asleep in Amsterdam and wakes up in a hotel room in Lisbon, the scene of a romantic past that he realizes he can never fully recapture.

Erich Maria Remarque *The Night in Lisbon* (Fawcett Books, US). Better known as author of *All Quiet On The Western Front*, German author Remarque writes with a similar detachment in this tale of a war-time refugee seeking an escape route from Europe. One night in Lisbon, he meets a stranger who has two tickets, and within hours their lives are inextricably linked in a harrowing and moving tale.

Antonio Tabucchi *Declares Pereira* (Harvill/New Directions); *Requiem: A Hallucination* (Harvill/New Directions). Tabucchi is a highly regarded Italian author and biographer of Pessoa, who lived in Portugal for many years. In *Declares Pereira* he has re-created the repressive atmosphere of Salazar's Lisbon, tracing the experiences of a newspaper editor who questions his own lifestyle under a regime which he can no longer ignore. The book has recently been made into a film by Roberto Faenza. *Requiem: A Hallucination* is an imaginative and dreamlike journey around Lisbon, with Tabucchi engaging in Saramago-esque conversations with people as diverse as a barman in the Museu de Arte Antiga and a Pessoa-like author. The unifying theme is food and drink, and the book even contains a note on recipes at the end.

Robert Wilson *A Small Death in Lisbon* (HarperCollins, UK). A policeman attempts to find the murderer of a girl found dumped on a beach on the train line to Cascais, opening up a can of worms stretching back to World War II. The novel presents an extremely evocative and accurate account of contemporary Lisbon – albeit its seedier side – though its potted summary of the Salazar years Is less convincing. This is, nevertheless, a gripping page-turner from a British author who lives in Portugal.

Richard Zimler *The Last Kabbalist of Lisbon* (Arcadia/Overlook Press, Peter Mayer Publishers). Kabbala is the magical art based on an esoteric interpretation of the Old Testament. American author Zimler, now a resident of Porto, writes an intense and compelling story of a Jewish kabbalist attempting to discover the mystery behind his uncle's murder during the massacre of New Christians in Rossio in 1506. Based on historical fact, the story has been a bestseller in Portugal, Italy and Brazil.

History and architecture

David Birmingham *A Concise History of Portugal* (Cambridge University Press, UK). One of the most recent histories of Portugal is also the best for the casual reader; concise, but providing straightforward and informative coverage from the year dot.

Damião de Góis *Lisbon in the Renaissance* (Italica Press, US). De Góis was a friend of Erasmus and lived in Lisbon when it was one of Europe's leading commercial and cultural centres. Written in 1554, the book is a celebration of the pre-earthquake city and its monuments, though the best bits of his work are the reports of mythical creatures such as *tagide* – sea monsters – living in the Tejo.

Paulo Santos *Lisbon: A Guide to Recent Architecture* (Ellipsis, UK). Neatly designed book detailing the hits and misses of the adventurous recent architecture in the city, from grand housing projects and the Expo site down to individual shops, bars, and even the public toilets in Parque Eduardo VII.

José Hermano Saraiva *Portugal: A Companion History* (Carcanet, UK). Highly accessible precis of the key moments in Portugal's history.

Travels, journals and observations

William Beckford *Recollections of an Excursion to the Monasteries of Alcobaça and Batalha*; *Travels in Spain and Portugal (1778–88)* (Centaur Press/Norwood Editions). Mad and enormously rich, Beckford lived for some time at Sintra and travelled widely in Estremadura. His accounts, told with a fine eye for the absurd, are a lot of fun.

Lord Byron *Selected Letters and Journals* (Pimlico/Belknap).

Only a few days of Portuguese travel but memorable ones – beginning with romantic enthusiasm, ending in outright abuse.

Henry Fielding *Journal of a Voyage to Lisbon*, with *A Journey From This World to the Next* (Oxford University Press, UK). In 1754 Fielding set sail to Lisbon in the hope that its climate would alleviate his ill health. Written with his usual satirical wit, the journal records the incidents and characters he meets on his voyage to the city where he was to meet his death, though there is little about Lisbon itself.

Paul Hyland *Backwards out of the Big World* (Flamingo, UK). Arriving on a cargo boat in the style of Henry Fielding, Hyland goes on to explore modern-day Lisbon before heading up through Portugal, meeting contemporary Portuguese writers, bullfighters, gypsies and the heir to the defunct throne en route. It's somewhat contrived, but with some interesting insights.

Marion Kaplan *The Portuguese: the Land and its People* (Penguin in UK & US). Published in 1991, this is a readable, all-embracing volume, covering everything from wine to the family, poetry and the land. The style is a bit old-fashioned, but it's the best general introduction to the country available.

Fernando Pessoa *Lisbon: What The Tourist Should See* (Livros Horizonte, Portugal). A somewhat dull insight into the city as Pessoa saw it. Written in English and Portuguese (but only available in Portugal), Pessoa's 1925 guidebook describes a Lisbon that is largely recognizable today. *Fernando Pessoa*, another book available only in Portugal (Hazan, Portugal), is a revealing collection of documents and photographs of the author at work, with an introduction by Antonio Tabucchi.

Fernão Mendes Pinto *The Peregrination* (Carcanet, UK). The autobiography and biography of a sixteenth-century explorer who followed Vasco da Gama's trail around the Orient. The trader, who called himself a soldier, pirate, agent and ambassador, was shipwrecked five times, captured thirteen times and enslaved sixteen times, but lived to tell the tale in all its gory detail.

Poetry

Luís de Camões *The Lusiads*
(Penguin, UK); *Epic and Lyric*
(Carcanet, UK). *The Lusiads* is
Portugal's national epic, celebrating the ten-month voyage
of Vasco da Gama, which
opened up the sea route to
India. This is a good translation.
Epic and Lyric includes extracts
from *The Lusiads* together with
other shorter poems.

Pedro Tamen *Honey and
Poison: Selected Poems*
(Carcanet, UK). Lisbon law
graduate Tamen is regarded as
one of Portugal's leading contemporary poets; his poems of
passion capture the distinctive
sights and emotions of a country which has moved from dictatorship to democracy during
his lifetime.

Food and drink

Maite Manjon *Gastronomy of
Spain and Portugal* (Prentice-
Hall, US). A comprehensive
collection of classic Iberian
recipes, including a glossary of
Portuguese and Spanish terms
and explanations of traditional
cooking techniques.
Particularly good on regional
specialities, including Lisbon
dishes and wines.

Portuguese Tourist Board
Wine Routes - Portugal
(Publicações Dom Quixote,
Portugal). Spiral-bound booklet
detailing touring routes round

Portugal's various wine-grow-
ing areas, including Sintra and
the Lisbon coast. Details on
individual places are sketchy,
but it is attractively illustrated
with excellent background
information on wines, grape
varieties and wine lodges.

Edite Vieira *The Taste of
Portugal* (Grub Street, UK). A
delight to read, let alone cook
from. Vieira combines snippets
of history and passages from
Portuguese writers (very well
translated) to illustrate her
dishes. Highly recommended.

Language

f you have some knowledge of Spanish, you won't have much problem reading **Portuguese**. Understanding it when it's spoken, though, is a different matter: pronunciation is entirely different and at first even the easiest words are hard to distinguish. Even so, it's well worth the effort to master at least the rudiments; once you've started to figure out the words it gets a lot easier very quickly.

A useful word is "**Tem**...?" (pronounced *taying*) which means "Do you have...?", or "**Queria**..." (I'd like...). And of course there are the old standards, "Do you speak English?" (*Fala Inglês?*) and "I don't understand" (*Não compreendo*).

Pronunciation

The chief difficulty with pronunciation is its lack of clarity – consonants tend to be slurred, vowels nasal and often ignored altogether. The **consonants** are, at least, consistent:

C is soft before E and I, hard otherwise unless it has a cedilla – açucar (sugar) is pronounced "assookar".

CH is somewhat softer than in English; chá (tea) sounds like Shah.

WORDS AND PHRASES

Basics

sim; *não*	yes; no
olá; *bom dia*	hello; good morning
boa tarde/noite	good afternoon/night
adeus, até logo	goodbye, see you later
hoje; *amanhã*	today; tomorrow
por favor/se faz favor	please
tudo bem?	everything all right?
está bem	it's all right/OK
obrigado/a*	thank you
onde; *que*	where; what
quando; *porquê*	when; why
como; *quanto*	how; how much
não sei	I don't know
sabe . . .?	do you know . . .?
pode . . .?	could you . . .?
desculpe; *com licença*	sorry; excuse me
este/a; *esse/a*	this; that
agora; *mais tarde*	now; later
mais; *menos*	more; less
grande; *pequeno*	big; little
aberto; *fechado*	open; closed
senhoras; *homens*	women; men
lavabo/quarto de banho	toilet/bathroom

*Obrigado agrees with the sex of the person speaking – a woman says *obrigada*, a man *obrigado*.

Getting around

esquerda, direita,	left, right, straight
sempre em frente	ahead
aqui; *ali*	here; there
perto; *longe*	near; far

Onde é a estação de camionetas?	Where is the bus station?
a paragem de autocarro para . . .	the bus stop for . . .
Donde parte o autocarro para . . .?	Where does the bus to . . . leave from?
A que horas parte?	What time does it leave?
(chega a . . .?)	(arrive at . . .?)
Pare aqui por favor	Stop here please
bilhete (para)	ticket (to)
ida e volta	round trip

Accommodation

Queria um quarto	I'd like a room
É para uma noite (semana)	It's for one night (week)
É para uma pessoa (duas pessoas)	It's for one person/two people
Quanto custa	How much is it?
Posso ver?	May I see/look around?
Há um quarto mais barato?	Is there a cheaper room?
com duche	with a shower

Shopping

Quanto é?	How much is it?
banco; câmbio	bank; change
correios	post office
(dois) selos	(two) stamps
Como se diz isto em Português?	What's this called in Portuguese?
O que é isso?	What's that?

Days of the week

domingo	Sunday	*quinta-feira*	Thursday
segunda-feira	Monday	*sexta-feira*	Friday
terça-feira	Tuesday	*sábado*	Saturday
quarta-feira	Wednesday		

Numbers

1	*um*	12	*doze*	40	*quarenta*
2	*dois*	13	*treze*	50	*cinquenta*
3	*três*	14	*catorze*	60	*sessenta*
4	*quatro*	15	*quinze*	70	*setenta*
5	*cinco*	16	*dezasseis*	80	*oitenta*
6	*seis*	17	*dezassete*	90	*noventa*
7	*sete*	18	*dezoito*	100	*cem*
8	*oito*	19	*dezanove*	101	*cento e um*
9	*nove*	20	*vinte*	200	*duzentos*
10	*dez*	21	*vinte e um*	500	*quinhentos*
11	*onze*	30	*trinta*	1000	*mil*

J is pronounced like the "s" in pleasure, as is G except when it comes before a "hard" vowel (A, O and U).

LH sounds like "lyuh".

Q is always pronounced as a "k".

S before a consonant or at the end of a word becomes "sh," otherwise it's as in English.

X is also pronounced "sh"– caixa (cash desk) is pronounced "kaisha".

Vowels are worse – flat and truncated, they're often difficult for English-speaking tongues to get around. The only way to learn is to listen: accents, Ã, Ô, or É, turn them into longer, more familiar sounds.

When two vowels come together they continue to be enunciated separately except in the case of **El** and **OU** – which sound like a and long o respectively. E at the end of a word is silent unless it has an accent, so that carne (meat) is pronounced "karn", while café sounds much as you'd expect. The **tilde over Ã or Õ** renders the pronunciation much like the French -an and -on endings only more nasal. More common is **ÃO** (as in pão, bread – são, saint – limão, lemon), which sounds something like a strangled yelp of "Ow!" cut off in midstream.

MENU READER

Basic words and terms

almoço	lunch
assado	roasted
colher	spoon
conta	bill
copo	glass
cozido	boiled
ementa	menu
estrelado/frito	fried
faca	knife
fumado	smoked
garfo	fork
garrafa	bottle
grelhado	grilled
jantar	dinner
mexido	scrambled
pequeno almoço	breakfast

Soups, salad and staples

arroz	rice
azeitonas	olives
batatas fritas	chips/french fries
caldo verde	cabbage soup
fruta	fruit
gaspacho	chilled vegetable soup
legumes	vegetables
manteiga	butter
ovos	eggs
pão	bread
pimenta	pepper
piri-piri	chilli sauce
queijo	cheese
sal	salt

salada	salad
sopa de legumes	vegetable soup
sopa de marisco	shellfish soup
sopa de peixe	fish soup

Fish and shellfish

arroz de marisco	seafood rice
atum	tuna
bacalhau à brás	salted cod with egg and potatoes
caldeirada	fish stew
camarões	shrimp
carapau	mackerel
cataplana	fish, shellfish or meat stewed in a circular metal dish
gambas	prawns
lagosta	lobster
lulas (grelhadas)	squid (grilled)
pescada	whiting
salmão	salmon
sardinhas na brasa	charcoal-grilled sardines
truta	trout

Meat

bife à portuguesa	thin beef steak with a fried egg on top
borrego	lamb
chouriço	spicy sausage
cozido à portuguesa	boiled casserole of meats and beans, served with rice and vegetables
espetada mista	mixed meat kebab
febras	pork steaks
frango no churrasco	barbecued chicken
pato	duck
porco à alentejana	pork cooked with clams
presunto	smoked ham
vitela	veal

INDEX

A

accommodation 115–135
  Caparica 290–291
  Cascais 279–281
  Estoril 274
  Guincho 279–280
  Queluz 269
  Sesimbra....................................295
  Sintra 259–262
  Sintra coast..............................266
accommodation price codes.........118
addresses.....................................118
Adrenalina...................................111
Aerobus 4
airlines 240
airport...3
Ajuda..75
Alcântara....................................73–75
  bars and clubs 186–188
  cafés 173
  eating 161–162
Aldeia do Meco............................292
Alfama.......................................45–47
  accommodation 123–126
  cafés 171
  eating 146–151
American Express.........................240
Amoreiras................................90–91
Antiga Confeitaria de Belém 81

antique shops 217–219
Aqueduto das Águas
  Livres 91–92
Arco da Rua Augusta 33
Armazéns do Chiado 38
Arrábida 297–299
arrival 3
Avenida 24 de Julho 73
  bars and clubs 189
Avenida Almirante Reis
  eating 165
Avenida João Crisóstomo 5
Avenida da Liberdade 87–90
  accommodation 128–130
  cafés 175
  eating 163–164
Azenhas do Mar 266
azulejos 55

B

Bairro Alto 58–64
  accommodation 126–127
  bars and clubs 182–185
  cafés 172–173
  eating 153–158
Baixa.......................................31–37
  accommodation 118
  bars and clubs 178–179

cafés 168–170
    eating 138–140
banks 19
Barreiro station 5
bars and clubs 176–189
Basílica da Estrela...........................67
beach (see Praia)
beaches 215
    Caparica 289–290
    Cascais...........................277–278
    Costa da Caparica 292–293
    Estoril..............................273
    Sesimbra..........................293
    Sintra coast.....................265–266
Beckford, William 257, 321
Belém 76–86
    cafés..............................174
    eating 162–163
Belenenses 211
Benfica 210–211
boat trips, Sesimbra 294
Boca do Inferno, Cascais 278
books 316–323
bookshops 219–220
Bowling Internacional de Lisboa 231
budget Lisbon.................................20
bullfights 209–210
bus pass, Stagecoach 277
bus stations 240–241
bus tours 17
buses 14
Byron, Lord...........................248, 321

C

Cabo da Roca 265
Cabo Espichel 293
Cacilhas 286–288
Café A Brasileira 38
Café Suíça 36
cafés 167–175
    with outdoor tables 174
    with views 172
Cais do Sodré 40
    bars and clubs 179–180
    cafés...............................171

eating 145
Câmara Escura 50
Campo de Golfe de Belas.............213
Campo de Santa Clara 53
    eating 151
Campo dos Mártires da Pátria 89
Campo Grande 100–102
campsites 134
Caparica 289–292
    accommodation 290–291
    eating and drinking 291–292
Capela de São João Baptista 60
car parks 6
car rental....................................7, 241
Carcavelos 272–273
Carnival, Lisbon 233
Cartão Lisboa (Lisbon Card) 11
Casa do Fado e da Guitarra
    Portuguesa (fado and Portuguese
    guitar museum)......................47
Casa dos Bicos 45
Casa Museu Dr Anastáccio Gonçalves
    (art collection and house
    museum) 94
Casa Museu Fernando Pessoa
    (Pessoa's house museum) 68–69
Cascais 275–284
    accommodation 279–281
    bars and clubs 283–284
    eating 281–283
casino, Estoril 273
Castelo
    accommodation 123–126
    bars and clubs 181
    eating 148–149
Castelo de São Jorge 49–50
Castelo dos Mouros, Sintra...........254
castle, Sesimbra 295
cathedral (Sé) 44
Cemitério dos Ingleses 68
Centro Artístico Infantil 230
Centro Colombo 232
Centro Cultural de Belém 207
Centro Cultural de Belém 81
Centro Cultural Olga Cadaval,
    Sintra....................................251

Centro da Ciência Viva (science
    museum) 109
Centro de Arte Moderna (modern art
    museum) 98
Chiado 37–40
    accommodation 123
    bars and clubs 178
    cafés 170
    eating 143–145
children's activities.................228–232
Christmas in Lisbon 238–239
churches (see Igreja)
cinema 205–206
City Hall 32
climate xv
clothes shops 220–222
clubbing 176–189
Colares 265
Coliseu dos Recreios 37
communications 21
Conceição Velho...............................32
Confeitaria Nacional 36
contemporary Lisbon 314–315
Convento da Arrábida 297–298
Convento do Carmo 61
Convento dos Capuchos 258–259
Cook, Sir Francis..................257–258
Costa da Caparica 292–293
costs 19
craft shops 217–219
crime 24
Cristo Rei 287
Cruz Alta, Sintra 255
Culturgest 204
cyber-cafés 23

D

development, urban 39
disabled access 116
disabled travellers 241
Discoveries Monument 82–83
Discoveries, the................305–306
diving 298
Doca de Alcântara...........................73
    bars and clubs 187

Doca de Belém................................83
Doca de Bom Sucesso...................83
Doca de Santo Amaro.....................74
    bars and clubs 188
Doca do Jardim do Tobaco.............48
docks (see Doca)
dolphin watching............................298
dress 241
drinks 177
driving..6
drugs 314

E

Earthquake, the Great......................30
eating 136–166
    Cacilhas 287–288
    Caparica 291–292
    Cascais 281–283
    Estoril 274–275
    Sintra 262–264
Eça de Queiroz 317
electricity 242
Elevador da Bica............................41
Elevador da Glória.....................37, 59
Elevador de Santa Justa 33–34, 62
Elevador do Lavra...........................37
Elevador Panorâmico da Boca do
    Vento, Cacilhas 287
email...23
embassies 242
emergencies 242
Estádio da Luz 211
Estádio do Restelo 211
Estádio José Alvalade 211
Estádio Nacional 211
Estoril 273–275
    accommodation 274
    eating and drinking 274–275
Estoril Golf Club 213
Estrela 67–69
    eating 160
Estufas (hot houses) 93
ethnic Lisbon 66
euro 19

European Community 312
European Football Championships
   2004 ....212, 315
exchange 20
Expo 98 ....82, 275

F

fado 47
Feira da Ladra market...................54
Feira Internacional de Lisboa (FIL) ..111
Feira Popular 101
ferries 16
Festa de Santo António 235
festivals.................................233-239
fiction, Lisbon in 316-320
Fielding, Henry 68, 321
film 205-206
fireworks.....................................273
Fonte da Telha.............................290
food shops 222-223
food terms 328
football 210-212
free admission, sites with 9
Fundação Arpad Siznes-Viera da Silva
   (art museum) 92-93
Fundação Calouste Gulbenkian ..94-99
Fundação Medeiros e Almeida (art
   collection and house museum)....90

G

gardens (see Jardim)
Gay and Lesbian Film Festival..190, 237
gay contacts..............................190
gay Lisbon 190-193
Gay Pride 190-191
golf 212-213
golf courses 213
Gonçalves, Nuno 69
Graça
   cafés.......................................171-172
Guincho 278-279
Gulbenkian, Calouste 95

H

Henriques, Afonso 305
history..............................303-315
horse and carriage ride 232
horse-riding 213
hospital...............................242

I

Igreja da Assunção, Cascais 277
Igreja de Madre de Deus.................57
Igreja de Santo António...................45
Igreja de São Domingos 35
Igreja de São Roque 60
Igreja dos Mártires 38
information 7
Instituto da Cinemateca
   Portuguesa 205-206
Instituto do Vinho do Porto 59
internet points..............................23
Internet sites 8

J

Jardim Botânico (Ajuda) 75
Jardim Botânico 64
Jardim da Água 109
Jardim da Estrela 67
Jardim da Tapada das
   Necessidades......................74-75
Jardim do Tobaco, eating 152
Jardim do Torel.............................89
Jardim do Ultramar........................81
Jardim Garcia de Orta...................110
Jardim Zoológico 102-103
João V 269
José Maria de Fonseca wine vaults
   and museum 299

K

kids' Lisbon 228-232

L

Lagoa de Albufeira 292
language.............................324–329
Lapa 73
  accommodation 127–128
  cafés.......................................173
  eating 160–161
Lapa Palace Hotel...........................73
Largo da Anunciada 37
Largo das Portas do Sol 49
Largo de São Domingos 35
Largo do Carmo 61
Largo do Chafariz de Dentro............46
Largo Martim Moniz 36
laundry 242
left luggage...................................242
Linha de Cascais
  (Cascais train line)....................272
Lisbon Card (Cartão Lisboa) 11
Lisbon Players 206
Lisbon Welcome Centre 7, 32
listings magazines............................9
live music 194–204
lost property 242
Lumiar 102
Lux 181

M

Mãe d'Água 92
Mafra......................................269–271
mail...21
Manuel I 306
Manueline architecture 79
maps..9
Marathon, Lisbon 214
Maria I...268
Marina de Cascais 277
markets..................................223–224
markets, Cascais 278
Martinho da Arcada 32
menu reader 328–329
Mercado da Ribeira.................41–42
Methuen Treaty 308
metro 13

metro map 12
mini-railway, Caparica 289–290
Miradouro da Graça 52
Miradouro da Santa Luzia 48
Miradouro de Santa Catarina 41
Miradouro de São Pedro de
  Alcântara 59
mobile phones 23
money 19
Monserrate, Sintra.................257–258
Moorish rule 304–305
Mosteiro dos Jerónimos 77–80
Mouraria 52
  eating 148–149
multicultural Lisbon 66
Museu Arqueológico do Carmo
  (archeological and ethnographical
  museum) 61
Museu Biblioteca Conde Castro
  Guimarães, Cascais
  (house museum) 277
Museu Calouste Gulbenkian
  (art museum) 95–98
Museu da Água (Santa Apolónia; water
  museum) 56
Museu da Cidade (city museum)....101
Museu da Ciência
  (science museum) 63
Museu da Electricidade
  (electricity/industrial museum) 85
Museu da Historia Natural
  (natural history museum) 63
Museu da Marinha
  (maritime museum) 80
Museu da Marioneta
  (puppet museum).....................231
Museu das Crianças
  (children's museum) 80
Museu de Água Príncipe Real (water
  museum) 63
Museu de Arqueologia
  (archeological museum) 80
Museu de Arte Moderna, Sintra
  (modern art museum) 251
Museu de Arte Popular
  (folk art museum) 83

Museu do Brinquedo, Sintra 253
Museu do Centro Científico e Cultural
    de Macau (Macau cultural
    museum) 85–86
Museu do Chiado
    (contemporary art museum) 40
Museu do Design
    (design museum) 82
Museu do Mar, Cascais
    (museum of the sea) 278
Museu do Teatro
    (theatrical museum) 102
Museu do Teatro Romano
    (Roman theatre museum)............48
Museu do Traje
    (costume museum) 102
Museu dos Coches
    (coach museum) 84
Museu Escola de Artes Decorativas
    (decorative arts museum) 48–49
Museu Militar (military museum) 56
Museu Nacional de Arte Antiga
    (National Gallery) 69–72
Museu Nacional do Azulejo
    (tile museum) 57
Museu Oceanográfico, Portinho da
    Arrábida (marine museum) 298
Museu Rafael Bordalo Pinheiro (art
    collection and house museum)..101
museum (see Museu, Casa Museu,
    Fundação)
music 194–204
    African and Brazilian 199–201
    classical 203–204
    fado and folk 195–199
    jazz 203
    rock and pop 202
    shops 225
    venues 204

N

Napoleonic wars 309
New Year's Eve events 238
newspapers 243
Noites de Bailado 235

Núcleo Arqueológico.......................33

O

Oceanário de Lisboa
    (oceanarium) 109–110
Olisipónia
    (historical multimedia museum) ..50
Olivais dock 108
Oriente station 5

P

Padrão dos Descobrimentos......82–83
Palácio-Convento de Mafra....269–271
Palácio da Ajuda..............................75
Palácio da Assembléia 66–67
Palácio da Pena, Sintra 254–255
Palácio da Seteais, Sintra 261
Palácio de Queluz 267–269
Palácio do Monteiro-Mor...............102
Palácio dos Marquêses da
    Fronteira 103–104
Palácio dos Milhões, Sintra 256
Palácio Nacional, Sintra 252
Palmela..237
Panteão Nacional 54
Pantheon of the Bragança
    dynasty 53
parks 230
Parliament building 66–67
Parque da Pena, Sintra 254
Parque de Gil 230–231
Parque do Estoril 273
Parque Eduardo VII 93
    accommodation 131–134
    cafés 175
    eating 164–165
Parque Infantil 93
Parque Monsanto 92
Parque Municipal da Gandarinha,
    Cascais 277
Parque das Nações...............105–112
    bars and clubs 189
    eating 165–166
Parque Natural da Arrábida 297–299

Pavilhão Atlântico
(Atlantic Pavilion) 112
Pavilhão da Realidade Virtual
(Virtual Reality Pavilion)..............109
Pavilhão das Exposições
(Exposition Pavilion) 108
Pavilhão de Macau 111
Pavilhão de Portugal 108
Penha Longa Golf Club................213
Pessoa, Fernando...................68, 317
pharmacies.................................243
Phoenicians................................303
Planetário Calouste Gulbenkian
(planetarium) 230
playgrounds 230–231
Pombal, Marquês de..............62, 308
Ponte Vasco da Gama 105
port...178
Portinho da Arrábida...................298
Porto Brandão 85
Portuguese colonial food 147
Portuguese dishes 136–137
Portuguese language 324–329
post 21
post offices 22
Pousada Dona Maria I, Queluz....268
Praça Afonso de Albuquerque 84
Praça da Figueira 36
Praça das Amoreiras....................91
Praça de Touros de Campo Pequeno
(bullring) 210
Praça do Comércio 31–32
Praça do Império 81
Praça do Município 32
Praça do Príncipe Real 62
bars and clubs 185–186
eating 158
Praça dos Restauradores 36
Praça Marquês de Pombal 90
Praia da Andraga 266
Praia da Conceição, Cascais 277
Praia das Maças 266
Praia de Santa Marta, Cascais 278
Praia do Guincho 278–279
Praia do Meco 292–293
Praia dos Lagosteiros 292

Praia Grande...............................266
Presidência da República
(President's house).....................81
Prince Henry the Navigator 305
public holidays 234
puppet shows..............................231

Q

Queluz 267–269
Quinta da Regaleira,
Sintra 255–257
Quinta de Marinha Golf Club 213

R

Rato, eating 159
Rego, Paula 99
Reserva da Mata Nacional dos
Medos 292
restaurants 138–166
price codes 138
with outdoor seating 150
with views 145
revolution 312
river cruises 17
Rodriguez, Amália.......................196
Roman Lisbon 303
Roman theatre 48
Rossio 34–35
accommodation 119
station....................................5
Rua das Portas de Santo Antão 37
eating 141
Rua de São João da Praça...............46
Rua do Arsenal 32
Rua do Carmo 38
Rua do Poço dos Negros 67
Rua do Século 62
Rua Garrett................................38
Rua Viera Portuense 81

S

Salazar, António do Oliveira 310–311

Saldanha...94
   accommodation 131
   cafés...175
   eating..164
Santa Apolónia 54
   clubs 181
   station 4
Santa Cruz 52
Santa Engrácia 54
Santos
   bars and clubs 189
   eating..145
Santos Populares 234
   (popular saints festival) 234–235
São Bento....................................66–67
   bars and clubs 185–186
   eating..160
São Vicente de Fora 53
Saramago, José 318
Sé (cathedral)...................................44
self-catering accommodation 131
Sesimbra....................................293–297
   accommodation 295
   bars and clubs 296–297
   eating..296
Severa, Maria 196
shopping....................................216–227
shopping centres 225–226
Siege of Lisbon................................51
sightseeing tours.............................17
Sintra......................................248–264
   accommodation 259–262
   coast..266
   eating and drinking 262–264
Sintra Music Festival 235
soccer....................................210–212
Sony Plaza 111
Spanish rule 306–307
Sporting Lisbon 211
sports....................................208–215
stamps...22
stations...5
supermarkets 227
surfing..214
swimming 215, 232

T

Tapada de Mafra............................271
taxi vouchers 3
taxis...18
Teatro Camões 109
Teatro Nacional de Dona Maria II
   ....34, 206
Teatro Nacional de São Carlos 38
Teatro Taborda 231
Teatro Virtual, Sintra 253–254
telephones 22
temperature xv
tennis 215
theatre 206–207
tickets....................................194–195
tiles (azulejos) 55
time 243
tipping 243
toilets...243
Torre de Belém.........................83–84
Torre Vasco da Gama 110
tourist office.......................................7
toy train, Belém...............................80
toy train, Cascais 278
toy train, Parque das Nações 108
Trafaria..85
trains..4
tram #28..52
tram tours...17
trams..14
transport, city 10
travel agents 243
travel passes 11
travellers' cheques 21

U

university...101

V

Vasco da Gama 306
Vasco da Gama, tomb of 78
vegetarian restaurants...................144

viewpoints (see Miradouro)

W

walks.............................17, 73, 89, 287
weather xv
Web sites 8
Wellington, Duke of.........................309
when to visit xiv
windsurfing 214

wine 178, 299
wine harvest festival 237

Y

youth hostels 124–125

Z

zoo 102–103

around the world

Alaska ★ Algarve ★ Amsterdam ★ Andalucía ★ Antigua & Barbuda ★
Argentina ★ Auckland Restaurants ★ Australia ★ Austria ★ Bahamas ★
Bali & Lombok ★ Bangkok ★ Barbados ★ Barcelona ★ Beijing ★ Belgium &
Luxembourg ★ Belize ★ Berlin ★ Big Island of Hawaii ★ Bolivia ★ Boston
★ Brazil ★ Britain ★ Brittany & Normandy ★ Bruges & Ghent ★ Brussels ★
Budapest ★ Bulgaria ★ California ★ Cambodia ★ Canada ★ Cape Town ★
The Caribbean ★ Central America ★ Chile ★ China ★ Copenhagen ★
Corsica ★ Costa Brava ★ Costa Rica ★ Crete ★ Croatia ★ Cuba ★ Cyprus ★
Czech & Slovak Republics ★ Devon & Cornwall ★ Dodecanese & East
Aegean ★ Dominican Republic ★ The Dordogne & the Lot ★ Dublin ★
Ecuador ★ Edinburgh ★ Egypt ★ England ★ Europe ★ First-time Asia ★
First-time Europe ★ Florence ★ Florida ★ France ★ French Hotels &
Restaurants ★ Gay & Lesbian Australia ★ Germany ★ Goa ★ Greece ★
Greek Islands ★ Guatemala ★ Hawaii ★ Holland ★ Hong Kong & Macau ★
Honolulu ★ Hungary ★ Ibiza & Formentera ★ Iceland ★ India ★ Indonesia
★ Ionian Islands ★ Ireland ★ Israel & the Palestinian Territories ★ Italy ★
Jamaica ★ Japan ★ Jerusalem ★ Jordan ★ Kenya ★ The Lake District ★
Languedoc & Roussillon ★ Laos ★ Las Vegas ★ Lisbon ★ London ★

in twenty years

London Mini Guide ★ London Restaurants ★ Los Angeles ★ Madeira ★ Madrid ★ Malaysia, Singapore & Brunei ★ Mallorca ★ Malta & Gozo ★ Maui ★ Maya World ★ Melbourne ★ Menorca ★ Mexico ★ Miami & the Florida Keys ★ Montréal ★ Morocco ★ Moscow ★ Nepal ★ New England ★ New Orleans ★ New York City ★ New York Mini Guide ★ New York Restaurants ★ New Zealand ★ Norway ★ Pacific Northwest ★ Paris ★ Paris Mini Guide ★ Peru ★ Poland ★ Portugal ★ Prague ★ Provence & the Côte d'Azur ★ Pyrenees ★ The Rocky Mountains ★ Romania ★ Rome ★ San Francisco ★ San Francisco Restaurants ★ Sardinia ★ Scandinavia ★ Scotland ★ Scottish Highlands & Islands ★ Seattle ★ Sicily ★ Singapore ★ South Africa, Lesotho & Swaziland ★ South India ★ Southeast Asia ★ Southwest USA ★ Spain ★ St Lucia ★ St Petersburg ★ Sweden ★ Switzerland ★ Sydney ★ Syria ★ Tanzania ★ Tenerife and La Gomera ★ Thailand ★ Thailand's Beaches & Islands ★ Tokyo ★ Toronto ★ Travel Health ★ Trinidad & Tobago ★ Tunisia ★ Turkey ★ Tuscany & Umbria ★ USA ★ Vancouver ★ Venice & the Veneto ★ Vienna ★ Vietnam ★ Wales ★ Washington DC ★ West Africa ★ Women Travel ★ Yosemite ★ Zanzibar ★ Zimbabwe

also look out for our maps, phrasebooks, music guides and reference books

RIGA
OUAGADOUGOU
SINGAPORE
ROUGH GUIDES TWENTY YEARS

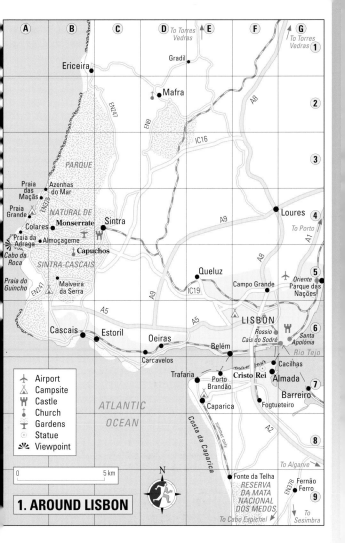

1. AROUND LISBON

			To Torres Vedras	To Torres Vedras

Ericeira

Gradil

Mafra

PARQUE

Praia das Maças
Azenhas do Mar

Praia Grande

NATURAL DE

Colares
Monserrate
Sintra

Loures

Praia da Adraga
Almoçagem

Capuchos

To Porto

Cabo da Roca

SINTRA-CASCAIS

Praia do Guincho

Malveira da Serra

Queluz

Campo Grande

Oriente
Parque das Nações

Cascais

Estoril

Oeiras

IC19

LISBON

Belém

Carcavelos

Rossio
Cais do Sodré

Santa Apolónia

Rio Tejo

Trafaria

Porto Brandão

Cristo Rei

Cacilhas

Almada

ATLANTIC
OCEAN

Caparica

Barreiro

Fogtueteiro

Costa da Caparica

summer only

To Algarve

Fonte da Telha

RESERVA DA MATA NACIONAL DOS MEDOS

Fernão Ferro

To Cabo Espichel

To Sesimbra

Legend

- ✈ Airport
- △ Campsite
- ♛ Castle
- ✝ Church
- ⚘ Gardens
- ⊙ Statue
- ☀ Viewpoint

0 — 5 km

N

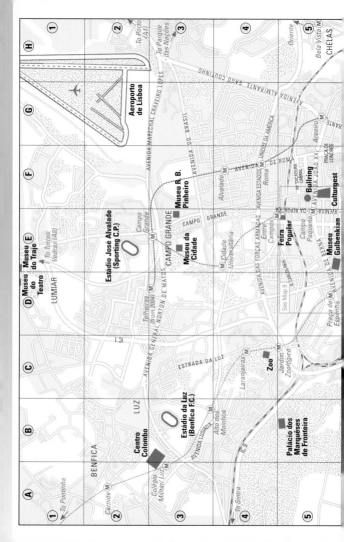

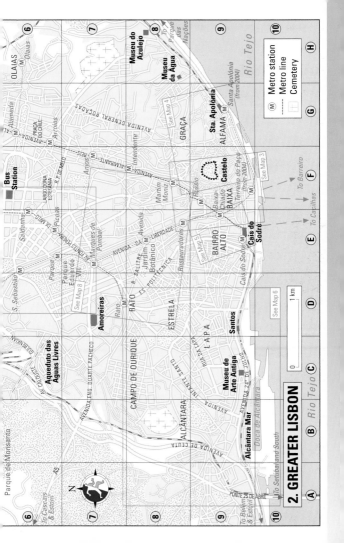

2. GREATER LISBON

Legend:

Ⓜ Metro station
---- Metro line
▨ Cemetery

Map labels:

Parque de Monsanto

Aqueduto das Aguas Livres

Amoreiras

Bus Station

OLAIAS

Ⓜ Olaias

Museu do Azulejo

Parque das Nações

Museu da Agua

Rio Tejo

GRAÇA

Sta. Apolónia

Ⓜ ALFAMA

Santa Apolónia (tram 2004)

Ⓜ Alameda

Ⓜ Arroios

Ⓜ Intendente

Ⓜ Martim Moniz

LARGO DONA ESTEFANIA

AVENIDA GENERAL ROÇADAS

AVENIDA ALMIRANTE REIS

R. P. DE MELO

Ⓜ Saldanha

Ⓜ Picoas

Ⓜ AV. DE MELO

S. Sebastião

Parque Eduardo VII

Ⓜ Parque

Ⓜ Marquês de Pombal

Ⓜ São Sebastião

AVENIDA DA LIBERDADE

Jardim Botânico

R. ES POLITÉCNICA

R. SAITRE

RATO

Ⓜ Rato

ESTRELA

LAPA

RUA DA LAPA

Santos

CAMPO DE OURIQUE

AV. GULBENKIAN

AV. AUGUSTE

AVENIDA DUARTE PACHECO

ALCÂNTARA

AVENIDA DE CEUTA

AVENIDA INFANTE SANTO

AVENIDA 24 DE JULHO

Museu de Arte Antiga

Alcântara Mar

Doca de Alcântara

PONTE 25 DE ABRIL

To Belém & Estoril

To Setúbal and South

To Cascais & Estoril

To Cascais & Estoril

A5

GULBENKIAN

Ⓜ Restauradores

BAIRRO ALTO

CHIADO

Ⓜ Chiado

BAIXA

Ⓜ Baixa-Chiado

Rossio

Ⓜ Rossio

Castelo

Terreiro do Paço (tram 2004)

Ⓜ Terreiro do Paço

Cais do Sodré

Ⓜ Cais do Sodré

To Capilhas

To Barreiro

See Map 5

See Map 6

See Map 3

See Map 4

See Map 8

Rio Tejo

N

0   1 km

A B C D E F G H

1 2 3 4 5 6 7 8 9 10

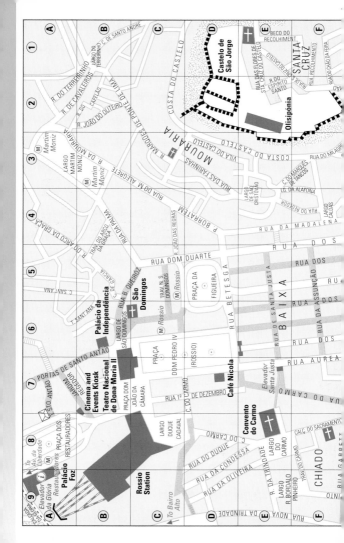

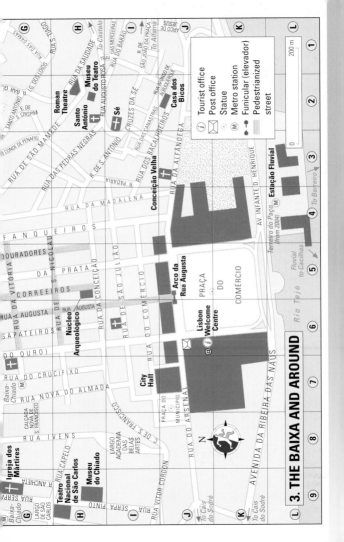

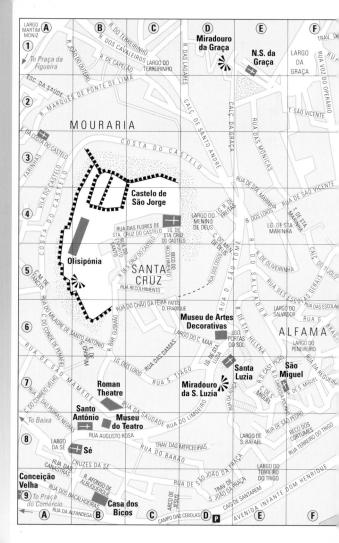

LARGO MARTIM MONIZ A 1

To Praça da Figueira

R. DO OUTEIRO

R. DO TERREIRINHO B

R. DOS CAVALEIROS

R. DE CAPELÃO C

LARGO DO TERREIRINHO

R. DAS LAGARES

Miradouro da Graça D

N.S. da Graça E

LARGO DA GRAÇA

TRAV. D F

RUA VOZ DO OPERARIO

ESC. DA SAÚDE 2

R. MARQUES DE PONTE DE LIMA

CALÇ. DE SANTO ANDRÉ

CALÇ. DA GRAÇA

T. SÃO VICENTE

E DA COSTA DO CASTELO

MOURARIA

COSTA DO CASTELO 3

FARINHAS

RUA DAS MÓNICAS

VILA DO CASTELO

RUA DE STA. MARINHA

RUA DE SÃO VICENTE

COSTA DO CASTELO 4

Castelo de São Jorge

LG. R DE FREITAS

LARGO DO MENINO DE DEUS

R. DOM. DE OLISÍPO

B. DOS LÓIOS

LG. DE STA. MARINHA

CALÇ. DO TIJOLO

C M DE TANCOS 5

Olisipónia

RUA DAS FLORES DE STA. CRUZ DO CASTELO

RUA DO CRUZ DO CASTELO

BECO DO RECOLHIMENTO

SANTA CRUZ

RUA DE SÃO TOMÉ

R. D. MEN. DE DEUS

R. D. SALVADOR

RUA DE OLIVEIRINHA

RUA DAS ESCOLAS GERAIS

RUA DAS ESCOLA

RUA DO MILAGRE DE SANTO ANTÓNIO

RUA RECOLHIMENTO

B. DE STA. HELENA

LARGO DO SALVADOR

RUA G

C. DO CONDE DE PENAFIEL 6

R. BAR GUSMÃO

RUA DO CHÃO DA FEIRA PATEO D. FRADIQUE

LARGO DO C. MAR

Museu de Artes Decorativas

LGO PORTAS DO SOL

ALFAMA

LARGO DO PENEIREIRO

BRAG

RUA DE SÃO MAMEDE

CRISPIM

LG. DOS LÓIOS

LG. DE STA. LUZIA

Santa Luzia

São Miguel

R. D. CAST BRANCO

R. DE S. MIGUEL

RUA DA REGUEIRA

RUA DO CORREIO VELHO 7

Roman Theatre

RUA DA SAUDADE

RUA DE S. TIAGO

Miradouro da S. Luzia

C. DE S. MIGUEL

C. DO LARGO DAS PEDRAS NEGRAS

Santo António

Museu do Teatro

RUA AUGUSTO ROSA

RUA DO LIMOEIRO

BECO DOS CORTUMES

RUA TERREIRO DO TRIGO 8

LARGO DA SÉ

Sé

CRUZES DA SÉ

TRAV. DAS MERCEEIRAS

RUA DO BARÃO

LARGO DE S. RAFAEL

RUA DE SÃO PEDRO

RUA DAS CANASTRAS

Conceição Velha

RUA AFONSO DE ALBUQUERQUE

LARGO DO TERREIRO DO TRIGO 9

To Praça do Comércio

RUA DOS BACALHOEIROS

Casa dos Bicos

RUA DA ALFANDEGA

ARCO DE SENS.

CAMPO DAS CEBOLAS

RUA DE SÃO JOÃO DA PRAÇA

TRAV. DE S. JOÃO DA PRAÇA

CAIS DE SANTAREM

AVENIDA INFANTE DOM HENRIQUE

A B C D E F

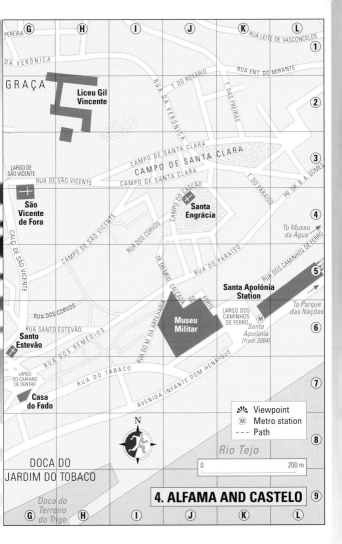

4. ALFAMA AND CASTELO

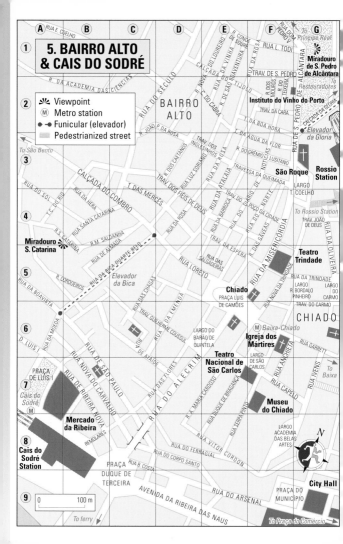

5. BAIRRO ALTO & CAIS DO SODRÉ

- ☆ Viewpoint
- Ⓜ Metro station
- •–• Funicular (elevador)
- ▨ Pedestrianized street

RUA E COELHO

RUA DA ACADEMIA DAS CIENCIAS

R. DA ACADEMIA DAS CIÊNCIAS

R. DO CONDE DE SOURE

RUA L. TODI

RUA DA VINHA

CALÇADA DO LOUREIRO

NOVA DO LOUREIRO

TRAV. DE S. PEDRO

R. DOS MOUROS

RUA DA ROSA TERREIRA

RUA DA BARROCA

RUA DA ATALAIA

TRAV. DE S. PEDRO DE ALCÂNTARA

To Príncipe Real

☆ Miradouro de S. Pedro de Alcântara

To Restauradores

Instituto do Vinho do Porto

TRAV. DA CARA

R. DA BOA HORA

T. DA ÁGUA DA FLOR

CALÇADA DA GLÓRIA

✚ Elevador da Glória

BAIRRO ALTO

R. DO SÉCULO

CALÇADA DO COMBRO

R. DA BICA DUARTE BELO

RUA DO SÉCULO

C. DO CABRA

R. JOÃO D. POBRE

TRAV. DOS INGLESINHOS

RUA DO GRÊMIO LUSITANO

RUA NOVA DO NORTE

✚ São Roque

LARGO T. COELHO

To Rossio Station

Rossio Station

TRAV. DOS FIÉIS DE DEUS

TRAV. LUZ SORIANO

RUA DA ROSA

RUA DIÁRIO DE NOTÍCIAS

TRAV. DO POÇO DA CIDADE

RUA DAS GÁVEAS

TRAV. DA QUEIMADA

RUA DA MISERICÓRDIA

TRAV. JOÃO DE DEUS

RUA DA OLIVEIRA

To São Bento

RUA DO SOL AO RIO

RUA DA HERA

T. C. DO RIO

T. DAS MERCÊS

R. DA SÉ

R.S. CATARINA

RUA SANTA CATARINA

R.M. SALDANHA

RUA DE ALMADA

☆ Miradouro S. Catarina

R. CORDOEIROS

RUA DA BOAVISTA

R. DA MOEDA

Elevador da Bica

RUA DAS CHAGAS

RUA DA EMENDA

TRAV. GUILHERME COUSSUL

RUA LORETO

RUA DAS SALGADEIRAS

RUA DA ESPERA

Chiado

PRAÇA LUÍS DE CAMÕES

Teatro Trindade

RUA DA TRINDADE

LARGO R. BORDALO PINHEIRO

RUA NOVA DA TRINDADE

LARGO DO CARMO

TRAV. DO CARMO

CHIADO

Ⓜ Baixa-Chiado

RUA GARRETT

✚ Igreja dos Mártires

LARGO DO BARÃO DE QUINTELA

Teatro Nacional de São Carlos

LARGO DE SÃO CARLOS

RUA ANCHIETA

RUA IVENS

To Baixa

RUA DE SÃO PAULO

RUA DE SÃO PAULO

RUA DAS FLORES

D. LUÍS I

PRAÇA DE LUÍS I

Cais do Sodré Ⓜ

RUA NOVA DO CARVALHO

RUA DE ATAÍDE

RUA DO ALECRIM

R. A. MARIA CARDOSO

RUA DUQUE DE BRAGANÇA

RUA CAPELO

Museu do Chiado

LARGO ACADEMIA DAS BELAS ARTES

Mercado da Ribeira

RUA DE RIBEIRA NOVA

REMOLARES

RUA SERPA PINTO

RUA VITOR CORDON

Cais do Sodré Station

RUA B. COSTA

PRAÇA DUQUE DE TERCEIRA

RUA DO FERRAGIAL

RUA DO CORPO SANTO

RUA DO ARSENAL

City Hall

PRAÇA DO MUNICÍPIO

AVENIDA DA RIBEIRA DAS NAUS

N

0 ____ 100 m

To ferry

To Praça do Comércio

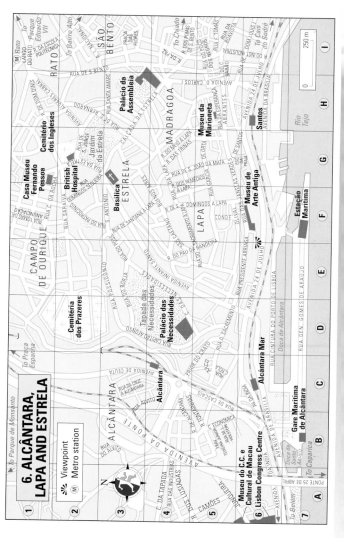

6. ALCÂNTARA, LAPA AND ESTRELA

- ⁂ Viewpoint
- Ⓜ Metro station

To Parque de Monsanto

To Praça de Espanha

To Belém

To Caparica

PONTE 25 DE ABRIL

Museu do C.C. e Cultural de Macau

Lisbon Congress Centre

Gare Marítima de Alcântara

Alcântara Mar

Alcântara

Cemitério dos Prazeres

Palácio das Necessidades

Tapada das Necessidades

Museu de Arte Antiga

Estação Marítima

Basílica da Estrela

British Hospital

Casa Museu Fernando Pessoa

Cemitério dos Ingleses

Palácio da Assembleia

Museu da Marioneta

Santos

CAMPO DE OURIQUE

ALCÂNTARA

ESTRELA

LAPA

MADRAGOA

RATO

SÃO BENTO

Jardim da Estrela

To Chiado

To Bairro Alto

To Rato

To Cais do Sodré

Rio Tejo

AVENIDA DA BRASÍLIA

AVENIDA 24 DE JULHO

AVENIDA DE BRASÍLIA

AVENIDA DA BRASÍLIA

RUA GEN. GOMES DE ARAUJO

RUA DA CINTURA DO PORTO DE LISBOA

Doca de Alcântara

Doca de Alc.(S)

PONTE DA PONTE

AVENIDA DA PONTE

Parque Eduardo VII

Largo do Rato

0   250 m

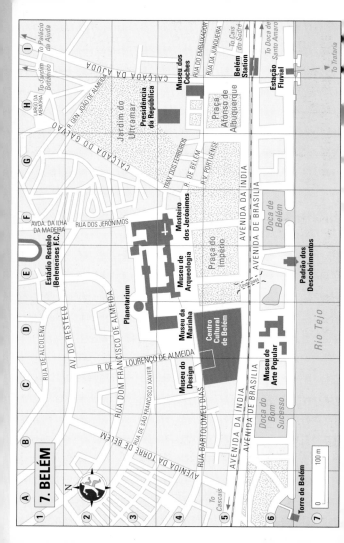

7. BELÉM

N

| A | B | C | D | E | F | G | H | I |

1

2

3

4

5

6

7

To Palácio da Ajuda

To Jardim Botânico

LARGO DA MEMÓRIA

R. GEN JOÃO DE ALMEIDA

CALÇADA DA AJUDA

Museu dos Coches

RUA DA JUNQUEIRA

To Cais do Sodré

Belém Station

Estação Fluvial

To Doca de Santo Amaro

To Trafaria

CALÇADA DO GALVÃO

Jardim do Ultramar

Presidência da República

Praça Afonso de Albuquerque

RUA DO EMBAIXADOR

AVDA. DA ILHA DA MADEIRA

RUA DOS JERÓNIMOS

Estádio Restelo (Belenenses F.C.)

RUA DE ALCOLENA

AV. DO RESTELO

RUA DOM FRANCISCO DE ALMEIDA

Planetarium

Museu de Arqueologia

Mosteiro dos Jerónimos

TRAV. DOS FERREIROS

R. DE BELÉM

AV. PORTUENSE

Praça do Império

AVENIDA DA ÍNDIA

AVENIDA DE BRASÍLIA

Doca de Belém

Underpass

R. DE LOURENÇO DE ALMEIDA

RUA DE SÃO FRANCISCO XAVIER

Museu do Design

Museu da Marinha

Centro Cultural de Belém

AVENIDA DE BRASÍLIA

Padrão dos Descobrimentos

AVENIDA DA ÍNDIA

RUA BARTOLOMEU DIAS

AVENIDA DA TORRE DE BELÉM

To Cascais

Museu de Arte Popular

AVENIDA DA ÍNDIA

AVENIDA DE BRASÍLIA

Doca do Bom Sucesso

Rio Tejo

Torre de Belém

0   100 m

8. AVENIDA DA LIBERDADE AND AROUND

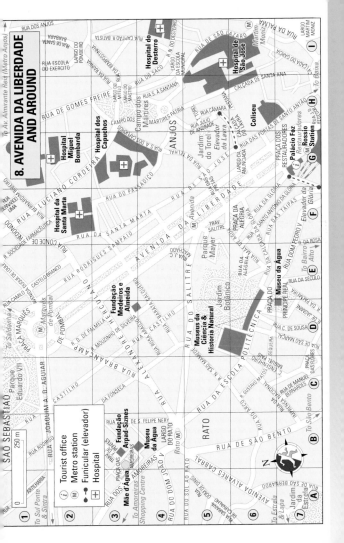

Legend:
- *(i)* Tourist office
- **(M)** Metro station
- Funicular (elevador)
- ✚ Hospital

0 ——— 250 m

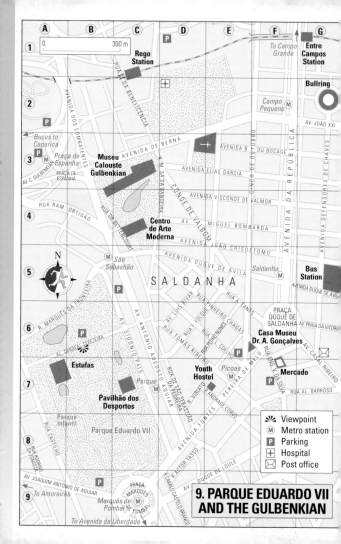

9. PARQUE EDUARDO VII AND THE GULBENKIAN

Legend

- ☀ Viewpoint
- Ⓜ Metro station
- Ⓟ Parking
- ✚ Hospital
- ✉ Post office

Map labels

0 — 300 m

Rego Station

Entre Campos Station

To Campo Grande

Bullring

Campo Pequeno

AV. JOÃO XXI

AVENIDA DOS COMBATENTES

Buses to Caparica

Praça de Espanha

AV. C. GULBENKIAN

PRAÇA DE ESPANHA

AVENIDA DE BERNA

RUA DA BENEFICENCIA

Museu Calouste Gulbenkian

AVENIDA B. DU BOCAGE

AVENIDA ELIAS GARCIA

RUA SA DA BANDEIRA

RUA RAM ORTIGÃO

RUA DR BETTENCOURT

AVENIDA VISCONDE DE VALMOR

CONDE DE VALBOM

MIGUEL BOMBARDA

AVENIDA DA REPÚBLICA

CINCO DE OUTUBRO

AVENIDA DEFENSORES DE CHAVES

Centro de Arte Moderna

AV. DE VALBOM

AVENIDA JOÃO CRISÓSTOMO

AVENIDA DUQUE DE ÁVILA

Ⓜ São Sebastião

SALDANHA

Saldanha Ⓜ

Bus Station

AVENIDA DUQUE DE ÁVILA

R. MARQUES DA FRONTEIRA

RUA A. EANES

AV. SIDÓNIO PAIS

AV. LUIS BIVAR

RUA PINHEIRO CHAGAS

RUA FOLQUE

RUA DR PEDRO NUNES

PRAÇA DUQUE DE SALDANHA

AV DA PRAIA DA VITORIA

AL. CARDEL FERREIRA

AV. ANTONIO AUGUSTO AGUIAR

RUA TOMÁS RIBEIRO

RUA LATINO COELHO

Casa Museu Dr. A. Gonçalves

RUA ENG VIEIRA DA SILVA

AV. CASAL RIBEIRO

Estufas

Parque

RUA DE S. SEBASTIÃO DA PEDREIRA

Youth Hostel

Picoas Ⓜ

R. VIRIATO

RUA ANDRADE CORVO

PEREIRA DE MELO

Mercado

RUA AL. BARROSO

Pavilhão dos Desportos

Parque Infantil

Parque Eduardo VII

RUA CASTILHO

AV. JOAQUIM ANTÓNIO DE AGUIAR

To Amoreiras

RUA RODRIGO DA FONSECA

AVENIDA FONTES

R. ACTOR TASSO

PRAÇA MARQUÊS

Marquês de Pombal Ⓜ

RICARDO CASTELO BRANCO

AV. DUQUE DE LOULÉ

To Avenida da Liberdade

N